SEQUENCE KNITTING

SEQUENCE KNITTING

SIMPLE METHODS FOR CREATING COMPLEX REVERSIBLE FABRICS

CECELIA CAMPOCHIARO

Copyright © 2015 by Cecelia Campochiaro

All rights reserved. No part of this book may be reproduced or transmitted in any form by any means, electronic, mechanical, photocopying, recording, or otherwise, without prior written permission from the publisher.

Book Design: Vanessa Yap-Einbund
Technical Editor: Renée Lorion
Photography: Cecelia Campochiaro

Published by Chroma Opaci Books
Sunnyvale, California
www.chromaopaci.com

First edition, third printing

ISBN: 978-0-9863381-0-6

Printed and bound in Malaysia by the Times Publishing Group

CONTENTS

chapter 1	**INTRODUCTION**	**1**
chapter 2	**1-ROW METHOD**	**25**
chapter 3	**SERPENTINE METHOD**	**97**
chapter 4	**SPIRAL METHOD**	**195**
chapter 5	**1-ROW SHAPED METHOD**	**281**
chapter 6	**DESIGN CONSIDERATIONS**	**331**
	APPENDIX	**359**
	INDEX	**377**

PREFACE

Sequence Knitting is a new approach to creating knitted fabrics by knitting the same sequence of stitches again and again. Sequence Knits are usually easy to make and reversible. The patterns are so simple they can often be written in just a few sentences.

My inspiration for Sequence Knitting was the scarf shown on the facing page, which I knit from Stephanie Pearl-McPhee's One Row Handspun Scarf pattern and Lisa Souza's handspun yarn. The simplicity of the 1-row pattern, based on the sequence [K3, P1], and the resulting beautiful, reversible, and complex texture, were revelations to me.

I was so delighted with Pearl-McPhee's scarf, I started making swatches to see what other fabrics I could create with a similar approach. For example, I would take the sequence [K3, P3] and work it on multiples of 6, 6+1, 6+2, 6+3, 6+4, and 6+5 to see what would happen. After a year of making swatches, reading, thinking and experimenting, the concepts of Sequence Knitting began to emerge in my mind.

One surprise for me was the rarity of these concepts in the knitting literature. Now that I have been immersed in Sequence Knitting for several years, it seems almost primal in its simplicity, so it was hard to me to believe that others had not already written about it.

There are some 1-row patterns like Pearl-McPhee's, there are the faggoting laces from Europe, the "mistake ribbing" created when [K2, P2] is knit across a multiple of 4+3 stitches, and swirled fabric knit in the round. But I could not find any systematic studies of 1-row patterns, nor any mention of some of the methods I had been developing.

In spite of not being able to find references I still feel that Elizabeth Zimmerman is right, these methods are unvention rather than invention, because they are so inherently simple.

The purpose of this book is to introduce a new and structured way to create knitted fabrics. This book is for knitters of all levels, but it is not a general introduction to knitting.

An understanding of standard concepts like reading charts and finishing techniques is presumed. Details like consistent tension, selvedges, cast-ons, cast-offs, and blocking all matter a great deal in how a finished piece is perceived, but this book does not attempt to cover these topics. Instead I refer you, gentle reader, to the many outstanding books already in the literature or to an expert at your local yarn shop. Use this book in conjunction with other books, articles, and patterns.

Chapter 1 is an introduction to Sequence Knitting.

Chapter 2 explores the fabrics you can create with 1-row patterns using knit and purl stitches.

Chapter 3 describes serpentine knitting where a single sequence of stitches is worked again and again, continuing from row to row without interruption. This method was a breakthrough for me and led to the discovery of many interesting fabrics that cannot be found in any existing stitch dictionaries.

Chapter 4 discusses Sequence Knitting in the round, with many newly discovered, uncovered, invented or unvented fabrics.

Chapter 5 covers 1-row patterns where increases or decreases are used to create triangular or parallelogram-shaped pieces, again with novel and interesting textures.

Chapter 6 is about using color and fiber together to develop new fabrics. With the simplicity of Sequence Knitting, choices of color and fiber become a bigger part of the creation process.

The Appendix has useful information about finishing, a glossary of terms, sources, references and a little math for those who might be interested. There is also a table of cast-on stitch counts for different pattern multiples, which is helpful for modifying patterns.

The charts throughout this book are worked in the usual way from right to left beginning with row 1 and show the fabric as viewed from the frontside, with knit stitches in white and purl stitches in gray. Initially I planned to use either the white box / dot or the vertical / horizontal line standards, but the patterns were too hard for me to see.

The pattern-repeat boxes on the charts show the row repeat and repeat length of each pattern, but do not themselves represent the pattern multiple, and thus must be used in the context of the entire chart. The numbers along the bottom will always show the pattern multiples in a sequence knitting chart.

I used many one-of-a-kind yarns, including my own hand-dyes in the book. The downside of this is that some of the patterns cannot be exactly replicated because my hand-dyes are unique, and some boutique or limited quantity yarns have become unavailable during the writing of the book. However, for every pattern, the weight and type of yarn is given, so you can make informed choices about yarns you want to use.

One joyous aspect of knitting today is having access to a wide variety of high-quality, hand-dyed, hand-spun, and exotic-fiber yarns. Knitters have never had as many wonderful and amazing choices for yarn as we do now, and I encourage you to explore the full gamut of possibilities.

I hope you will take the concepts presented here and expand upon them. There are a vast number of wonderful fabrics and patterns yet to be discovered!

This book is dedicated to the Crow sisters: my late mother Rachel Crow Campochiaro, and my aunts Anne Crow Gilleran, Martha Crow, Mary Crow and Nancy Crow.

THANK YOU

To Vanessa Yap-Einbund for her design advice, technical help and all-around great support and to Renée Lorion for expertly finding my many mistakes. These gracious women have been integral to the creation process and both have taught me a great deal about creating a document of this scale.

To Nancy Marchant for her conviction that this project would matter to the knitting community, for her mentorship, and for pushing me to complete the project.

To Catherine Lowe for her kind, thoughtful advice. So many ideas came from seeds planted by Catherine in one of her amazing workshops and in our one-on-one conversations.

To my faithful and supportive knitting team: Aimee Aurelio, Deborah Bennett, Fely Berrara, Catherine Boxwell, Martha Earl, Liz McKee, Elianna Meyerson, Shelly Miyasato, Chris Sapyta, Cassandra Vlahos, Carol Walther and Rebecca Williams. Shelly and Catherine knit all the swatches. Aimee, Fely, Liz, Shelly, Chris, Carol and Rebecca all knit multiple pieces, many of which are in the book. Working with them, in some cases over many iterations of a piece, was all important to the design process.

To Cat Bordhi, Annemor Sundbø, and Susanna Hanson for taking time with me to discuss the project. Cat was the first person I reached out to in the knitting community to discuss the idea of Sequence Knitting. Annemor spent an afternoon with me in her village in Norway talking about the ideas and about possible historical references. Susanna is a great encourager who helped me decide to self-publish. She also recommended that I seek out Annemor and the "labor of love" that is the Östergötlands Ullspineri.

To Nancy Crow, John Stitzlein, Jan Newbury and Alison Boxwell for helping me learn how to dye fiber and textiles. My education began with a shibori dyeing workshop taught by Jan at Nancy and John's Timberframe Barn in Ohio in 2008. Nancy and John kindly let me have the run of their dyeing studio a couple years later so I could experiment by myself. More recently, Alison and I worked together to learn and develop our own approaches for hand painting and kettle dyeing yarn.

To my colleagues Karen Biagini, who helped me understand some of the mathematics behind the sequences, plus Patrick P. Lee and Keith Bartholomew who helped me develop the charts.

And to my dear friends and family for unwavering support and without whom I could never have completed this book.

CHAPTER 1

INTRODUCTION

1-Row, Serpentine, Spiral, and Shaped 1-row Methods

WHAT IS SEQUENCE KNITTING?

Sequence Knitting is just like it sounds: knit a sequence of stitches repeatedly using some kind of rule to create a fabric. Many of these fabrics are well-known, and many more are new.

There are many benefits to Sequence Knitting. It enables knitters to create complex pieces with very little mental effort. This makes Sequence Knitting ideal for social knitting, travel knitting, or any time when a simple approach is desired.

The repetition of the stitches in the sequence has a soothing, meditative quality. Knitters of all levels from beginners to experts can explore and experiment with Sequence Knitting. Many Sequence Knits are reversible and if they are worked back and forth, they lie flat with minimal blocking.

Since a sequence is repeated again and again, the instructions for this kind of knitting are very simple. They do not require following a chart or multi-row pattern.

If a piece of fabric can be created with Sequence Knitting, it can also be created with traditional knitting. Let's look at 2 examples for describing the pattern for a simple 2x2 ribbed scarf. The square brackets denote the sequence of stitches to be repeated.

Example A:

Cast on a multiple of 4 stitches. On every row, [K2, P2] until the piece measures 70 inches. Bind off, wash and block.

Example B:

Cast on a multiple of 4+2 stitches.

Row 1: [K2, P2], K2

Row 2: P2, [K2, P2]

Repeat rows 1 and 2 until the piece measures 70 inches. Bind off, wash and block.

Example A is written as a Sequence Knitting pattern. There is a sequence of stitches, [K2, P2], and they are worked according to a simple rule or algorithm. Example B is written as a 2-row pattern. In both cases the resulting piece is a scarf knit in 2x2 ribbing, but the mindset for the Sequence Knit is different as you don't have to track the rows. This freedom from following a chart or a multi-row pattern becomes very important when the row-repeat is larger than 2 and the patterns are more complex.

Charts are included in this book to aid the knitter in visualizing the resulting fabric, and also for adapting the patterns to situations where Sequence Knitting cannot be used in its pure form, such as shaping a sleeve cap.

Sequence Knitting is a broad and general way to think about knitting. The result is a huge number of new fabrics that can be created with relative ease. There are an infinite number of sequences, they can contain any kind of stitches, and the rules for how a sequence is repeated can vary. The example above is a 1-row rule — start the sequence fresh on every row. Over the course of the book we will explore different kinds of rules that can be applied to both flat and circular knitting.

SEQUENCES AND SEQUENCE LENGTHS

Sequence Knitting is taking a sequence of stitches and a simple rule or algorithm and applying it again and again.

A sequence can contain knits, purls, slip stitches, increases, decreases, or any number of fancy stitches.

The simplest sequences are:

[K1] or [P1]

The brackets indicate that the stitches inside are the sequence to be repeated. These basic sequences have a length of 1 stitch and when worked flat will result in knit-garter or purl-garter. In circular knitting they will result in stockinette or reverse stockinette.

An example of a more complex sequence is:

[K1, P1]

Here the sequence length is 2. Knitting this sequence can result in either 1x1 ribbing or seed stitch.

Here is an example of a very complex sequence that includes different kinds of stitches:

[K1, P1, K3, slip 1, YO, K2tog]

The increase is paired with the decrease, resulting in a sequence length of 8. If the increases and decreases were not paired, the fabric would grow or shrink on every row. Thus the only rule for a sequence is that it must be a fixed length.

Sequence	Sequence Length
[K1]	1
[K1,P1]	2
[K2,P3,K3,K1b]	9
[K3,S1WYIB,K3,P3,S1WYIF,P3]	14
[8(K1,P1),4(K2,P2)],2(K1,P1)]	36
[K8,P7,K6,P5,K4,P3,K2,P1]	36
[K1,YO,K2tog]	3
[K3,YO,P3,YO,K3tog]	9
[K3,YO,P3]	6 and growing
[K3,P3,K2tog]	8 and shrinking

The table above gives some examples of different sequences with their lengths. While a sequence can be any length, the spirit of Sequence Knitting is to keep it simple so the pattern can be easily remembered. Of the two examples that are 36 stitches long, one is far easier to remember than the other. A sequence that is very long or very complicated might not be much fun to actually knit.

PATTERN MULTIPLES

Once you decide on the sequence, the next important factor is the pattern multiple. The pattern multiple is defined as the sequence length plus some number of extra stitches.

When the pattern multiple is varied, the stitches line up with each other differently from row-to-row, resulting in different fabrics. For any sequence of a given length, there are the same number of possible pattern multiples. For the sequence [K1, P1], the sequence length is 2, and there are 2 unique pattern multiples, 2 and 2+1.

Similarly for the complex sequence [K1, P1, K3, slip 1, YO, K2tog], where the sequence length is 8, there are 8 possible pattern multiples: 8, 8+1, 8+2, 8+3, 8+4, 8+5, 8+6, and 8+7.

The following examples are all equivalent ways to express the same pattern multiple:

- 3+2 or 3-1
- 8+6 or 8-2
- 4+1 and 4+3 or 4+/-1

The table at right summarizes the possible pattern multiples using the more succinct +/- nomenclature. This shortened way of writing the pattern multiple is a better way to explain some behaviors of Sequence Knitting. Both ways are used interchangeably throughout the book.

The extra stitches beyond the sequence length are the remainder. To know the remainder, use the +/- way to describe the pattern multiple. For example, the sequence [K3, P3] on 6+2 has a sequence length of 6 and a remainder of 2. If I were to work the sequence [K3, P3] on 6+4, the remainder is also 2, because 6+4 is also 6-2.

Sequence Length	Possible Pattern Multiples
1	1
2	2, 2+1
3	3, 3+/-1
4	4, 4+/-1, 4+2
5	5, 5+/-1, 5+/-2
6	6, 6+/-1, 6+/-2, 6+3
7	7, 7+/-1, 7+/-2, 7+/-3
8	8, 8+/-1, 8+/-2, 8+/-3, 8+4
n (even)	n, n+/-1, ... , n+/-(n/2 – 1), n+n/2
n (odd)	n, n+/-1, ... , n+/-((n-1)/2)

SEQUENCE KNITTING METHODS

There are 4 methods for Sequence Knitting covered in this book: 1-row, serpentine, spiral, and shaped 1-row.

1-Row

In this method the sequence is worked across every row and every row is the same. For example, if the sequence is [K3, P3] and the pattern multiple is 6, every row will be:

[K3, P3]

If there is a remainder, work a partial repeat of the sequence. For example, if the pattern multiple is 6+4, every row will be:

[K3, P3], K3, P1

The 1-row method has some very common examples, like ribbing and mistake ribbing.

Serpentine

In this case the sequence is worked independent of the number of stitches in the row. At the beginning of a new row you do not restart the sequence, but rather you continue the sequence from where you left off on the last row. For example, if the sequence is [K2, P2] and the pattern multiple is 4+3, the first row will be:

Row 1: [K2, P2], K2, P1

Instead of restarting the sequence on the second row, the second row *continues* from the first:

Row 2: P1, [K2, P2], K2

The third and fourth rows follow in similar fashion:

Row 3: P2, [K2, P2], K1

Row 4: K1, P2, [K2, P2]

The fifth row restarts the entire sequence, so this example is a 4-row pattern. The serpentine method is exciting because it yields complex designs that would normally require following a chart. With Sequence Knitting these complex fabrics can be created just by repeating a simple sequence of stitches.

Spiral

Spiral knitting is similar to serpentine, but worked in the round. The sequence does not restart every round, but continues in a spiral. Amazing textures can be created as the stitches line up very differently depending on the sequence and the pattern multiple.

Shaped 1-row

The last method is a 1-row approach with increases or decreases at the beginnings or ends of rows. For example, a pattern could be: Cast on 200 stitches. On every row, work the sequence [K3, P3] to the last 2 stitches, then knit 2 stitches together.

3 METHODS COMPARED

As an illustration of the power of Sequence Knitting, these pages show how 3 very different fabrics can be created with the sequence [K3, P3] and a pattern multiple of 6+1 using the 1-row, serpentine, and spiral methods.

In the 1-row method, every row is the same. In this example, each row is [K3, P3], K1. The pattern forms an accordion where the 2-stitch ribs are separated by single columns of knit or purl garter stitch. All 1-row patterns have a 2-row repeat.

In the serpentine method the first row is the same as the 1-row method: [K3, P3], K1. But unlike 1-row knitting, the second row now follows from the first: K2, P3, [K3, P3], K2. The third row will begin with K1, P3. Thus the sequence is continued unbroken from row to row. The row repeat for this pattern is 6 rows.

In serpentine knitting you can't always "read" your knitting the way you can with a 1-row fabric, but the knitting is easy - as long as you always complete the sequence before you put your needles down.

The third chart illustrates the spiral method, which is worked in the round. This swatch is worked in the round and then cut open as for a steek. The sequence shifts 1 stitch every row to create a right-leaning swirl pattern. This pattern has a 6-row repeat.

The next page shows 13 scarves worked with 1-row and serpentine methods.

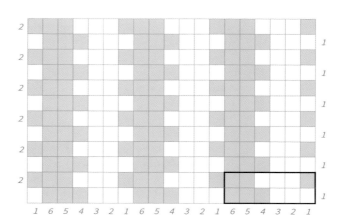

1-Row

The sequence [K3, P3] is worked on every row. Since the number of stitches cast on is a multiple of 6+1, every row ends on K1.

PAGE 6

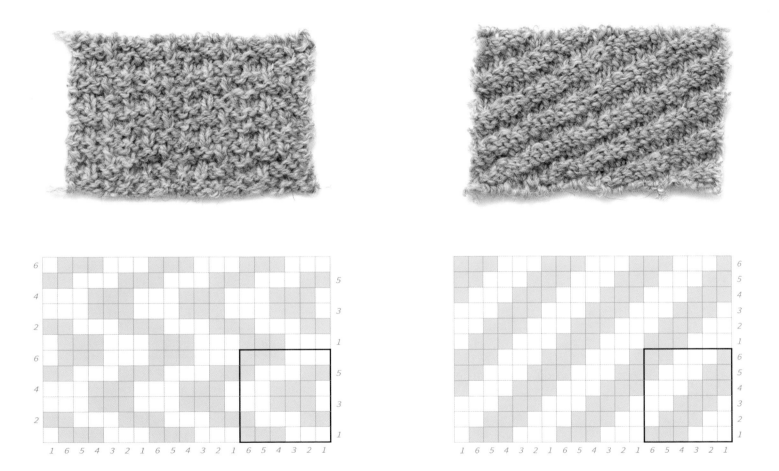

Serpentine

The same sequence worked on a multiple of 6+1 using the serpentine method becomes a completely different fabric.

Spiral

Worked in the round in the spiral method, but shown as a flat swatch, this same sequence on a multiple of 6+1 again yields a completely different fabric.

13 SEQUENCE KNITTING SCARVES

13 different scarves are shown on the facing page, corresponding to the patterns below from left to right. Each scarf is worked either with the 1-row method or the serpentine method, which are simple enough that all 13 patterns can fit on 1 page. The yarn used for the samples is a cashmere-mohair blend from School Products in New York that is no longer available. However, any smooth, luxurious aran-weight yarn will do.

All scarves use 300-350 g of aran-weight wool and size 7 (4.5 mm) needles with a gauge of 4.5 stitches/inch in stockinette. In each case, work until the scarf measures 70 inches. Bind off. Wash, block and weave in ends.

Marlett

Cast on 44 stitches (6+2). Work [K1, P1, K2, P2], K1, P1 using the 1-row method.

Enders

Cast on 36 stitches (6). Work [K2, 2(P1, K1)] using the 1-row method.

Morant

Cast on 36 stitches (6). Work [K1, P1, K2, P2] using the 1-row method.

Lyden

Cast on 38 stitches (6+2). Work [K1, P1, K2, P2] using the serpentine method.

Piland

Cast on 37 stitches (4+1). Work [K3, P1] using the serpentine method.

Ruddock

Cast on 34 stitches (8+2). Work [K6, P2] using the serpentine method.

Askin

Cast on 34 stitches (8+2). Work [3(K1, P1), K2] using the serpentine method.

Murley

Cast on 35 stitches (8+3). Work [3(K1, P1), K2] using the serpentine method.

Kenner

Cast on 36 stitches (5+1). Work [P1, K3, P1] using the serpentine method.

Drewes

Cast on 34 stitches (9+7). Work [K3, P3, K3] using the serpentine method.

Wortham

Cast on 42 stitches (10+2). Work [2(K2, P2), K2] using the serpentine method.

Falbo

Cast on 44 stitches (10+4). Work [2(K2, P2), K2] using the serpentine method.

Andrus

Cast on 38 stitches (12+2). Work [K3, P6, K3] using the serpentine method.

PERMUTATIONS: 1 ROW AND SERPENTINE

Consider a sequence of 4 stitches. How many fabrics are possible and why? Let's take the example of [K2, P2]. First consider that this sequence has 4 permutations, where a permutation is the same sequence with a different starting point:

K2, P2

K1, P2, K1

P2, K2

P1, K2, P1

Next you have the choice of 4 possible pattern multiples:

4

4+1

4+2

4+3

Thus [K2, P2] has 4 permutations, each of which can be knit using 4 pattern multiples, resulting in 16 fabrics per method.

The facing page shows 2 sets of charts for this sequence. The upper half is based on the 1-row method and the lower half is based on the serpentine method.

A few observations can be made from these 2 sets of charts. Many of the charts in both blocks are similar. The 1-row charts only show 3 distinct classes of fabrics: 2x2 ribbing, 2x2 broken garter, and an accordion design where the columns of knit and purl ribs are separated by alternating columns of knit-garter and purl-garter. Within the 16 unique fabrics, 13 of the 16 are variations of these 3, with differences at the edges. This is also true of the lower block of charts, but in this case the accordion design is swapped for 2x2 blocks of knit and purl stitches.

Also observe that the top row of each block of charts are identical. When the pattern multiple equals the sequence length, the serpentine method is the same as the 1-row method.

Delving a little deeper, observe that the 1-row charts contain 4 examples of 2x2 ribbing. However, in each case the selvedges are different. Depending on the purpose of the piece, these selvedge variations might be important. For example, symmetry might matter for a scarf, or the 2 frontsides of a cardigan might need to mirror each other.

As the sequences become longer, more complexities are possible and many new and interesting fabrics can be created.

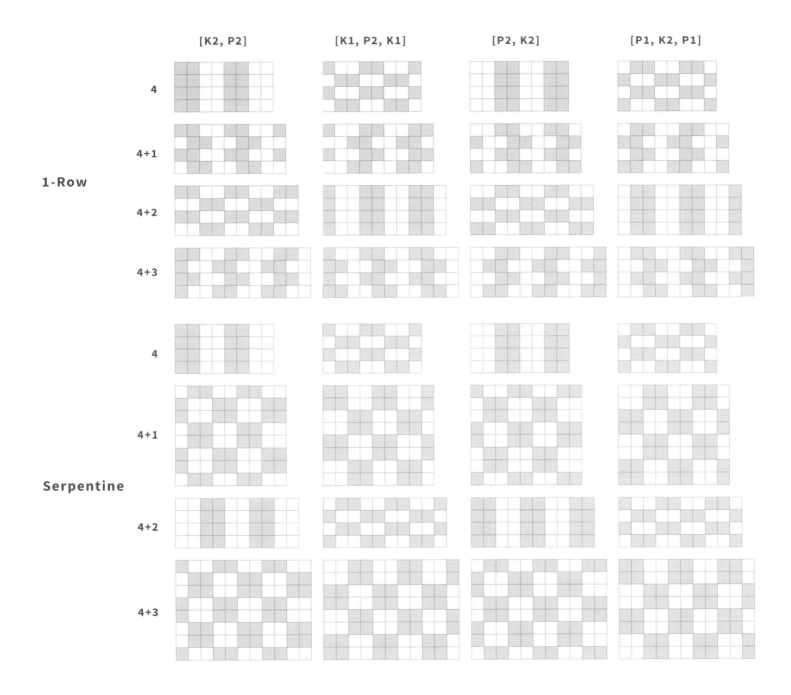

Fabrics that can be created with [K2, P2]

The top 16 charts use the 1-row method, and the bottom 16 charts use the serpentine method. The rows show the pattern multiples, the columns show the permutations of the sequence.

PERMUTATIONS: SPIRAL

The spiral fabrics are different than 1-row or serpentine fabrics because the spiral character of circular knitting lets the stitches in the sequence align differently from round to round. A swirl, like that shown in the center of the 3 pictured swatches, is especially common in spiral Sequence Knitting.

The chart on the facing page is analogous to the charts on the previous page. [K2, P2] yields 3 fabrics in spiral knitting: 2x2 ribbing, 2x2 broken garter and a swirl that can lean to the right or to the left.

Notice that every column in the chart looks very similar. Permutations are less important in spiral knitting because it is circular - there is no clear beginning and ending. The only differences across the rows are where the rounds begin. Spiral knitting will be discussed in more detail in Chapter 4.

Spiral Swatches

Shown from left to right are [K2, P2] on 4, 4+1, and 4+2.

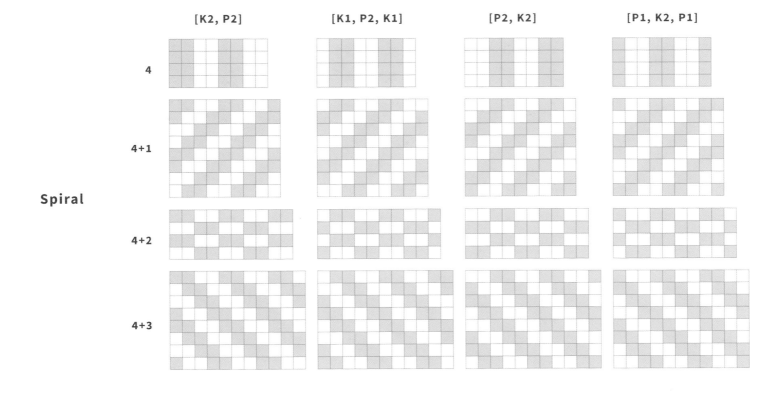

Fabrics that can be created with [K2, P2] using the spiral method

The rows show the pattern multiples, the columns show the permutations of the sequence.

GAUGE

Gauge can vary widely in Sequence Knitting. Patterns deviating by only 1 stitch can have very different gauges. Familiar swatches of garter stitch, seed stitch, and 1x1 ribbing are shown here. These swatches were knit with the same needles, the same yarn, and by the same person. The stitch counts for each swatch are almost the same:

Garter stitch: 24 stitches x 26 rows
Seed stitch: 25 stitches x 26 rows
1x1 Ribbing: 24 stitches x 26 rows

The difference between seed stitch and 1x1 ribbing is the most dramatic as the sequence [K1, P1] is the same, as is the row count. However, a difference of 1 stitch, 24 vs. 25, results in a ribbed swatch only 65% as wide as the seed stitch swatch, but 30% taller. A 5 or 10% difference may be acceptable in the width of a scarf, but probably not in a sock or a sweater. Making swatches is always advised to ensure the desired result.

If I am unsure of the gauge, or if the cast-on is especially long, such as for a scarf worked lengthwise, I usually do a provisional cast-on. I leave a long tail, with enough yarn to work the row, wound into a butterfly. After the piece is done I remove the provisional cast on and bind off using the yarn from the butterfly. This way, both top and bottom edges of the piece look the same and I can control the tension.

Garter Stitch

Seed Stitch or 1x1 Broken Garter

1x1 Ribbing

REVERSIBILITY

Many of the fabrics created with Sequence Knitting are reversible, but "reversible" is a loosely-used term in the knitting community. It can mean many things, but more often than not it means that someone found both sides of a knitted fabric attractive. For most knitted fabrics this subjective definition does not tell the knitter how the backside relates visually to the frontside.

Understanding the level of reversibility of a fabric or pattern is an important part of the design and something to understand before embarking on a project. If I am making a scarf, I have different criteria for what I want in terms of reversibility than I do for a sweater, where the inside will not be seen by others. In most patterns, even scarf patterns, the backside is not discussed or even represented in photographs. When investing time and materials in a project that will be seen from both sides, the appearance of the backside is an important consideration.

In this book the following four definitions are used to describe reversibility from high to low: perfectly reversible, shift reversible, shift-flip reversible, and aesthetically reversible.

Perfectly reversible

There are not many examples in this special category. In this case, the front and back are identical, including the selvedges, when the piece is flipped over from side to side. These rare examples include simple variations of symmetric ribbing and broken garter worked with the 1-row method.

Shift reversible

This category would be called "reversible" by most. The frontside and backside are the same except for the edges. The repeat matches on both sides, but is shifted. All 1-color, knit-purl, 1-row patterns that are not perfectly reversible are in this category.

Shift-flip reversible

In this case the bulk of the frontside and backside are the same if the view of the back can be shifted *and mirrored or flipped* from right to left. Many of the shaped 1-row fabrics are in this category. The selvedges may differ, depending on the specific method used for the increases or decreases.

Aesthetically reversible

This category includes all remaining fabrics. The front and backsides are different, and claiming reversibility is an aesthetic decision that belongs to each of us. Many Sequence Knits that are aesthetically reversible are still very similar on both sides, which is one reason why images of the backsides of all the swatches are shown.

A Sequence Knit that is perfectly, shift or shift-flip reversible when worked in 1 color may be less reversible when worked in 2 colors.

In circular knitting the backside is the inside of the cylinder. To view the backside of a circular swatch, cut a steek and flip it over from side to side. Spiral method fabrics will be always aesthetically reversible if the sequence contains different numbers of knits and purls. Even if the sequence contains an equal number of knits and purls, it may still be aesthetically reversible because of the pattern, or because the tension of the knits and purls is different.

If a sequence only contains knits and purls, then swapping the knits and purls is equivalent to working the backside of a fabric. For this reason, only the knit dominant sequences are included throughout the book. For example, [K5, P1] is included, but not [P5, K1].

The following pages show some examples of fabrics with different kinds of reversibility.

FRONTSIDE   BACKSIDE

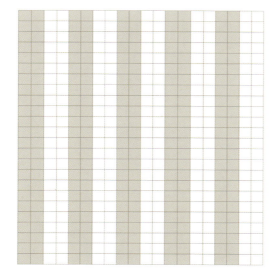
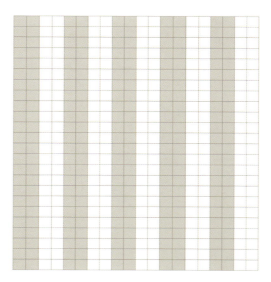

Perfect reversibility example

2x2 ribbing worked on a multiple of 4 stitches is perfectly reversible. The selvedges on the left and right edges of the swatches are the same, and the charts for the frontside and backside are identical.

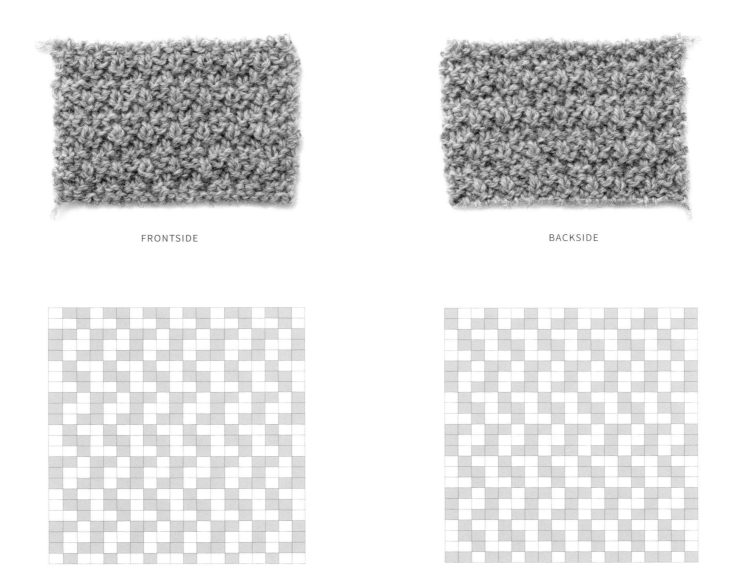

FRONTSIDE　　　　　　　　　　　　　　BACKSIDE

Shift reversibility example

This shift reversible example is based on [K2, P1] on 3+1 worked with the serpentine method. The swatches appear the same on both sides, but the pattern is shifted by 3 rows.

FRONTSIDE   BACKSIDE

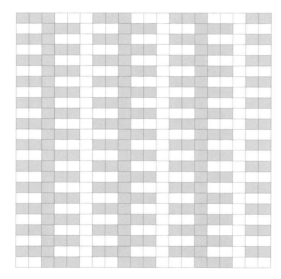
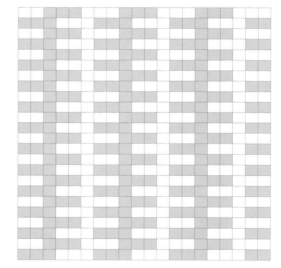

Shift-flip reversibility example

This shift-flip accordion is created by working [K3, P3] in 2 colors with the 1-row method. The columns of knit- and purl-garter stitch affect the reversibility. See page 36 for more information on the reversibility of garter stitch and color work.

FRONTSIDE

BACKSIDE

Aesthetic reversibility example

This example is based on [K3, P3, K1, P1] on 8+1 worked with the serpentine method. There is no way to shift or flip the backside image to match the frontside image, so they are fundamentally different. However, they appear similar.

FRONTSIDE   BACKSIDE

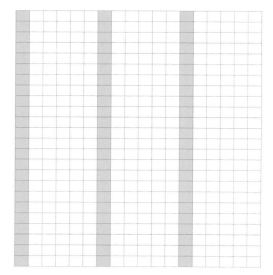
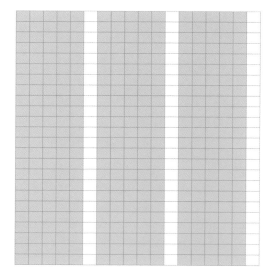

Aesthetic reversibility example

This example is based on [K5, P1] on a multiple of 6 worked in the spiral method. The "backside" is the inside, as this fabric is knit in the round, and looks completely different than the frontside.

SEQUENCE KNITTING AND SCIENCE

It isn't necessary to be familiar with science to enjoy Sequence Knitting, but you may find interesting the relationship between Sequence Knitting and some important scientific concepts. Sequence Knits are created with a short set of rules: repeat a sequence of stitches on a given pattern multiple in a specific way. Depending on the rules, the stitches line up in one way or another. In other words, depending on the rules, the design in the fabric *self-assembles*.

This concept of self-assembly is crucial for Sequence Knitting, and it is also an important phenomenon in nature. For example, molecules line up differently on the surfaces of solids or liquids because the forces at the surface are different than in the bulk material. Proteins and nucleic acids self-assemble in predictable ways depending on their molecular structure and external factors such as the acidity of their environment.

Debbie New, in her book *Unexpected Knitting,* introduced a related concept with Cellular Automaton Knitting where a set of rules leads to prescribed choices about how to modify a stitch pattern as it is worked. She applied the concepts of Cellular Automaton Knitting to both colorwork and textural patterns.

Chaos theory, which looks at the behavior of systems where initial conditions dramatically affect outcomes, is also related to Sequence Knitting. A common example cited in chaos theory is weather prediction, where a butterfly beating its wings in one part of the world can cause a massive storm across the globe. The [K1, P1] example from page 15 demonstrates this effect, as 1 extra stitch makes the difference between 1x1 ribbing and seed stitch: Small changes in the pattern multiple can lead to significant changes in the resulting fabric.

CHAPTER 2

THE 1-ROW METHOD

1-Row Patterns Created with a Single Sequence

WHAT IS THE 1-ROW METHOD?

The 1-row method is just like it sounds — a method where every row is worked the same. Each row consists of the same sequence of stitches worked from the beginning to the end. If the number of stitches in the row is not a multiple of the sequence length, the last sequence in the row will be incomplete. For example, if the sequence [K3, P3] is worked on 6+3, the last 3 stitches of every row will be K3.

Stephanie Pearl-McPhee's One Row Handspun Scarf is a 1-row pattern, and there are many other examples. 1x1 and 2x2 ribbing, seed stitch, and mistake ribbing are all examples of knit fabric that can be created with the 1-row method using just knit and purl stitches. If you go beyond knits and purls, there are many other possible fabrics including the family of lace stitches called faggotting where the 1-row structure creates fabrics with vertical columns of eyelets.

1-row patterns are a pleasure to knit because they are easy to remember and usually easy to "read." All the 1-row fabrics are either perfectly reversible or shift-reversible when knit in 1 color, and many are shift-reversible when knit in 2 colors where the colors are changed every other row.

This chapter focuses on the 1-row fabrics that can be created with knit and purl stitches.

THE STRUCTURE OF 1-ROW FABRICS

If you make a chart of a 1-row knit-purl fabric, you quickly realize that the chart requires precisely 2 rows because there is a frontside row and a backside row which interact to create the pattern. Since each stitch is either a knit or a purl, and the chart is only 2 rows high, each column in the chart is either a knit stitch over a knit stitch, a purl stitch over a purl stitch, a purl stitch over a knit stitch or a knit stitch over a purl stitch. These make columns of knit ribs, purl ribs, knit-garter, and purl garter, respectively. All 1-row knit-purl fabrics are comprised of some mix of these 4 kinds of columns. The fabrics could just have ribs, or just garter, or a mix of both.

The chart at right was shown in Chapter 1. It shows the 1-row accordion fabric created by the sequence [K3, P3] on 6+1 and it nicely illustrates the properties of a 1-row fabric. The first column, on the far right of the chart is knit-garter. The next 2 columns are stockinette, which together create a 2-stitch rib. The fourth column is purl-garter, and columns 5 and 6 are reverse-stockinette and create a rib facing the back of the fabric. The stitch repeat is 6 columns x 2 rows.

Some interesting facts about Sequence Knitting created with the 1-row method are:

- All fabrics are either perfectly reversible or shift-reversible when worked in 1 color.
- If you work a 1-row fabric in 2 colors where the color is changed every 2 rows, the fabric will only be reversible if there are equal numbers of knit-garter and purl-garter stitches.
- All ribbing-only fabrics will be shift-reversible in 2 colors because the number of knit-garter and purl-garter columns is zero.
- Ribs always come in knit-purl pairs. To be reversi-

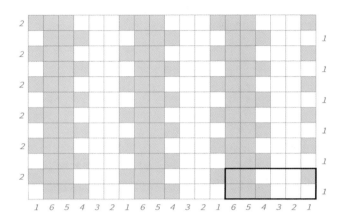

Illustration of 1-row fabric structure

[K3, P3] on a multiple of 6+1.

ble, a knit rib on the frontside must have an opposing purl rib that looks like a knit-rib when viewed from the backside. Mock ribbing is not possible with a 1-row fabric because it requires a knit-rib on the frontside, but no corresponding purl-rib on the backside.

- The stitch repeat is always the same as the sequence length and the row repeat is always 2 for 1-color fabrics and 4 for 2-color fabrics.

1-ROW FABRIC CLASSES

Classes are fabrics with common qualities or traits. With 1-row Sequence Knitting, using only knit and purl stitches, columns of ribs and garter can be combined to create 5 classes of fabrics: ribbing, garter/broken garter, mistake ribbing, accordions, and pleats.

Ribbing

Ribbing is fabric that only contains ribs.

Garter / Broken garter

Garter/Broken garter is a fundamental class of fabrics. Garter stitch is the simplest example, which can be created by either knitting or purling every stitch. In broken garter there is a mix of knit-garter and purl-garter. The most common form of broken garter is seed stitch, which could also be called 1x1 broken garter, and is comprised of alternating single columns of knit garter and purl garter. You will see a lot of examples of broken garter in this chapter. Unlike ribbing, the columns of knit and purl garter do not have to come in even pairs.

Mistake ribbing

Mistake ribbing in this book is defined as a fabric consisting of adjacent knit/purl rib pairs separated by any combination of garter columns. These fabrics have the properties of ribbing in that they look like ribbing, they lay flat, and they are stretchy, albeit less stretchy than pure ribbing. There are fabrics commonly called "mistake ribbing" where the pattern is just 1 stitch off what would be ribbing, but the resulting fabric is actually an accordion.

Accordion

An accordion is a fabric where knit and purl rib columns are separated by garter columns. This separation gives the fabrics an accordion-like shape that is much more three dimensional than mistake ribbing.

Box pleat

Finally, box pleats are like accordions, but rather than the ribs going knit-purl, knit-purl, they go knit-knit, purl-purl. This makes the box pleats fabrics even more three dimensional than an accordion.

We'll explore these concepts more on the following pages.

THE 5 CLASSES OF 1-ROW FABRICS

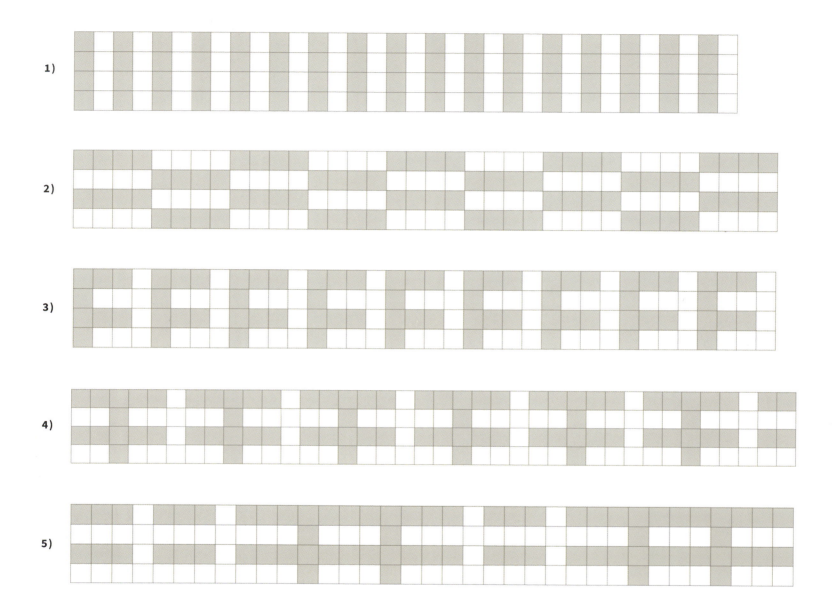

Charts showing the 5 classes of 1-row fabrics:
1. Ribbing ([K1, P1] on 2)
2. Broken garter ([K4, P4] on 8+4)
3. Mistake ribbing ([K3, P1] on 4)
4. Accordion ([K5, P1] on 6+2)
5. Box pleat ([K3, P1, K3, P1, K8] on 16+3)

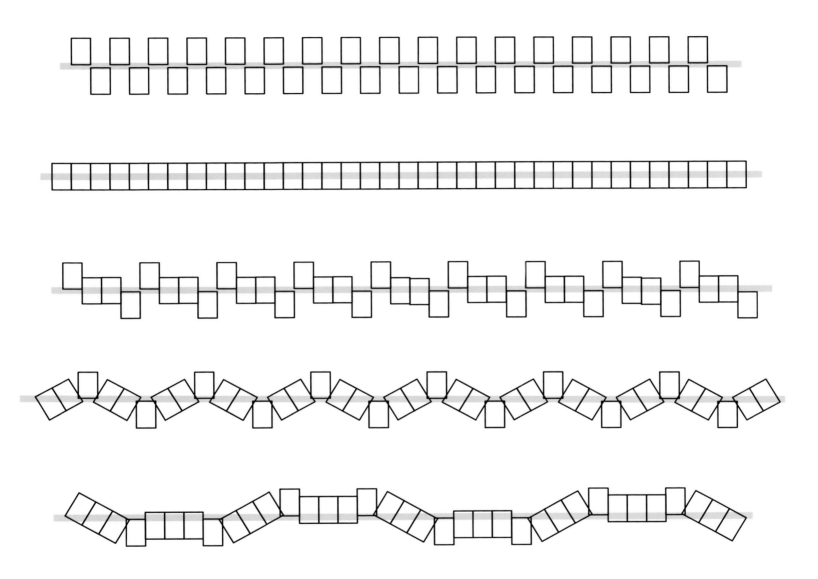

Diagrams corresponding to the facing page showing the 3D shape of a fabric as if you were looking down from its top edge. Each box indicates a column of stitches, so a box below the gray line is a rib protruding forward, a box centered on the line is either knit- or purl-garter, and a box above the line is a rib receding from the frontside of the fabric. In ribbing all the columns either protrude or recede from the center plane, in broken garter they lay close to the center plane, and mistake ribbing is a mix. Accordions and pleats are more three dimensional.

RIBBING AND MISTAKE RIBBING

Ribbing is already simple and familiar to most knitters, and it is not necessary to use Sequence Knitting to create it. But understanding ribbings is still important in the context of understanding the 1-row method.

Ribbing can only be achieved in a 1-row patttern when the sequence length is an even number of stitches, because every knit stitch needs to be mated with a purl stitch on the next row and vice versa. A sequence with a odd number of stitches like [K2, P1] cannot satisfy this requirement.

All 1-row ribbings are perfectly reversible. When viewed from the frontside or backside, one edge is a knit rib column and the other edge is a purl rib column.

The symmetric ribbings such as 1x1, 2x2 and 3x3 are worked by casting on a pattern multiple equal to the sequence length and working the sequence. Asymmetric ribbings can also be created, per the table on the facing page. In the asymmetric ribbings the order of the knit and purl columns can vary.

Mistake ribbing is much more interesting. Mistake ribbing is a fabric comprised of adjacent columns of knit/purl rib pairs separated by garter or broken garter columns. The swatch on the right is the simplest mistake ribbing, a 1x1 rib pair followed by a column of knit-garter. This fabric is created by working the sequence [K2, P1] on a multiple of 3+1.

The table on the facing page shows how to create some of the simpler mistake ribbings: pairs of single or double ribs with either knit-garter or alternating knit- and purl-

[K2, P1] on 3+1

garter spacers. The fabrics with alternating knit- and purl-garter columns will be shift-reversible when worked with 2 colors, while those with only knit-garter (or only purl-garter) will be aesthetically reversible.

Both ribbing and mistake ribbing have more horizontal stretch than vertical. Mistake ribbing has less stretch than ribbing and is wider and shorter than ribbing worked over the same number of stitches. Mistake ribbing is well-behaved; it requires minimal blocking and tends to lie flat.

Ribbing	Rib Width (stitches)	Sequences
Symmetric 1x1	1	[K1,P1] on 2
Symmetric 2x2	2	[K2,P2] on 4
Symmetric 3x3	3	[K3,P3] on 6
Symmetric 4x4	4	[K4,P4] on 8
Asymmetric 2x1	2, 1	[P1,K1,P2,K2] on 6+2 [K1,P1,K2,P2] on 6+2
Asymmetric 2x1x1	2, 1, 1	[2(K1,P1),K2,P2] on 8+4 [2(P1,K1),P2,K2] on 8+4
Asymmetric 3x1	3, 1	[K3,P3,K1,P1] on 8+6 [P3,K3,P1,K1] on 8+6

Mistake Ribbing	Rib Width (stitches)	Spacer Width (stitches)	Sequences
Single rib pairs with single knit-garter spacers	1	1	[K2, P1] on 3 or 3+1
Single rib pairs with double knit-garter spacers	1	2	[K3, P1] on 4 or 4+2
Single rib pairs with single knit- and purl-garter spacers	1	1	[K2, P2, K1, P1] on 6+1 [K2, P1, K1, P2] on 6+3 [K3, P1, K1, P1] on 6
Single rib pairs with double knit- and purl-garter spacers	1	2	[K3, P3, K1, P1] on 8+2
Double rib pairs with single knit-garter spacers	2	1	[K3, P2] on 5 or 5+1
Double rib pairs with double knit-garter spacers	2	2	[K4, P2] on 6 or 6+2

WILDE

Wilde is a 1-row mistake ribbing pattern worked in 2 different colors of fingering-weight yarn. The fabric is comprised of 2x2 ribs separated by 2-stitch columns of knit-or purl-garter, making the pattern shift-reversible. The sample shown is knit with handpainted fingering merino. Color A is navy blue and color B is panel-dyed in yellows and greens. Both solid and variegated fingering weight yarns will work well for this pattern.

Materials and supplies

100 g of fingering yarn in color A

100 g of fingering yarn in color B

Size 3 (3.25 mm) needles

Gauge

7 stitches / inch in stockinette

Dimensions

9 x 70 inches after blocking (23 x 178 cm)

Pattern Notes

1. This pattern has the character of ribbing and will widen after blocking.
2. Even though this is a 1-row pattern, it can be hard to read. To check for mistakes while working, view both sides at a distance and at different angles.

Directions

Cast on 74 stitches (12+2) with A and work 2 rows of the sequence:

[K4, P4, K2, P2], K2.

Change to B and work 2 rows of the sequence. Repeat the last 4 rows, taking care to always bring the new yarn in front of the dropped yarn. When the scarf measures 70 inches (178 cm) or desired length, end with 2 rows of A and bind off with A.

Wash, block, and weave in ends.

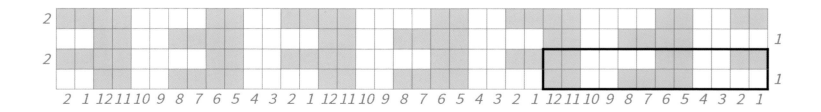

GARTER, BROKEN GARTER AND REVERSIBILITY

The facing page shows 2 columns of charts for the frontsides and backsides of 4 different fabrics:

- Knit garter in 1 color
- Knit garter in 2 colors
- 2x2 broken garter in 1 color
- 2x2 broken garter in 2 colors

Viewing charts for both sides of the fabrics helps to understand their reversibility. This is something to consider when making a scarf, a blanket or a shawl where the backside will be visible.

Look carefully at the top row of knit-garter charts. Garter stitch is usually considered reversible, but the ridges are shifted half a row up from front to back so it can be more precisely described as shift-reversible.

If you change colors while working garter, the backside where the new color is joined looks different from the frontside. And if you change colors every 2 rows, the front and back look completely different, as shown in the charts in the second row. On the left chart, the ridge is always centered between 2 rows of the same color, but on the backside chart, the ridge is always centered between 2 rows of different colors. This means each ridge is a pure color on the frontside, but a blend on the backside.

The charts in the third row show the frontside and backside of symmetric 2x2 broken garter in 1 color. Broken garter takes the frontside and backside of garter and jumbles them together. This is why symmetric broken garter is shift-reversible in 2 colors as illustrated in the fourth row.

Broken garter fabrics are uncommon, especially compared to garter stitch, ribbing and even mistake ribbing. Perhaps this is because they can look plain when worked in a solid color, and they do require purling. But when broken garter is worked in 2 colors it is not only shift-reversible, but also quite striking.

Frontside of 1-color knit-garter

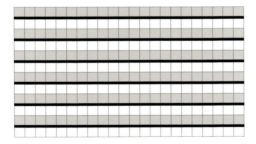

Backside of 1-color knit-garter

Frontside of 2-color knit garter

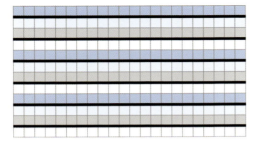

Backside of 2-color knit-garter

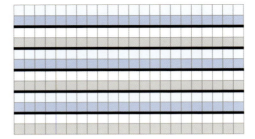

Frontside of 1-color, 2x2 broken garter

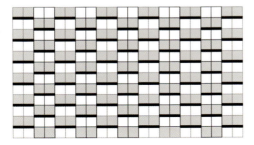

Backside of 1-color, 2x2 broken garter

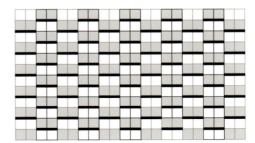

Frontside of 2-color, 2x2 broken garter

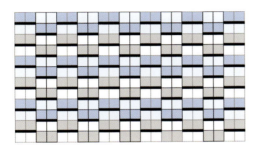

Backside of 2-color, 2x2 broken garter

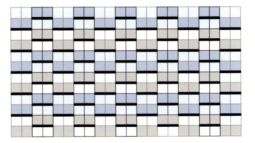

BROKEN GARTER

Broken garter is any fabric where each column of stitches can be described as either knit-garter or purl-garter. Seed stitch, also known as 1x1 broken garter, is the most common example.

The top 2 swatches on the facing page show 3x3 symmetric broken garter in 1 color on the left and 2 colors on the right. Both the 1- and 2-color fabrics are shift-reversible, and both have a similar look and feel to garter stitch. The table at right shows how to create symmetric broken garter using the 1-row method.

The lower 2 swatches show the asymmetric broken garter obtained when the sequence [K2, P1, K1, P1] (also written as [K1, 2(K1, P1)]) is worked as a 1-row pattern on a multiple of 5+2. In this case there are 2-stitch columns of knit garter alternated with a 3-stitch column of seed stitch. This fabric is shift-reversible in 1 color, and aesthetically reversible in 2 colors.

All the broken garter fabrics that can be created for sequences of 6 stitches or fewer with a 1-row pattern are included in the stitch dictionary at the end of this chapter. Many more can be created with sequences longer than 6 stitches.

The patterns on the next few pages feature 2-color symmetric broken garter fabrics.

Column widths	1-row pattern	Pattern multiple
1x1	[K1, P1], K1	2+1
2x2	[K2, P2], K2	4+2
3x3	[K3, P3], K3	6+3
4x4	[K4, P4], K4	8+4
5x5	[K5, P5], K5	10+5
6x6	[K6, P6], K6	12+6
7x7	[K7, P7], K7	14+7
8x8	[K8, P8], K8	16+8
9x9	[K9, P9], K9	18+9
10x10	[K10, P10], K10	20+10
11x11	[K11, P11], K11	22+11
12x12	[K12, P12], K12	24+12

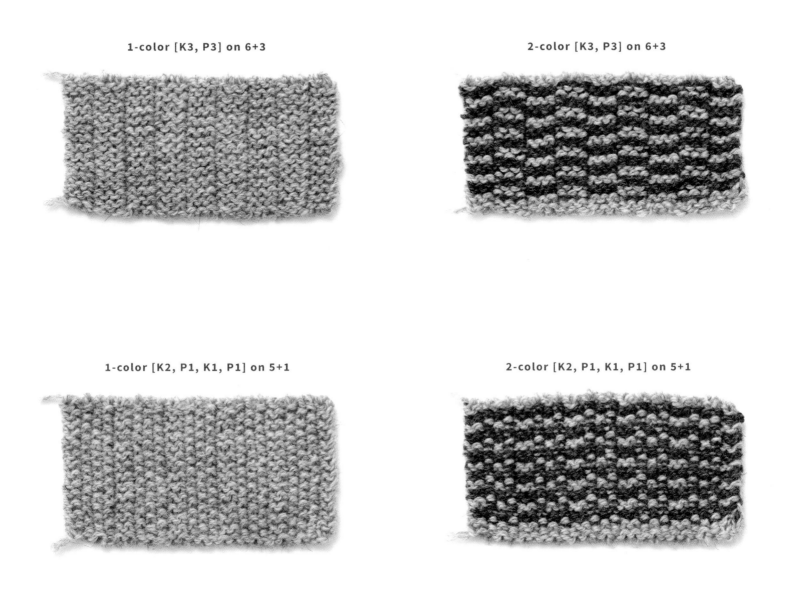

1-color [K3, P3] on 6+3

2-color [K3, P3] on 6+3

1-color [K2, P1, K1, P1] on 5+1

2-color [K2, P1, K1, P1] on 5+1

Examples of how broken garter looks different in 1 and 2 colors

The top 2 swatches are [K3, P3] on 6+3 in 1 color and 2 colors, where the colors are changed every 2 rows. The lower 2 swatches are a more complex form of broken garter created by working the sequence [K2, P1, K1, P1] on 5+1. Broken garter is very subdued in 1 color, but becomes bold in 2 colors.

BROKEN GARTER (BG) SCARVES

This series of scarves illustrates how broken garter looks different as the size of the repeat is varied from 2 to 22 as shown on the facing page from left to right. Samples are in Aslan Trends Royal Alpaca in Andean Coal and Grey. Each scarf is shift-reversible, easy to knit, and appropriate for both men and women.

Materials

200 g dk-weight yarn in color A
200 g dk-weight yarn in color B
Size 5 (3.75 mm) needles

Gauge

5 stitches / inch in stockinette

Dimensions

7.5 x 70 inches (19 x 178 cm)

Pattern notes

1. Always introduce the new color in front of the dropped color at side edge for a neat selvedge.
2. These patterns are easy to adapt to almost any yarn. To change the width, just vary the stitch count by multiples of the sequence length.

Directions

With A, cast on as instructed for each scarf. Following the pattern sequence, work 2 rows in A, then work 2 rows in B. Repeat last 4 rows until scarf measures 70 inches and ends with 2 rows of A. With A, bind off. Wash, block and weave in ends.

BG 1: Cast on 33 stitches (2+1)
Every row: [K1, P1], K1

BG 2: Cast on 34 stitches (4+2)
Every row: [K2, P2], K2

BG 3: Cast on 33 stitches (6+3)
Every row: [K3, P3], K3

BG 5: Cast on 35 stitches (10+5)
Every row: [K5, P5], K5

BG 7: Cast on 35 stitches (14+7)
Every row: [K7, P7], K7

BG 11: Cast on 33 stitches (22+11)
Every row: [K11, P11], K11

KOZAK

Kozak is a warm hat knit firmly in royal alpaca. The brim is folded up twice in the sample, which is worked in Aslan Trends Royal Alpaca in Bone and Chocolate.

Materials

100 g dk-weight yarn in color A

100 g dk-weight yarn in color B

Size 5 (3.75 mm) needles

Size 5 (3.75 mm) double pointed needles, set of 5

Gauge

Approximately 6 stitches / inch in stockinette

Pattern Notes

1. A is the color that will be used for the top of the hat and the accent line in the 3-needle bind-off.

2. When picking up the stitches for the crown, use the slipped stitches every 2 rows.

Directions

Cast on 42 (4+2) stitches with scrap yarn using a provisional cast on.

Setup row with A: [K2, P2], K2

Row 1, with A: Slip 1 as if to purl through the back of the stitch, K1, P2, [K2, P2], K2.

Rows 2 and 3 with B: Repeat row 1.

Row 4 with A: Repeat row 1.

Making sure to bring the new yarn in front when changing colors, repeat rows 1–4 until piece measures 21 inches (53 cm). End with a row 1 in A. Keep live stitches on the needle — do not bind off.

Remove provisional cast on and carefully place stitches on a double-pointed needle. With A, join cast-on edge to final row using a 3-needle bind-off. Do not cut yarn.

With the right side facing, double-pointed needles, and attached A, pick up and knit 1 stitch for every 2 rows along side edge of brim. Join for working in the round. Knit 2 rounds, working decreases if necessary to get an equal number of stitches on each of 4 double-pointed needles.

Decrease round: [K2tog, K to end of needle] 4 times.

Repeat the decrease round until 8 stitches remain. Cut yarn, draw through the remaining stitches, tighten and weave in ends.

Variation

Work the pattern in a solid worsted wool for A and Noro Kureyon for B. Cast on 34 stitches with a size 8 (5 mm) needle, and follow pattern beginning with the setup row.

COLORMILL

Colormill is a scarf or shawl pattern ideal for blending 2 different colored yarns. This simple and shift-reversible pattern is 5x5 broken garter worked lengthwise with 2 colors switched every 2 rows. The sample shown is the shawl version made with Rohrspatz & Wollmeise in Pistachio (color A) and my own hand-dyed yarn (color B). This pattern is suitable for any 2 solid or variegated yarns.

Go to page 352 to see the prototype for this piece and page 345 for variations with merino and silk mohair. The numbers in parentheses are for the scarf version.

Materials for the shawl (scarf)

150 (100) g fingering weight yarn in color A
150 (100) g fingering weight yarn in color B
Size 3 (3.25 mm) 60 inch (150 cm) circular needles

Gauge

6 stitches / inch in stockinette

Dimensions

11.5 x 70 inches (29 x 178 cm) for shawl
7 x 70 inches (18 x 178 cm) for scarf

Pattern Note

The only tricky aspect of this pattern is the long cast-on. If doing a long cast-on with even tension is a concern, use a provisional cast on (see page 364).

Directions

Cast on 405 stitches (multiple of 10+5) in color A. Work 2 rows in color A according to the pattern as follows:

[K5, P5], K5

Change to color B and work 2 rows. Continue in the sequence alternating A and B every 2 rows, always bringing the new yarn in front of the working yarn and taking care with tension, until piece measures 11-14 inches (28-36 cm) for a shawl or 7-8 inches (18-20 cm) for a scarf.

With A, bind off. Wash, block and weave in ends.

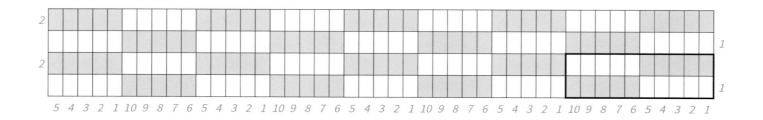

ACCORDIONS

Accordions are great fun to knit and to wear. They have a three dimensional quality that looks rich and luxurious, much like a brioche or fisherman's rib. The separation of the knit- and purl-rib columns shapes the fabric into furrows. The spring of the accordion can be made even stronger by using slip stitches instead of traditional knit-purl ribs.

The ribs of the accordion can be single, double, triple, or a mix, and the spaces can be narrow or wide, simple or complex. The most common accordion is often referred to as mistake ribbing. It is 1 stitch off 2x2 ribbing and can be created by working [K2, P2] on a multiple of 4 +/-1.

The table below shows the simplest 1-row patterns for accordions. All of these fabrics are shift-reversible in 1 color. In 2 colors, only the patterns that have an equal mix of knit- and purl-garter will be shift reversible, as illustrated on the facing page. The top 2 images show [K2, P2] on 4+1, which is shift-reversible in 2 colors. The bottom row shows [K3, P1] on 4+2, which is aesthetically reversible in 2 colors.

Turn the page to see a pattern for Derain, a scarf based on a fancy accordion where the spacers are seed stitch.

Accordion Type	Rib Width (stitches)	Spacer Width (stitches)	Sequence	Pattern multiples
Single ribs with knit-garter spacers	1	1	[K3, P1]	4+1
Single ribs with alternating knit- and purl-garter spacers	1	1	[K2, P2]	4+1, 4+3
Double ribs with single knit-garter spacers	2	1	[K4, P2]	6+1
Double ribs with alternating knit- and purl-garter spacers	2	1	[K3, P3]	6+1, 6+5
Single ribs with knit-garter spacers	1	2	[K5, P1]	6+2, 6+4
Single ribs with alternating knit- and purl-garter spacers	1	2	[K3, P3]	6+2
Single ribs with knit-garter spacers	1	3	[K7, P1]	8+3
Single ribs with alternating knit- and purl-garter spacers	1	3	[K4, P4]	8+3, 8+5
Double ribs with knit-garter spacers	2	2	[K6, P2]	8+2
Double ribs with alternating knit- and purl-garter spacers	2	2	[K4, P4]	8+2, 8+6
Triple ribs with knit-garter spacers	3	1	[K5, P3]	8+1
Triple ribs with alternating knit- and purl-garter spacers	3	1	[K4, P4]	8+1, 8+7

Frontside of [K2, P2] on 4+1

Backside of [K2, P2] on 4+1

Frontside of [K3, P1] on 4+1

Backside of [K3, P1] on 4+1

An example of reversibility in 2-color accordion fabrics
In the top row the accordion fabric has an even mix of knit- and purl-garter spacers and is shift reversible in 2 colors, while in the bottom row all the spacers are knit garter so the fabric is aesthetically reversible.

DERAIN

Derain is a 1-row accordion where the panels between the ribs are in seed stitch. The example shown is knit in a variegated cashmere from Koigu for String Yarns, color C458 2.

Materials

200 g sport weight cashmere

Size 4 (3.5 mm) needles

Gauge

6.5 stitches / inch in stockinette

Dimensions

9.5 x 70 inches (24 x 178 cm)

Pattern notes

1. A provisional cast on is recommended. This provides a couple of benefits. It ensures that the gauge at the edge is the same as the gauge of the fabric, which is important because cashmere is less springy than wool. It also allows both edges to be "cast off" so they will look the same.
2. This pattern is shift-reversible in 2 colors and would be well suited to combining 2 different solid or variegated yarns.

Stitch glossary

S1WYIF is to slip 1 stitch purlwise with the yarn in front. This is denoted S in the chart.

Directions

Cast on 53 (12+5) stitches with scrap yarn using a provisional cast on. Make a butterfly with enough working yarn to cast off the 53 stitches later. Work the setup row as follows:

Setup row: [3(K1, P1), 3(P1, K1)], 2(K1, P1), K1

Pattern row: [3(K1, P1), 3(P1, K1)], 2(K1, P1), S1WYIF

Repeat pattern row until the piece measures 70 inches (178 cm) and bind off. Remove the provisional cast on and bind off using the butterfly of yarn.

Gently wash, block and weave in ends.

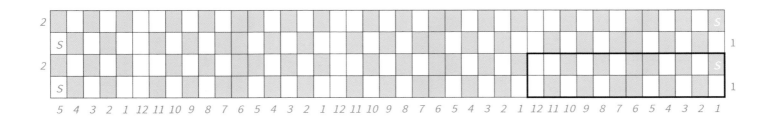

BOX PLEATS

As sequence lengths increase, box pleats are another fabric type that can be created with the 1-row method. Box pleats have the characteristic of knit-rib, spacer, knit-rib, spacer, purl-rib, spacer, purl-rib, spacer.

The smallest box pleat requires a sequence at least 8 stitches to fit 4 ribs and 4 spacers. The table on the facing page gives the patterns for box pleats with varying rib and spacer widths.

Like all 1-row fabrics these are shift-reversible in 1 color. In 2 colors the fabrics with an equal mix of knit- and purl-garter will be shift reversible, and those with just knit-garter will be aesthetically reversible.

Turn the page to see the Nebraska Winter Shawl, which is based on a shift-reversible box pleat.

Box Pleat Type	Rib Width (stitches)	Spacer Width (stitches)	Sequence	Pattern multiple
Single ribs with knit-garter spacers	1	1	[K5, P1, K1, P1]	8+1
Single ribs with alternating knit- and purl-garter spacers	1	1	[K2, P1, K2, P3]	8+1
Double ribs with single knit-garter spacers	2	1	[K7, P2, K1, P2]	12+1
Double ribs with alternating knit- and purl-garter spacers	2	1	[K3, P1, K3, P5]	12+1
Single ribs with knit-garter spacers	1	2	[K8, P1, K2, P1]	12+2
Single ribs with alternating knit- and purl-garter spacers	1	2	[K3, P2, K3, P4]	12+2
Single ribs with knit-garter spacers	1	3	[K11, P1, K3, P1]	16+3
Single ribs with alternating knit- and purl-garter spacers	1	3	[K4, P3, K4, P5]	16+3
Double ribs with knit-garter spacers	2	2	[K10, P2, K2, P2]	16+2
Double ribs with alternating knit- and purl-garter spacers	2	2	[K4, P2, K4, P6]	16+2
Triple ribs with knit-garter spacers	3	1	[K9, P3, K1, P3]	16+1
Triple ribs with alternating knit- and purl-garter spacers	3	1	[K4, P1, K4, P7]	16+1

NEBRASKA WINTER

The fabric of this warm shawl is a box pleat pattern and it has a subtle drape following the lines of the pleats. The sample is worked in Lisa Souza BFL in Mahogany and Mountain Colors Mountain Goat in Bitterroot Rainbow.

Materials and supplies

200 g worsted weight yarn in color A

200 g worsted weight yarn in color B

Size 6 (4 mm) needles

Gauge

5 stitches / inch in pattern

Dimensions

13 x 63 inches (33 x 160 cm)

Pattern note

Block gently to avoid flattening out the pleats.

Stitch glossary

S1WYIB is to slip 1 stitch purlwise with the yarn in back, denoted S in the chart.

Directions

Cast on 67 stitches (multiple of 16+3) in color A and work the setup row and row 2:

Setup row: [K4, P3, K4, P5], K3

Row 2: [K3, S1WYIB, P3, S1WYIB, K3, P5], K3

Change to color B and repeat Row 2 twice. Continue working row 2, changing colors every 2 rows, and taking care to always bring the new color from the front. When shawl is 70 inches long, end on 2 rows of color A.

Bind off with A. Wash, block and weave in ends.

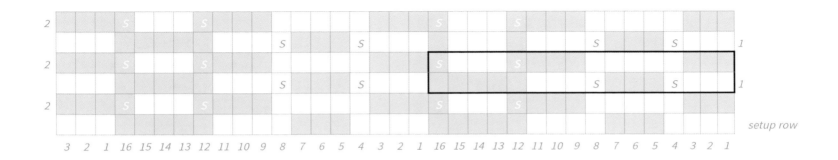

SELVEDGES IN 1-ROW KNITTING

Depending on the permutation and the pattern multiple of a 1-row fabric, both the bulk fabric and the selvedge will vary. The facing page shows all the 1-row charts for the sequence [K3, P3], including all the permutations and all the pattern multiples. The left column of charts contains 4 unique fabric types that can be achieved with the sequence [K3, P3]: 3x3 ribbing; an accordion with ribs that are 2 stitches wide separated by single columns of garter; an accordion with ribs 1 stitch wide separated by double columns of garter; and 3x3 broken garter. The 3x3 ribbing examples are highlighted with boxes around the charts to show how this fabric type can be created with any of the permutations, although the pattern multiples and the selvedges will be different. The selvedges can be 1-, 2- or 3-stitch ribs.

I dislike the edges of my knitting curling unless I am intentionally creating a rolled edge. Even with blocking it is very difficult to get stockinette stitch to lie flat. All of the 3x3 ribbing examples on the opposite page will curl at the side edges, because each rib is a little column of stockinette. A good solution is to add a garter selvedge. The charts on this page show how the 3x3 ribbing pattern changes as the garter selvedge goes from 1 to 3 stitches wide. Add the selvedge stitches at the beginning and end of each row and increase the pattern multiple accordingly.

The selvedges of non-ribbing fabrics are easier to handle than ribbing because they all contain columns of garter, and the permutation and pattern multiple of the 1-row pattern can be chosen so the columns of garter stitch are the selvedges. For example, if I want to knit an accordion with single ribs I can choose [K3, P3] on 6+2 and get a 2-stitch garter selvedge, rather than working the same sequence on 6+4, which results in single ribs at each edge. With some planning, the desired selvedge can be created for all 1-row patterns.

[K3, P3] on 6

K1, [K3, P3], K1 on 6+2

K2, [K3, P3], K2 on 6+4

K3, [K3, P3], K3 on 6

Adding selvedges

From top to bottom, the 1-row 3x3 ribbing pattern with no selvedge, 1-, 2- and 3-stitch knit-garter selvedges added.

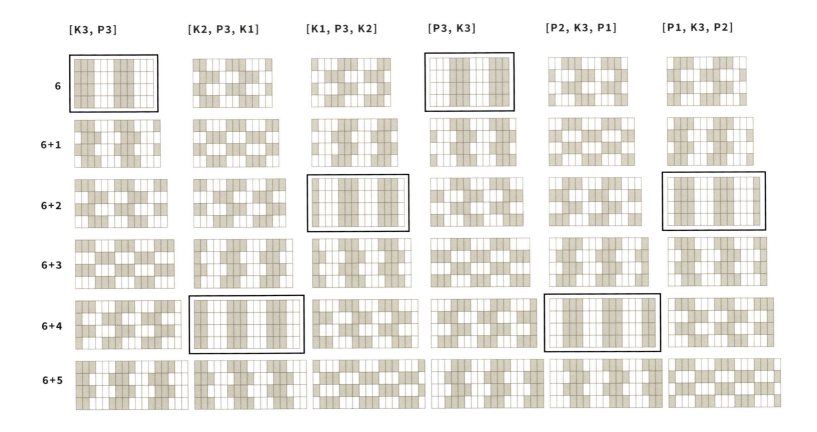

Effect of permutations on selvedges

This is a grid of charts for the sequence [K3, P3] for all permutations and pattern multiples. Note how each column has the same six fabrics, but the selvedges are different depending on the permutation and the pattern multiple. The 3x3 ribbings are highlighted with black boxes to make it easier to see how their selvedges vary. All the other fabrics have similarly varying selvedges.

FABRIC TYPES AND IRREGULAR FABRICS

The charts on the facing page show the 3 classes of 1-row fabrics that can be created with the sequence [K5, P1] worked on the multiples 6 through 6+5. The classes from top to bottom are:

- Mistake ribbing
- Accordion
- Accordion
- Accordion
- Mistake ribbing
- Broken garter

So there are 3 classes in all.

The 2 mistake ribbings are both 1x1 rib pairs separated by 3-stitch columns of knit garter, but the order of the stitches is different. The fabrics will be mirror images of each other. These fabrics are the same type, but different actual fabrics.

The third fabric is a symmetric accordion with single rib columns separated by 2-stitch columns of knit garter. There is no other fabric like this one in the set, so it is its own type. The same is true of the last fabric, a broken garter with 1-stitch columns of purl garter and 5-stitch columns of knit garter.

The second and forth charts are both accordions, and like the mistake ribbings, they are mirror images of each other. These are a third type.

Thus the sequence [K5, P1] can be used to create 6 unique fabrics in 4 distinct fabric types, that fall into 3 pattern classes.

The accordions in the second and fourth charts have another interesting property: they are irregular. The spacing between the ribs varies between 1 and 3. There are many possible irregular fabrics that can be created with the 1-row method. These have not been included in this book, but one could imagine using them for the two fronts of a cardigan for an interesting effect.

Another extension of the 1-row method that is beyond the scope of this book is the discussion of composite fabrics. As sequence lengths grow longer it is possible to get fabrics that can be classified as both a mistake ribbing and an accordion.

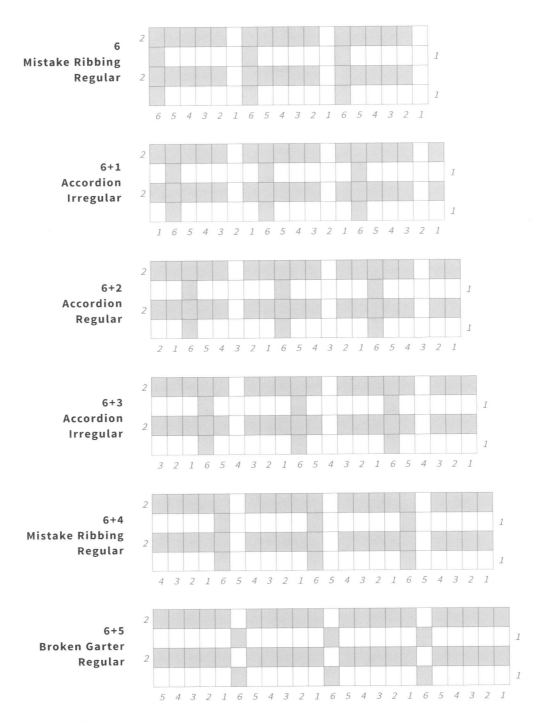

[K5, P1] on the multiples 6 through 6+5

These charts show the 1-row fabrics from the sequence [K5, P1] worked on 6 through 6+5. There are 4 fabric types: the first and fifth, the second and fourth, the third and the last. The second and forth are irregular because the spacers between the ribs are different widths.

1-ROW STITCH DICTIONARY

All the regular 1-row fabric types for sequence lengths 1–6 are given here, 36 fabrics in total. Each entry in the stitch dictionary contains the following:

- The sequence and the pattern multiple. If a permutation is used for the swatch, the more fundamental sequence is given in parentheses. For example, if the swatch uses the sequence [P1, K2, P1], the more fundamental sequence is [K2, P2].
- A comment on the reversibility of the fabrics.
- The frontsides (left column) and backsides (right column) of 1 and 2 color swatches. In the 2-color swatches, the colors change every 2 rows.
- A chart of the frontside of the fabric.

One example of each fabric type is given, and that example has a specific selvedge. If desired, the selvedge can be changed in two ways (see also page 55):

- By adding stitches to each side
- By changing both the pattern multiple and the permutation

In the latter case, making a chart is helpful to work out the different possibilities.

All the swatches in the stitch dictionaries in Chapters 2–5 are worked in Cascade 220 sport with size 4 (3.5 mm) needles. All cast-ons are Hiatt's Stranded Cast-On (The Principles of Knitting, second edition, page 55) to avoid distorting the shape of the swatches. After the swatch is complete, the equivalent cast off is to pull the working yarn through the live stitches to secure them.

1-ROW STITCH PATTERNS FOR SEQUENCE LENGTHS 1–6

Sequence Length (n)	Pattern multiple	Specific sequence	Fundamental sequence	Class	1-color reversibility	2-color reversibility
1	1	K1	K1	Garter	Shift	Aesthetically
2	2	K1, P1	K1, P1	Ribbing	Perfectly	Perfectly
2	2+1	K1, P1	K1, P1	Broken Garter	Shift	Shift
3	3+1	K2, P1	K2, P1	Mistake Ribbing	Shift	Aesthetically
3	3+2	K2, P1	K2, P1	Broken Garter	Shift	Aesthetically
4	4+1	K3, P1	K3, P1	Accordian	Shift	Aesthetically
4	4+2	K3, P1	K3, P1	Mistake Ribbing	Shift	Aesthetically
4	4+3	K3, P1	K3, P1	Broken Garter	Shift	Aesthetically
4	4	K2, P2	K2, P2	Ribbing	Perfectly	Perfectly
4	4+1	K2, P2	K2, P2	Accordian	Shift	Shift-flip
4	4+2	K2, P2	K2, P2	Broken Garter	Shift	Shift
5	5+3	K4, P1	K4, P1	Mistake Ribbing	Shift	Aesthetically
5	5+4	K4, P1	K4, P1	Broken Garter	Shift	Aesthetically
5	5+1	K3, P2	K3, P2	Mistake Ribbing	Shift	Aesthetically
5	5+3	K3, P2	K3, P2	Broken Garter	Shift	Aesthetically
5	5+1	K2, P1, K1, P1	K2, P1, K1, P1	Mistake Ribbing	Shift	Aesthetically
5	5+2	K2, P1, K1, P1	K2, P1, K1, P1	Broken Garter	Shift	Aesthetically
5	5+3	2(K1, P1), K1	K2, P1, K1, P1	Mistake Ribbing	Shift	Aesthetically
6	6	K3, P1, K2	K5, P1	Mistake Ribbing	Shift	Aesthetically
6	6+1	K3, P, K2	K5, P1	Broken Garter	Shift	Aesthetically
6	6+2	K2, P1, K3	K5, P1	Accordion	Shift	Aesthetically
6	6	K4, P2	K4, P2	Mistake Ribbing	Shift	Aesthetically
6	6	K2, P2, K2	K4, P2	Broken Garter	Shift	Aesthetically
6	6+1	K4, P2	K4, P2	Accordian	Shift	Aesthetically
6	6	K3, P3	K3, P3	Ribbing	Perfectly	Perfectly
6	6+1	K3, P3	K3, P3	Accordian	Shift	Aesthetically
6	6+2	K3, P3	K3, P3	Accordian	Shift	Shift-flip
6	6+3	K3, P3	K3, P3	Broken Garter	Shift	Shift
6	6	K3, P1, K1, P1	K3, P1, K1, P1	Mistake Ribbing	Shift	Aesthetically
6	6	K2, 2(P1, K1)	K3, P1, K1, P1	Mistake Ribbing	Shift	Aesthetically
6	6+1	K2, 2(P1, K1)	K3, P1, K1, P1	Broken Garter	Shift	Aesthetically
6	6	K1, P1, 2(P1, K1)	K2, P2, K1, P1	Mistake Ribbing	Shift	Aesthetically
6	6+1	K2, P2, K1, P1	K2, P2, K1, P1	Mistake Ribbing	Shift	Shift
6	6	2(K1, P1), P1, K1	K2, P1, K1, P2	Mistake Ribbing	Shift	Aesthetically
6	6+1	2(K1, P1), P1, K1	K2, P1, K1, P2	Mistake Ribbing	Shift	Shift
6	6+2	P1, K1, P2, K2	K2, P1, K1, P2	Ribbing	Perfectly	Perfectly

1-ROW: GARTER
[K1] ON ANY NUMBER OF STITCHES

Shift Reversible in 1 color, Aesthetically Reversible in 2 colors

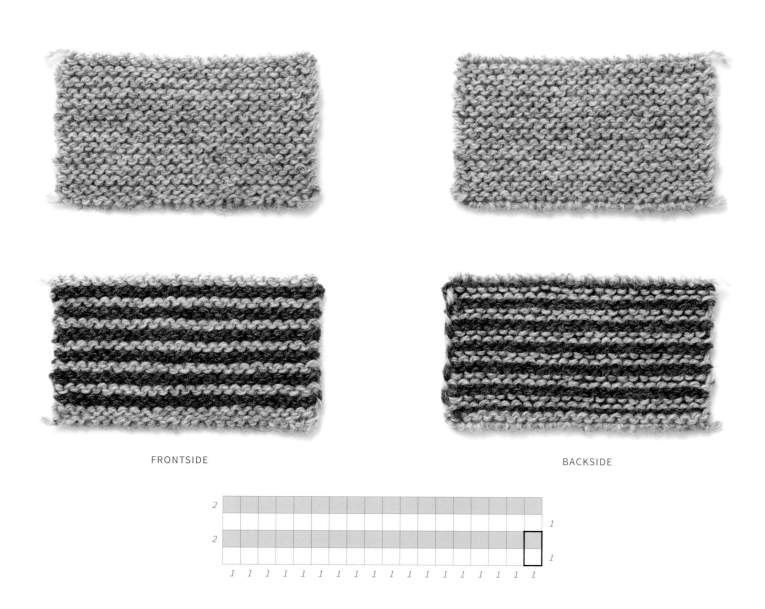

FRONTSIDE

BACKSIDE

1-ROW: RIBBING
[K1, P1] ON 2

Perfectly reversible in 1 and 2 colors

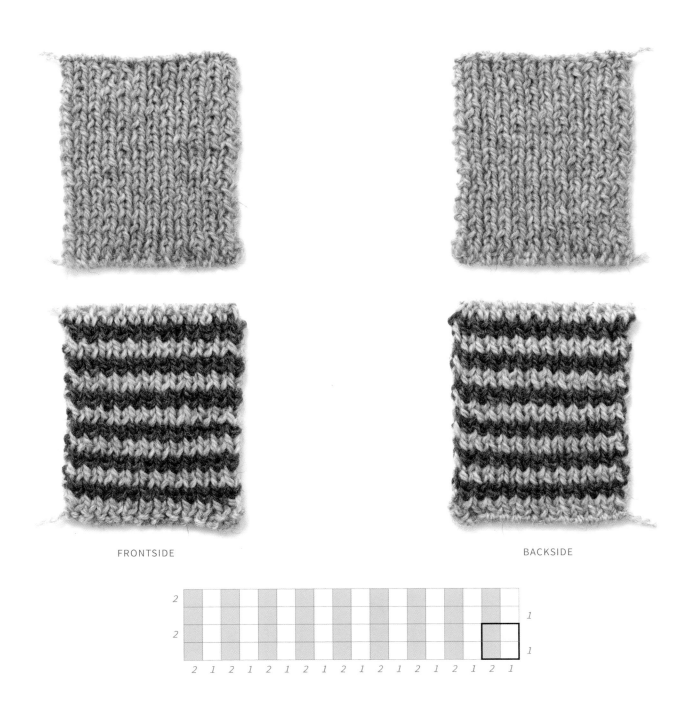

FRONTSIDE

BACKSIDE

1-ROW: BROKEN GARTER (SEED STITCH)
[K1, P1] ON 2+1

Shift Reversible in 1 and 2 colors

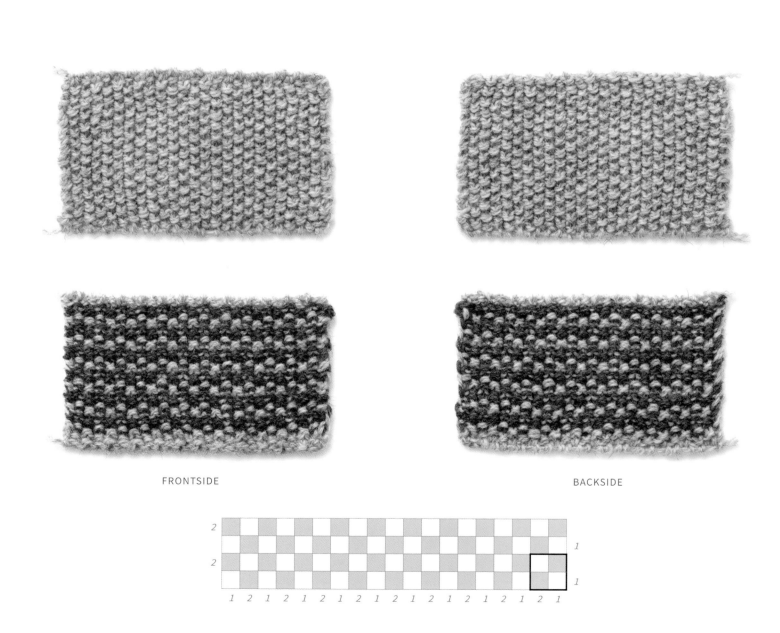

FRONTSIDE BACKSIDE

1-ROW: MISTAKE RIBBING
[K2, P1] ON 3+1

Shift Reversible in 1 color, Aesthetically Reversible in 2 colors

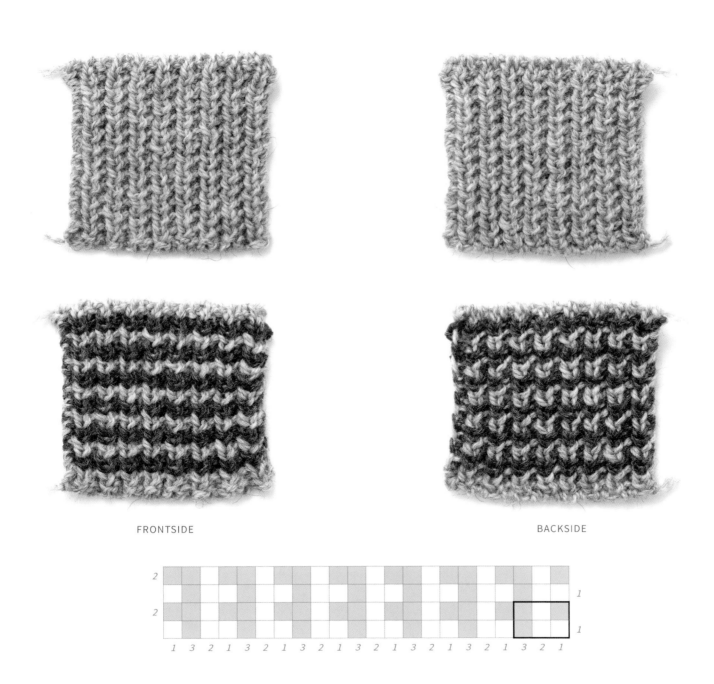

FRONTSIDE   BACKSIDE

1-ROW: BROKEN GARTER
[K2, P1] ON 3+2

Shift Reversible in 1 color, Aesthetically Reversible in 2 colors

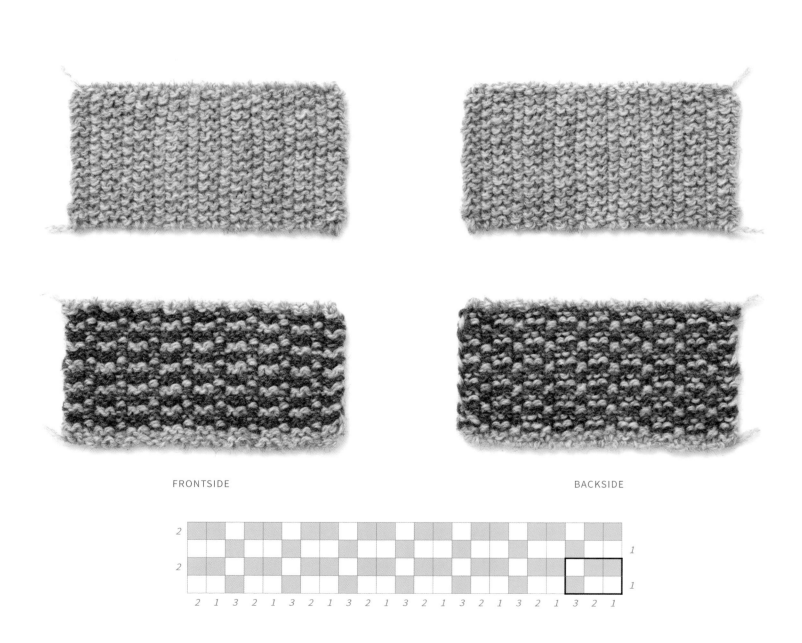

FRONTSIDE   BACKSIDE

1-ROW: ACCORDION
[K3, P1] ON 4+1

Shift Reversible in 1 color, Aesthetically Reversible in 2 colors

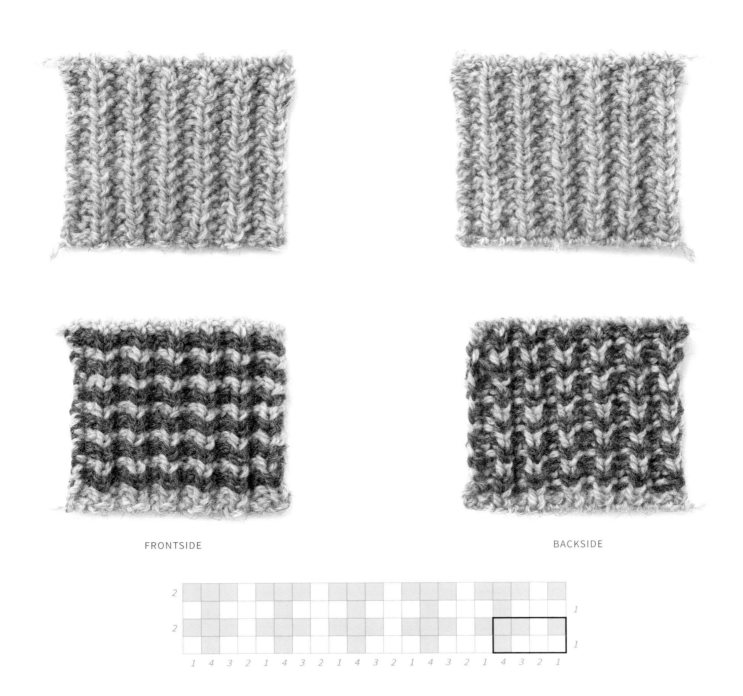

FRONTSIDE

BACKSIDE

1-ROW: MISTAKE RIBBING
[K3, P1] ON 4+2

Shift Reversible in 1 color, Aesthetically Reversible in 2 colors

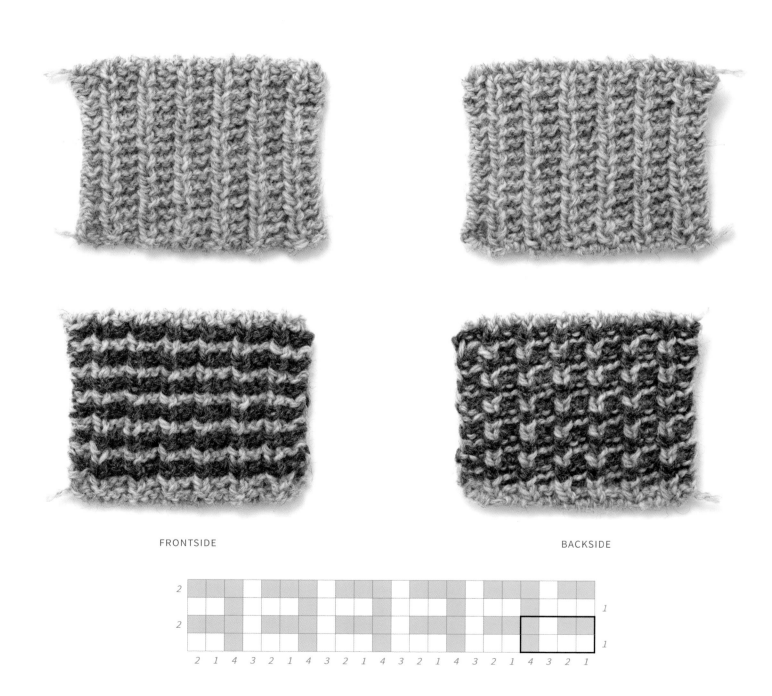

FRONTSIDE   BACKSIDE

1-ROW: BROKEN GARTER
[K3, P1] ON 4+3

Shift Reversible in 1 color, Aesthetically Reversible in 2 colors

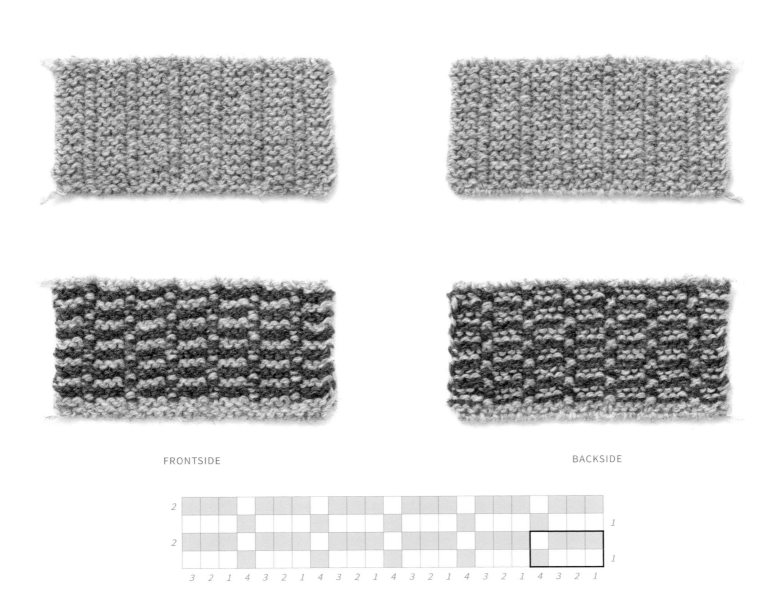

FRONTSIDE   BACKSIDE

1-ROW: RIBBING [K2, P2] ON 4

Perfectly Reversible in 1 and 2 colors

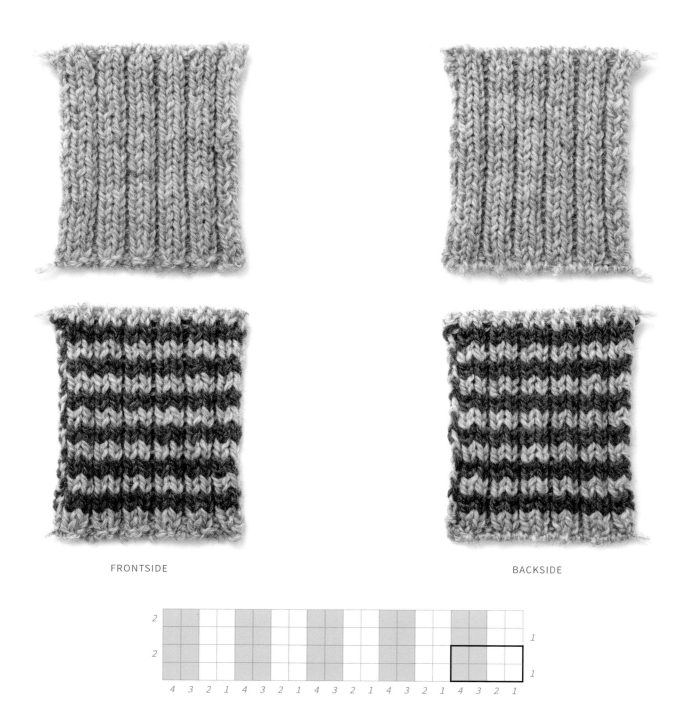

FRONTSIDE

BACKSIDE

1-ROW: ACCORDION
[K2, P2] ON 4+1

Shift Reversible in 1 color and Shift-flip Reversible in 2 colors

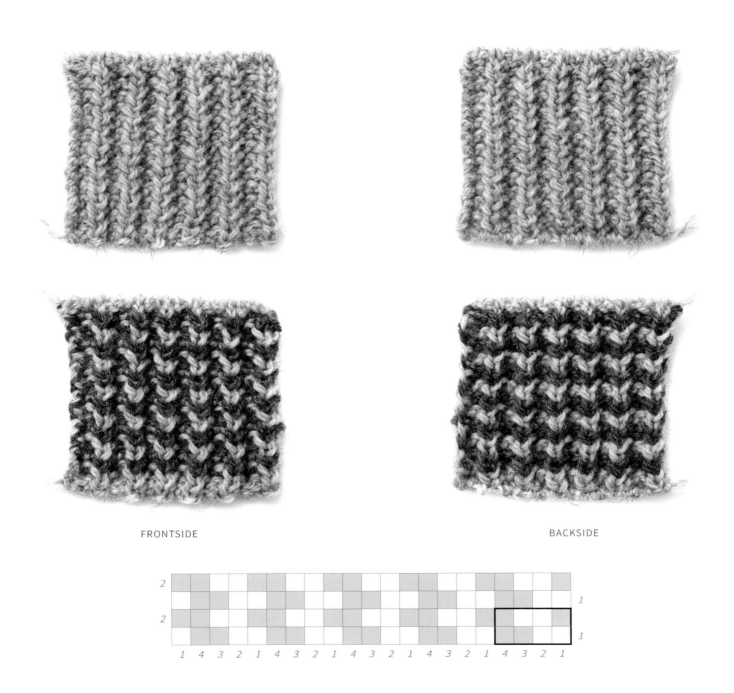

FRONTSIDE

BACKSIDE

PAGE 69

1-ROW: BROKEN GARTER
[K2, P2] ON 4+2

Shift Reversible in 1 and 2 colors

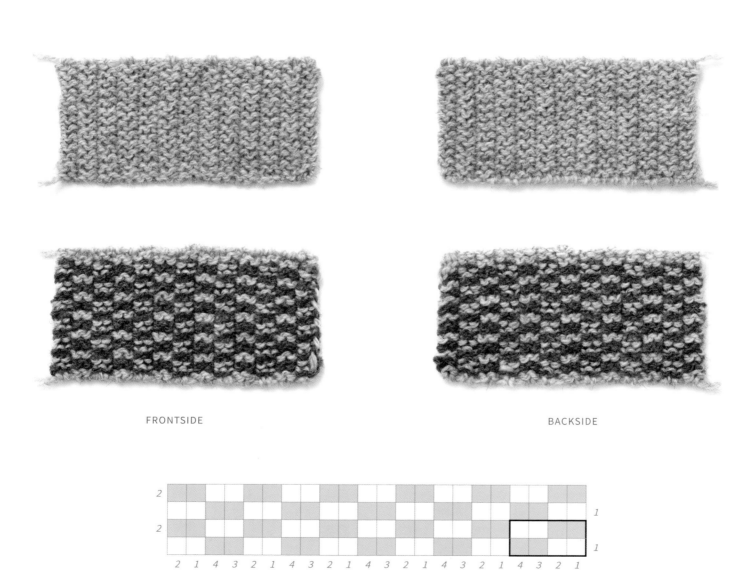

FRONTSIDE　　　　　　　　　　BACKSIDE

1-ROW: MISTAKE RIBBING
[K4, P1] ON 5+3

Shift Reversible in 1 color, Aesthetically Reversible in 2 colors

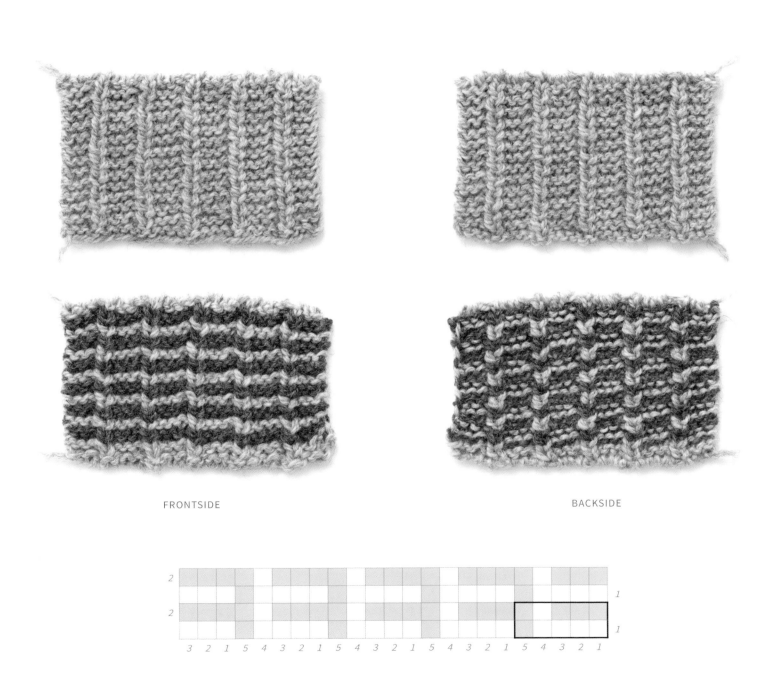

FRONTSIDE

BACKSIDE

1-ROW: BROKEN GARTER
[K4, P1] ON 5+4

Shift Reversible in 1 color, Aesthetically Reversible in 2 colors

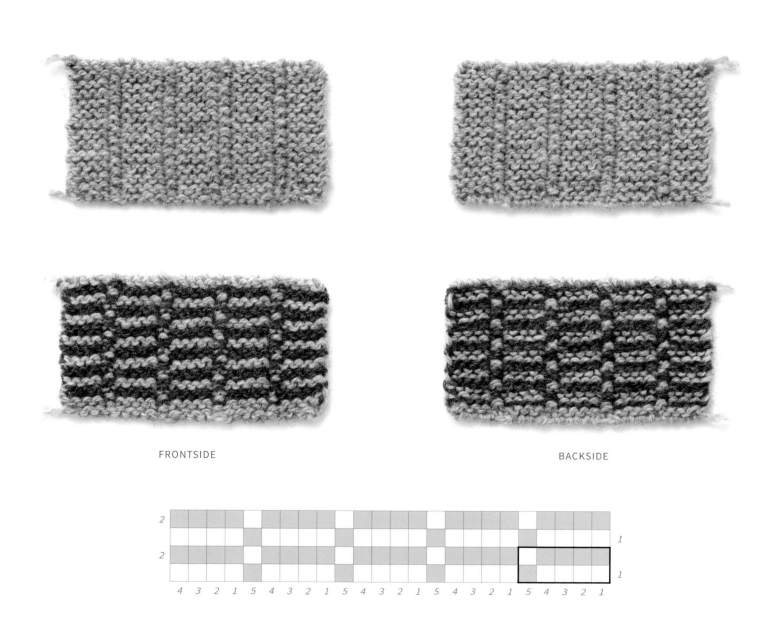

FRONTSIDE　　　　　　　　　　　　BACKSIDE

1-ROW: MISTAKE RIBBING
[K3, P2] ON 5+1

Shift Reversible in 1 color, Aesthetically Reversible in 2 colors

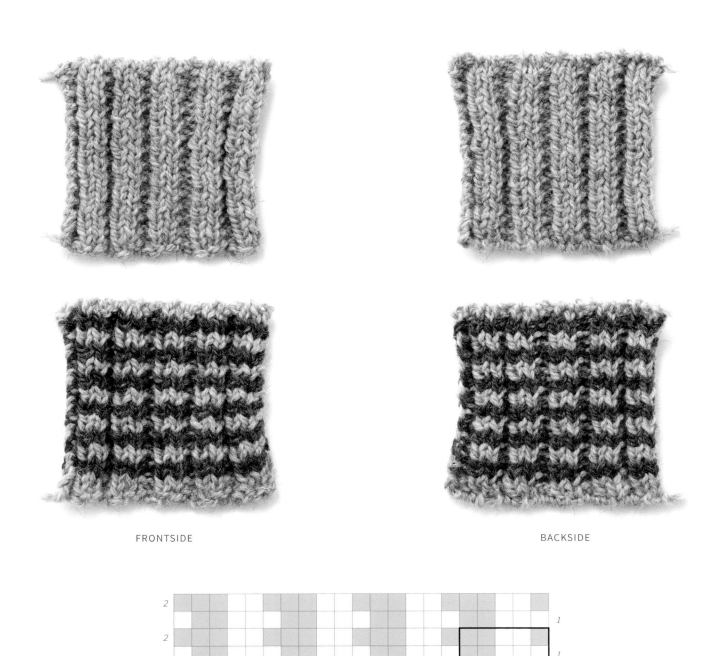

FRONTSIDE   BACKSIDE

1-ROW: BROKEN GARTER
[K3, P2] ON 5+3

Shift Reversible in 1 color, Aesthetically Reversible in 2 colors

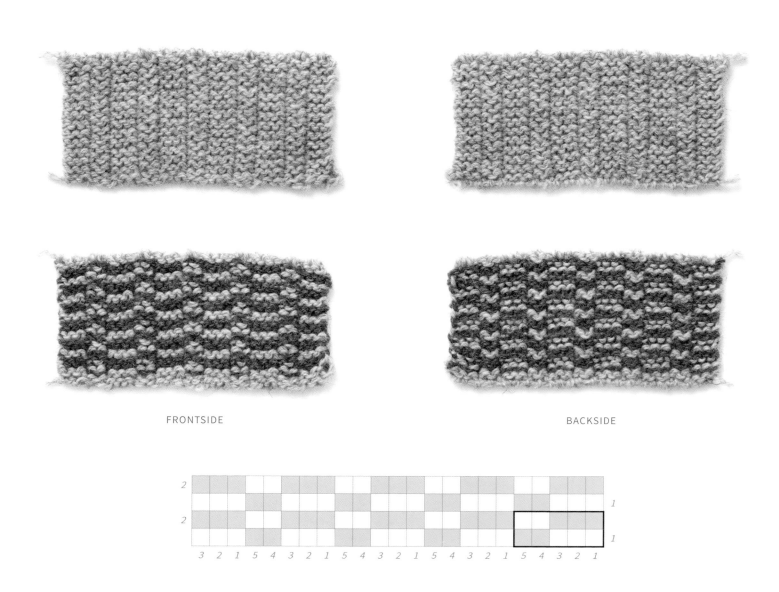

FRONTSIDE

BACKSIDE

1-ROW: MISTAKE RIBBING
[K2, P1, K1, P1] ON 5+1

Shift Reversible in 1 color, Aesthetically Reversible in 2 colors

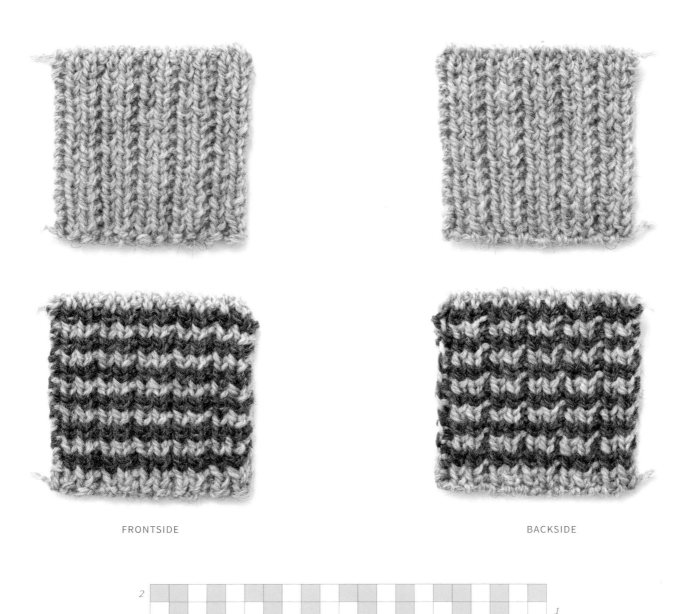

FRONTSIDE · BACKSIDE

1-ROW: BROKEN GARTER
[K2, P1, K1, P1] ON 5+2

Shift Reversible in 1 color, Aesthetically Reversible in 2 colors

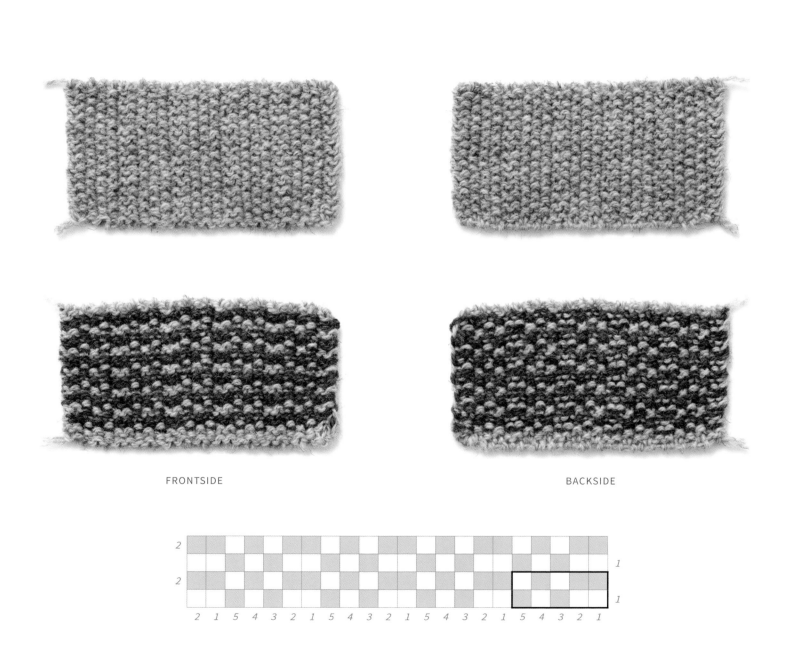

FRONTSIDE   BACKSIDE

PAGE   76

1-ROW: MISTAKE RIBBING
[2(K1, P1), K1] ON 5+3 (K2, P1, K1, P1)

Shift Reversible in 1 color, Aesthetically Reversible in 2 colors

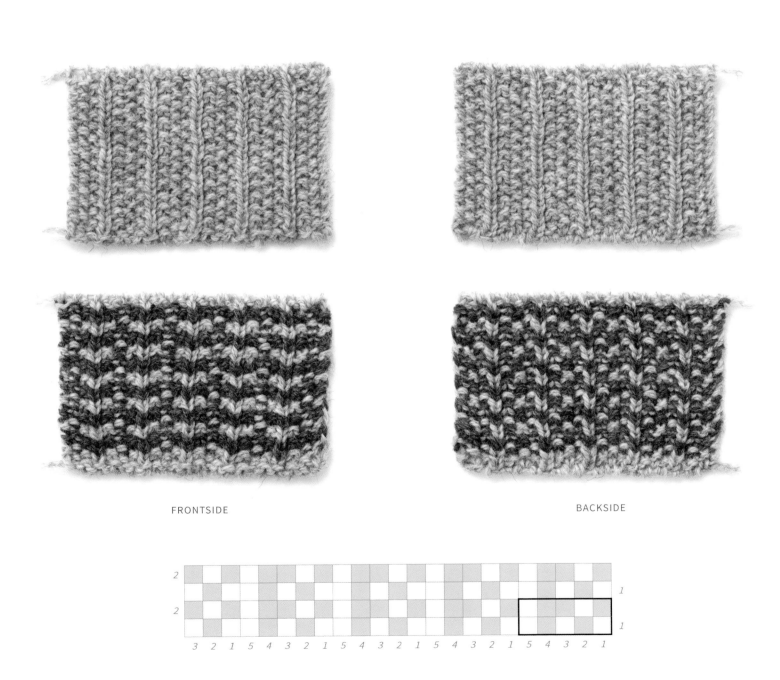

FRONTSIDE

BACKSIDE

1-ROW: MISTAKE RIBBING
[K3, P1, K2] ON 6 (K5, P1)

Shift Reversible in 1 color, Aesthetically Reversible in 2 colors

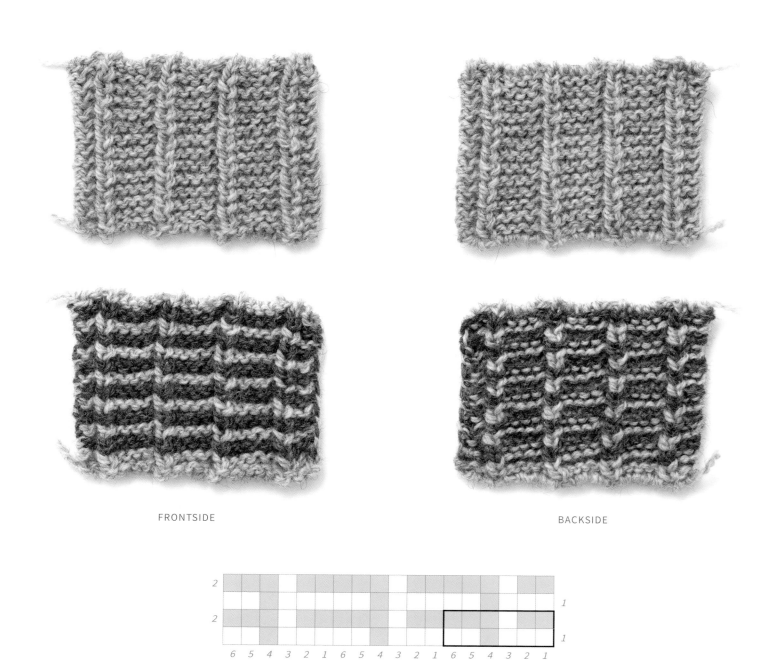

FRONTSIDE

BACKSIDE

1-ROW: BROKEN GARTER
[K3, P1, K2] ON 6+1 (K5, P1)

Shift Reversible in 1 color, Aesthetically Reversible in 2 colors

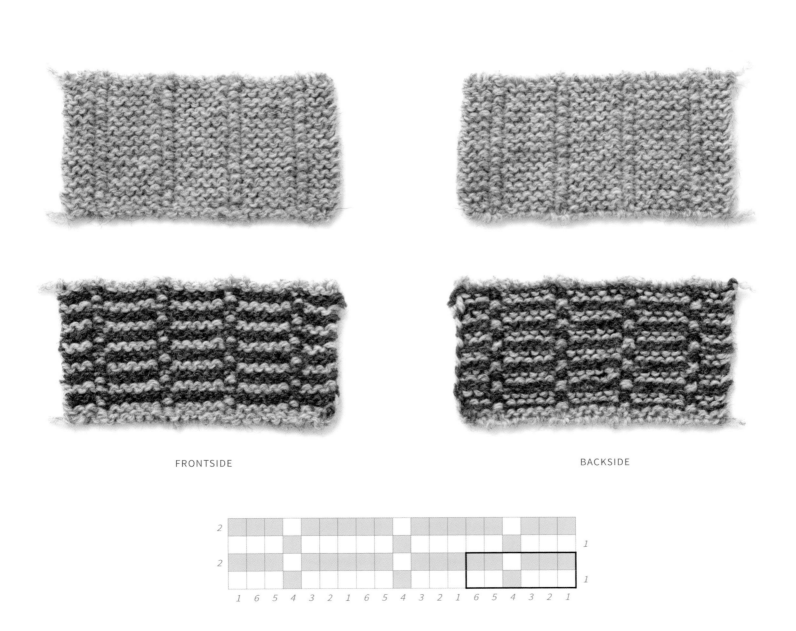

FRONTSIDE						BACKSIDE

1-ROW: ACCORDION
[K2, P1, K3] ON 6+2 (K5, P1)

Shift Reversible in 1 color, Aesthetically Reversible in 2 colors

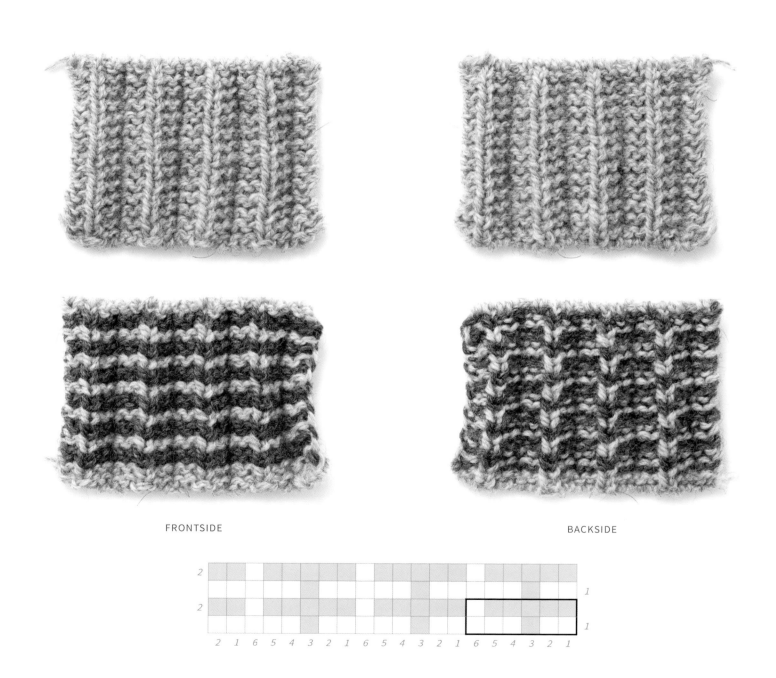

FRONTSIDE

BACKSIDE

PAGE 80

1-ROW: MISTAKE RIBBING
[K4, P2] ON 6

Shift Reversible in 1 color, Aesthetically Reversible in 2 colors

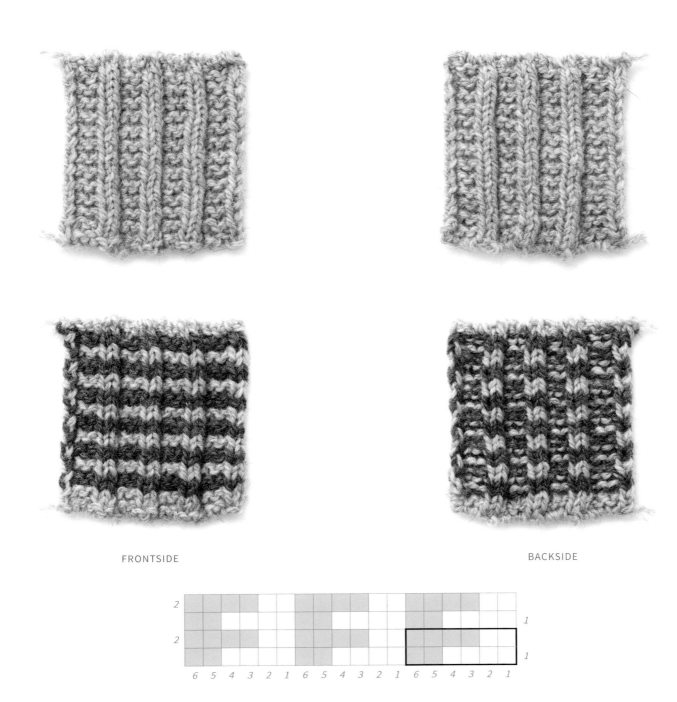

FRONTSIDE

BACKSIDE

1-ROW: BROKEN GARTER
[K2, P2, K2] ON 6 (K4, P2)

Shift Reversible in 1 color, Aesthetically Reversible in 2 colors

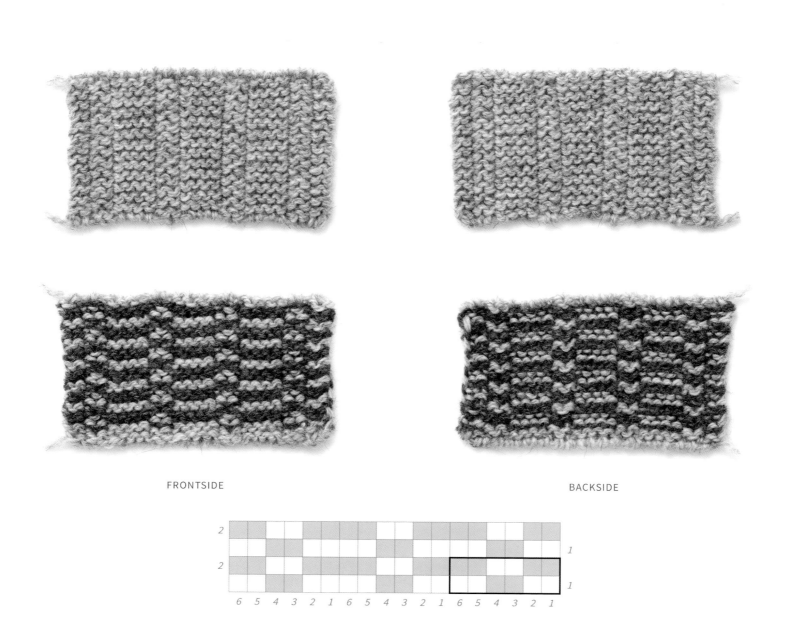

FRONTSIDE

BACKSIDE

1-ROW: ACCORDION
[K4, P2] ON 6+1

Shift Reversible in 1 color, Aesthetically Reversible in 2 colors

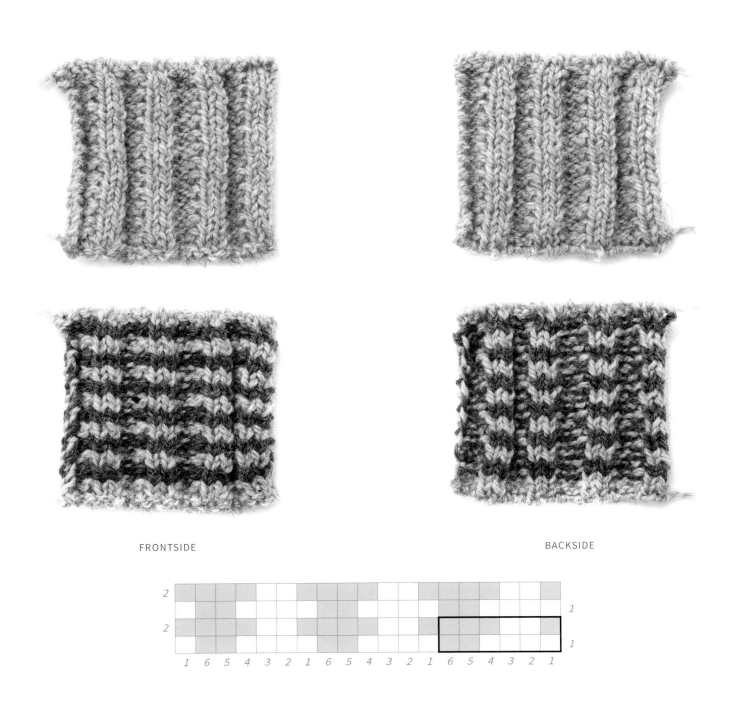

FRONTSIDE

BACKSIDE

1-ROW: RIBBING
[K3, P3] ON 6

Perfectly Reversible in 1 and 2 colors

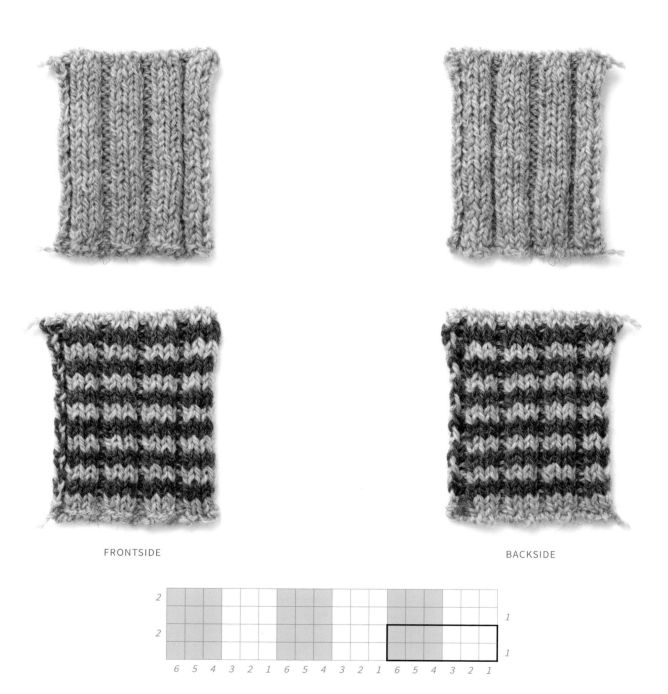

FRONTSIDE

BACKSIDE

1-ROW: ACCORDION
[K3, P3] ON 6+1

Shift Reversible in 1 color, Aesthetically Reversible in 2 colors

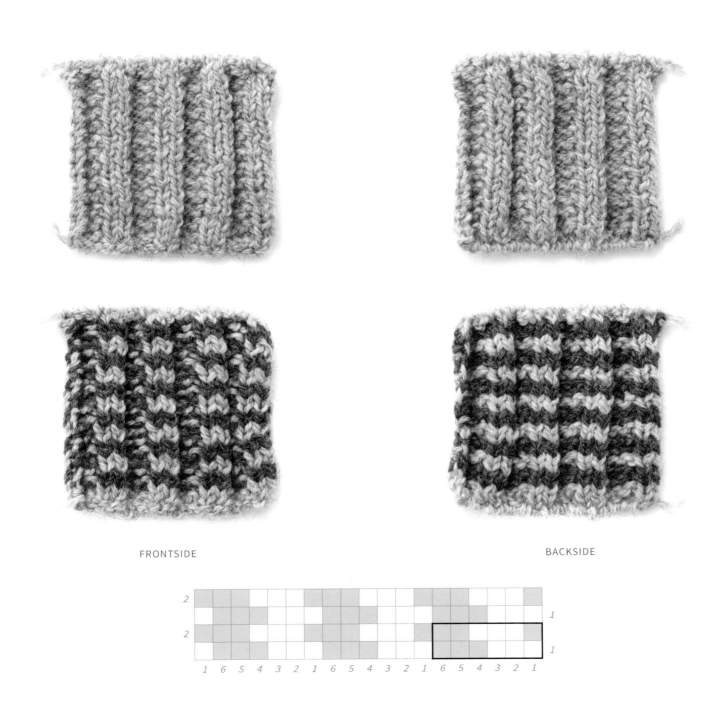

FRONTSIDE

BACKSIDE

1-ROW: ACCORDION
[K3, P3] ON 6+2

Shift Reversible in 1 color and Shift-flip Reversible in 2 colors

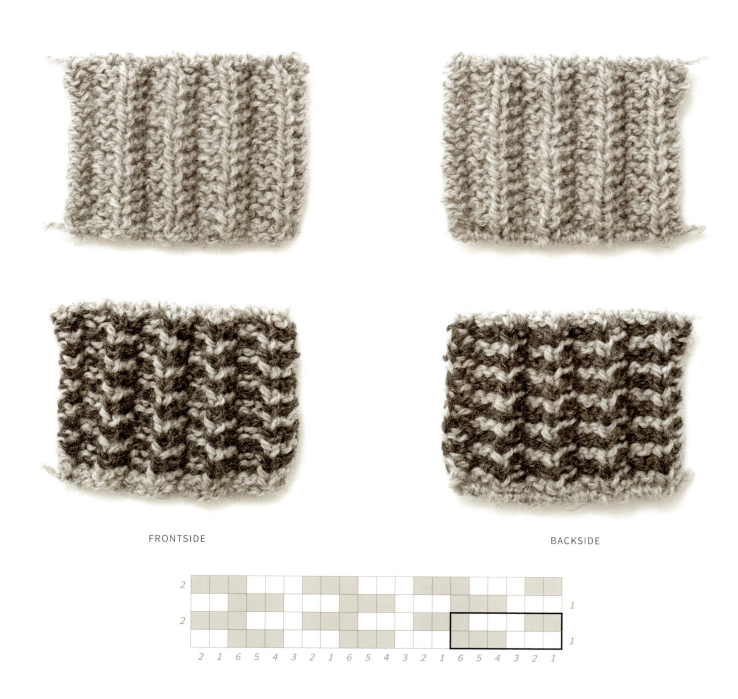

FRONTSIDE

BACKSIDE

PAGE 86

1-ROW: BROKEN GARTER
[K3, P3] ON 6+3

Shift Reversible in 1 and 2 colors

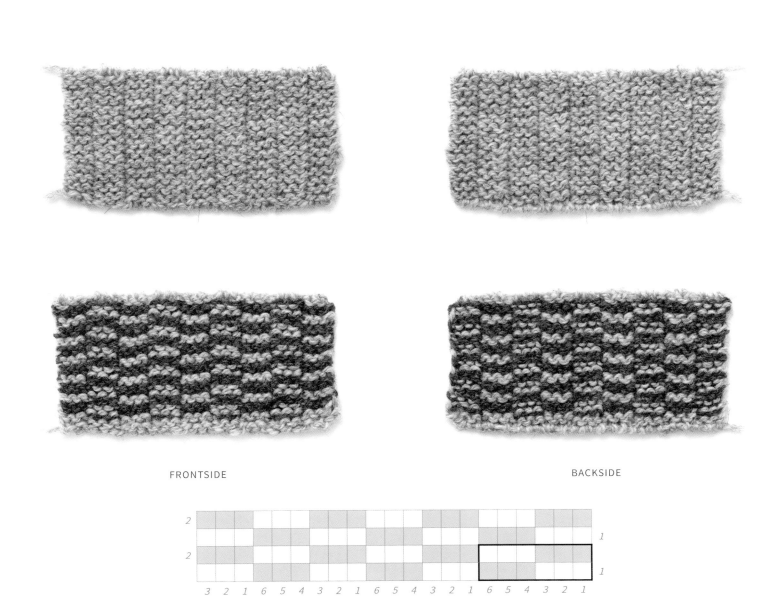

FRONTSIDE

BACKSIDE

1-ROW: MISTAKE RIBBING
[K3, P1, K1, P1] ON 6

Shift Reversible in 1 color, Aesthetically Reversible in 2 colors

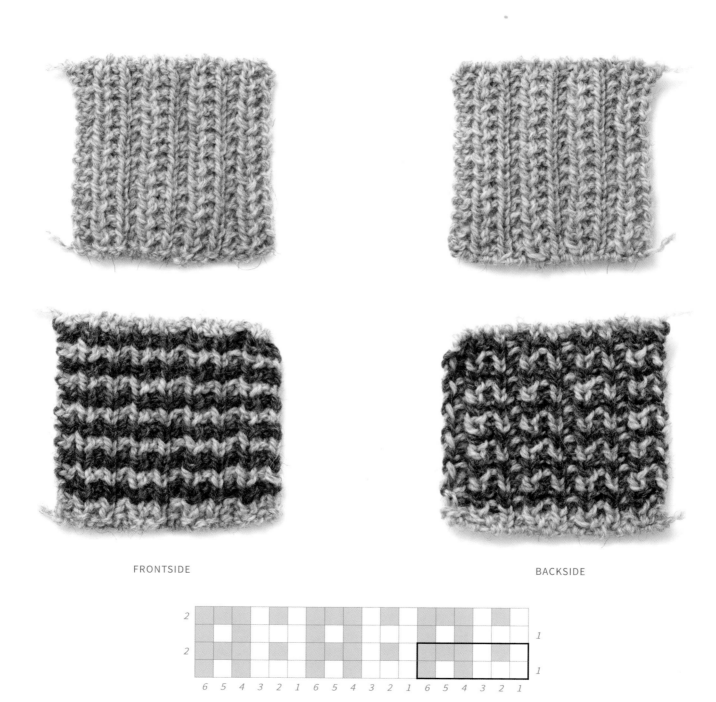

FRONTSIDE

BACKSIDE

1-ROW: MISTAKE RIBBING
[K2, 2(P1, K1)] ON 6 (K3, P1, K1, P1)

Shift Reversible in 1 color, Aesthetically Reversible in 2 colors

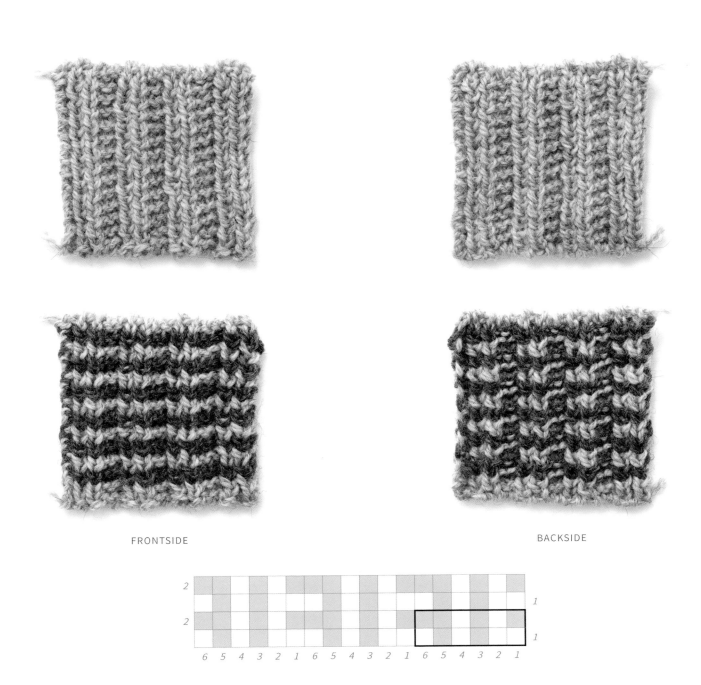

FRONTSIDE

BACKSIDE

1-ROW: BROKEN GARTER
[K2, 2(P1, K1)] ON 6+1 (K3, P1, K1, P1)

Shift Reversible in 1 color, Aesthetically Reversible in 2 colors

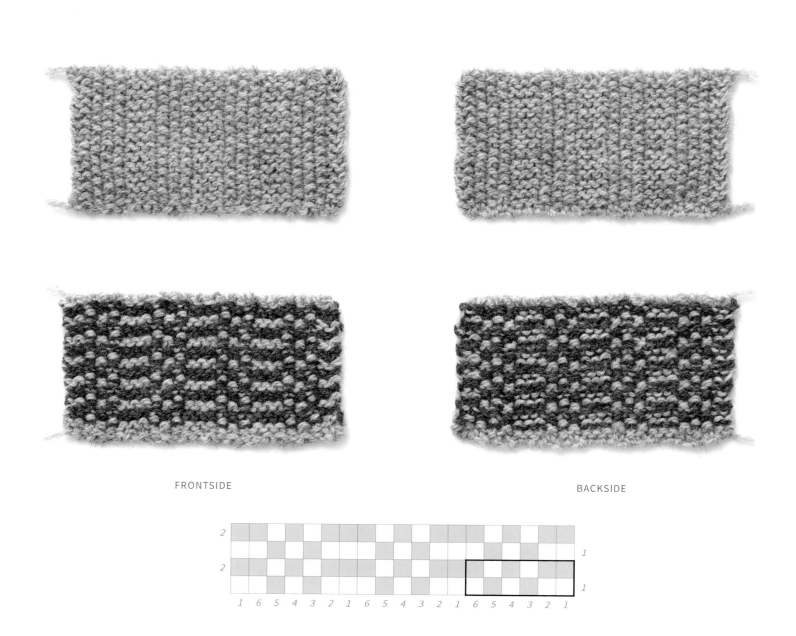

FRONTSIDE

BACKSIDE

1-ROW: MISTAKE RIBBING
[K1, P1, 2(P1, K1)] ON 6 (K2, P2, K1, P1)

Shift Reversible in 1 color, Aesthetically Reversible in 2 colors

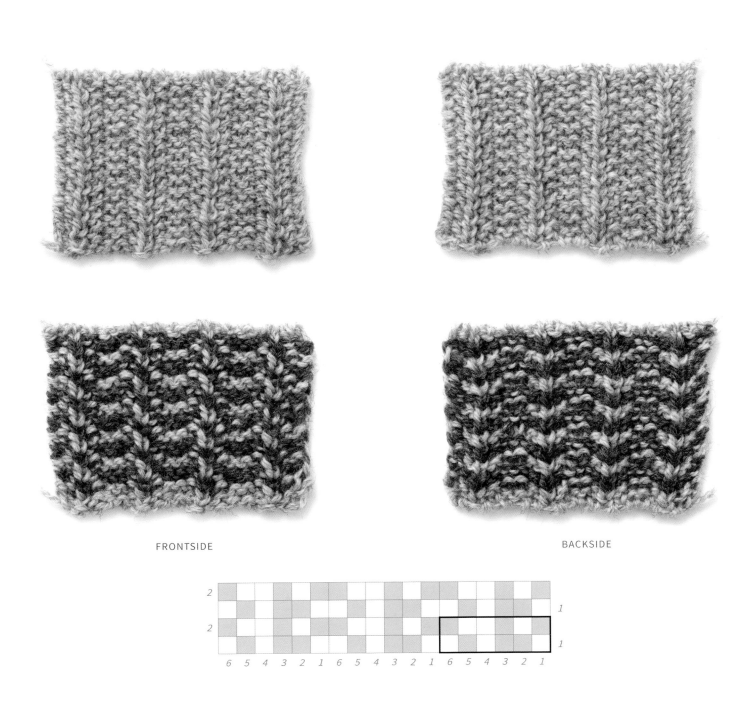

FRONTSIDE

BACKSIDE

1-ROW: MISTAKE RIBBING
[K2, P2, K1, P1] ON 6+1

Shift Reversible in 1 and 2 colors

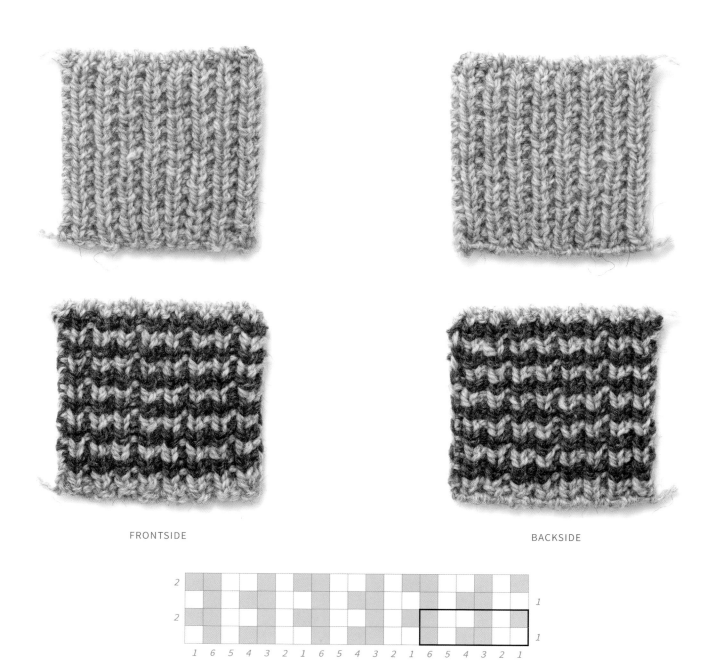

FRONTSIDE

BACKSIDE

1-ROW: MISTAKE RIBBING
[2(K1, P1), P1, K1] ON 6 (K2, P1, K1, P2)

Shift Reversible in 1 color, Aesthetically Reversible in 2 colors

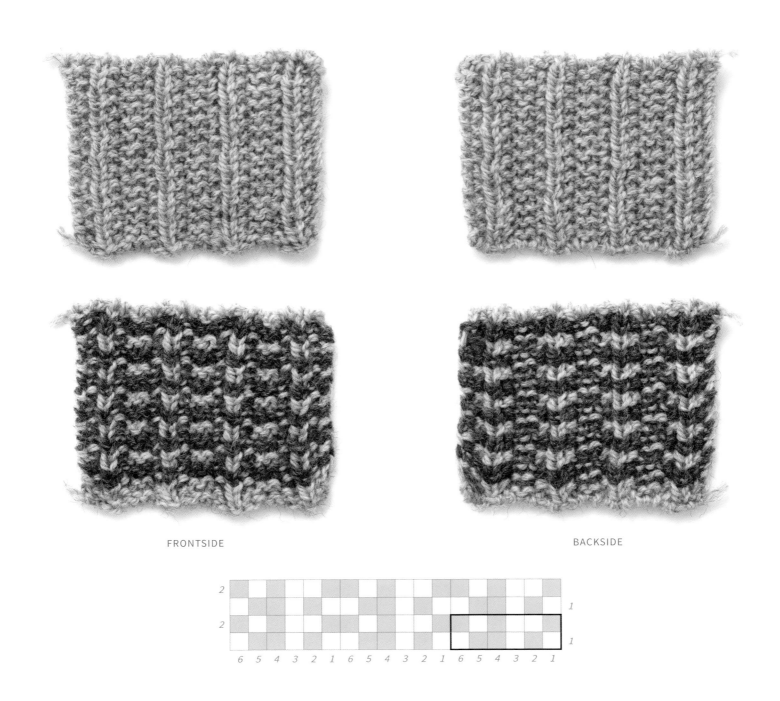

FRONTSIDE

BACKSIDE

1-ROW: MISTAKE RIBBING
[2(K1, P1), P1, K1] ON 6+1 (K2, P1, K1, P2)

Shift Reversible in 1 and 2 colors

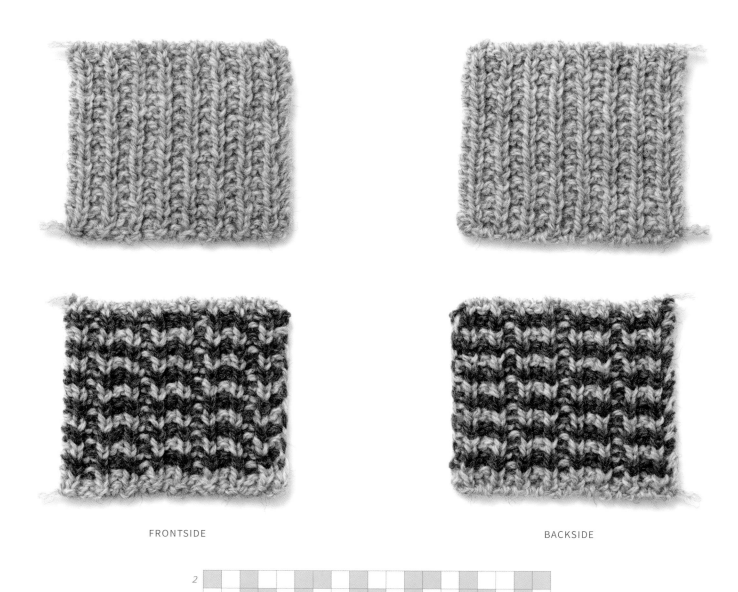

FRONTSIDE

BACKSIDE

1-ROW: RIBBING
[P1, K1, P2, K2] ON 6+2 (K2, P1, K1, P2)

Perfectly Reversible in 1 and 2 colors

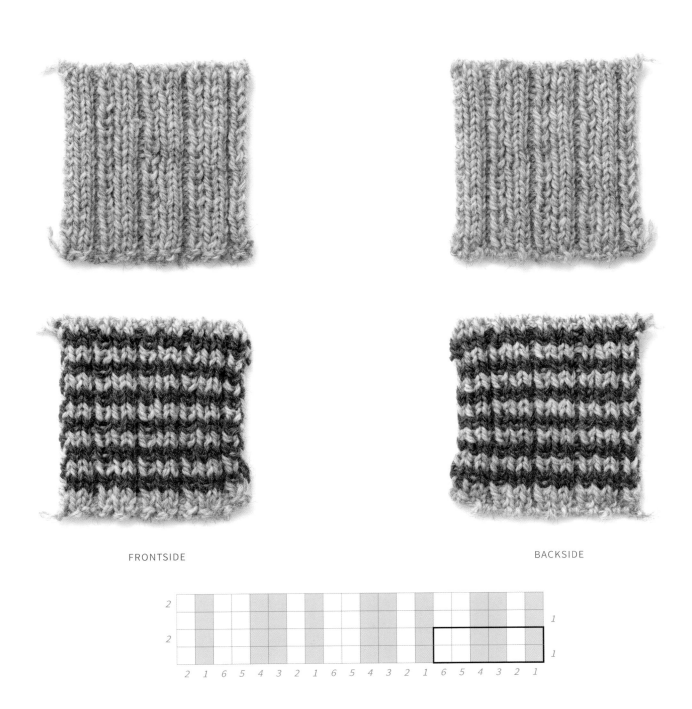

FRONTSIDE

BACKSIDE

CHAPTER 3

THE SERPENTINE METHOD

Complex, Multi-row Patterns Created with a Single Sequence

THE SERPENTINE METHOD

The serpentine method is a way to create a complex fabric with a single sequence. Unlike the 1-row method, the serpentine method lets you get off the grid without giving up the simplicity of a 1-row pattern. What do I mean by "get off the grid?" Fabrics created with 1-row patterns are always comprised of columns of ribs and garter. They are rectilinear. But the fabrics created with serpentine knitting are different, like the detail from the Mayes scarf on the facing page.

The idea is very simple: work a sequence of stitches across a row. If the number of stitches in the row is not a multiple of the sequence length, the end of the row will have an incomplete sequence. The next row then begins by completing the sequence from the prior row. For example, if a sequence length of 5 is worked over 37 stitches there will be 2 stitches left at the end of the first row. Begin the sequence again over these 2 stitches, then complete the sequence over the first 3 stitches of the next row. The sequence wraps around from row to row, like a serpent—hence the name *serpentine method*.

With the serpentine method 2 additional classes beyond the 1-row method classes are possible: *mock ribbing* and *all over*. Mock ribbing is different from mistake ribbing because it has knit ribs on 1 side which are purl ribs on the other. It does not have pairs of knit and purl ribs, so it is always aesthetically reversible and less stretchy than ribbing or mistake ribbing. All over is a vast class of fabrics and includes many sub-categories. I have only named a few of them like zig zag, disrupted garter and rib and seed diamonds.

The serpentine fabrics lie flat and do not require much blocking. They are almost always reversible in 1 color, but not usually reversible in 2 colors. As you can see from the stitch dictionary at the end of this chapter, the gauge can

vary widely, just as for the 1-row method.

You can also create these fabrics by following the provided charts, which might be the best approach for some situations like creating a fully fashioned sleeve or working in the round.

Because the edges are worked in pattern, the variation in the stitch pattern can make picking up stitches for seaming challenging. One possible solution is to add selvedge stitches, but to do this you will either have to follow a chart or remember to stay in pattern within the selvedge stitches.

This chapter includes 8 patterns, more detailed information about serpentine fabrics, and a stitch dictionary with 64 unique fabrics.

MAYES

Like many serpentine patterns, Mayes is shift reversible, and it does not need much blocking because it naturally lays flat. This scarf would normally require an 18-row chart, but it can be made by casting on a multiple of 9+1 stitches and working the sequence [K1, P2, K3, P2, K1] over and over again, wrapping the sequence from row to row. The sequence can be written in any of its 9 permutations such as [K3, P2, K2, P2] or [K2, P2, K3, P2], but I prefer to write it as [K1, P2, K3, P2, K1] because the sequence structure of 1, 2, 3, 2, 1, is easy for me to remember.

Even though the chart is not needed for the knitting, it is helpful to see it to understand the structure and to know the row repeat, which is 18, with a 9-row zig that leans to the right and a 9-row zag that leans to the left. This behavior is typical of serpentine fabrics created with odd sequence lengths. When working this pattern, rows 9 and 18 will end with a complete sequence, which is helpful for confirming that you are on pattern.

The sample shown used 2 hanks of Brooklyn Tweed Shelter in Truffle Hunt.

Materials and supplies

200 g worsted weight yarn

Size 7 (4.5 mm) needles

Gauge

5 stitches/inch in stockinette

Dimensions

9 x 70 inches (23 x 178 cm)

Directions

Cast-on 46 stitches (9+1). Work the sequence [K1, P2, K3, P2, K1] using the serpentine method until the scarf is 70 inches (178 cm) long.

Bind off. Wash, block and weave in ends.

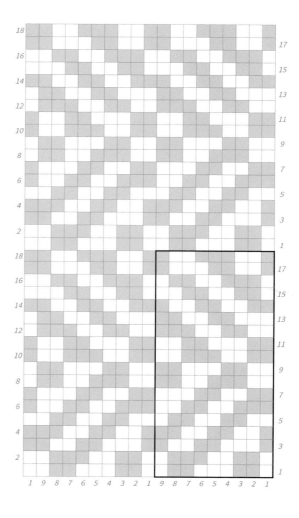

A SERIES OF SERPENTINE PATTERNS: DISRUPTED GARTER

[K2, P1] on 3+1

[K3, P1] on 4+1

[K6, P1] on 7+1

[K7, P1] on 8+1

It is interesting to compare different fabrics created with the serpentine method. These 8 swatches show the fabrics that result when 1 purl stitch is added to garter, disrupting the garter pattern. Read the swatches from left to right across the top row then left to right across the bottom row. For [K2, P1], a purl stitch replaces every third knit stitch, so the resulting fabric is radically different than garter. But for [K9, P1] the purl stitch only replaces every tenth knit stitch and the resulting fabric looks like a lot like garter.

[K4, P1] on 5+1

[K5, P1] on 6+1

[K8, P1] on 9+1

[K9, P1] on 10+1

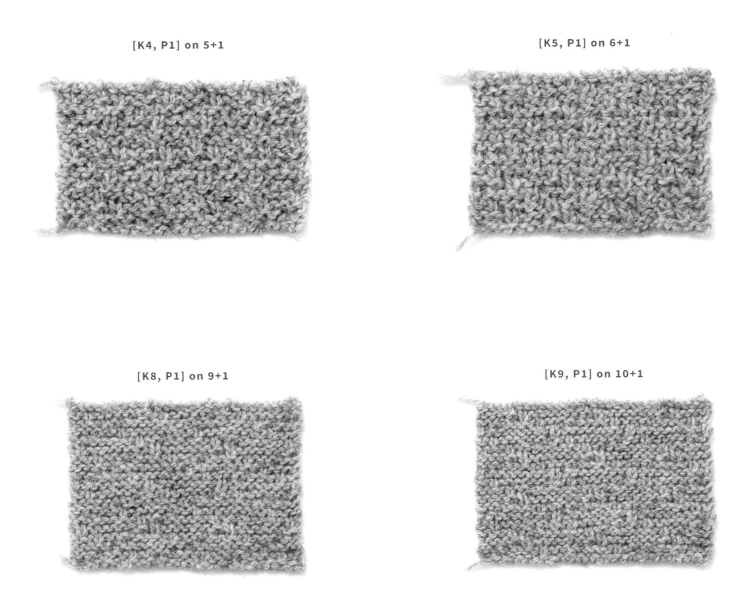

3 EXAMPLES OF SERPENTINE FABRICS

As an introduction to the serpentine method it is helpful to consider a few examples. The swatches and charts at right are for the sequence [K4, P4, K2, P2]. The left-most is worked on 12+1, the center is worked on 12+2, and the third is also worked on 12+2, but is the permutation [K3, P4, K2, P2, K1].

The fabric worked on 12+1 on the left is very flat and has a pebbly feel, almost as if it were knit with a bouclé yarn, while the fabric in the center is deeply crenelated. The way the stitches line up from row to row is what creates the different fabrics. Recalling that the only difference between 1x1 ribbing and seed stitch is the pattern multiple, we see here again how a tiny change — 1 extra stitch in the beginning — leads to a huge change in the resulting fabric. The permutation on the right is yet another completely different fabric.

With the 1-row method, the row repeats are always 2, but in serpentine knitting they can vary widely. The range of row repeats in the serpentine fabrics is as small as 2 rows and as large as double the sequence length. In the stitch dictionary at the end of this chapter there are fabrics where the sequence is 11 stitches long and the row repeat is 22. In the examples at right, the left fabric has a 12-row repeat, while the others have a 6-row repeat.

The Hadrians Wall pattern on the next page is based on the middle fabric.

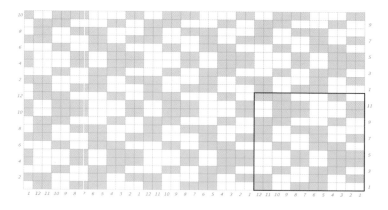

[K4, P4, K2, P2] Serpentine on 12+1

This fabric lies flat and is aesthetically reversible.

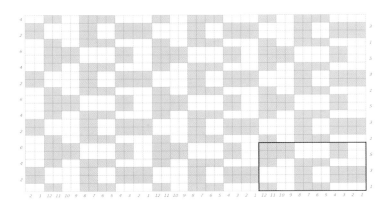

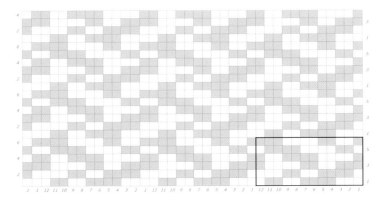

[K4, P4, K2, P2] Serpentine on 12+2

This shift-reversible fabric is deeply textured and almost has the feeling of a cabled rib.

[K3, P4, K2, P2, K1] serpentine on 12+2

This completely different fabric is created with another permutation of the sequence.

HADRIANS WALL

This serpentine knitting design creates a ribbing-like fabric with deep grooves and textures. The sample is made with Studio Donegal Soft Donegal, a merino yarn spun in Ireland, in Grey.

Materials

225 g of worsted weight yarn

Size 7 (4.5 mm) needles

Gauge

5 stitches / inch in stockinette.

Dimensions

8 x 70 inches (20.5 x 178 cm)

Directions

Cast on 38 (multiple of 12+2) stitches and work the following sequence using the serpentine method:

[K4, P4, K2, P2]

When the piece is 70 inches (178 cm) long, bind off.

Wash, block and weave in ends.

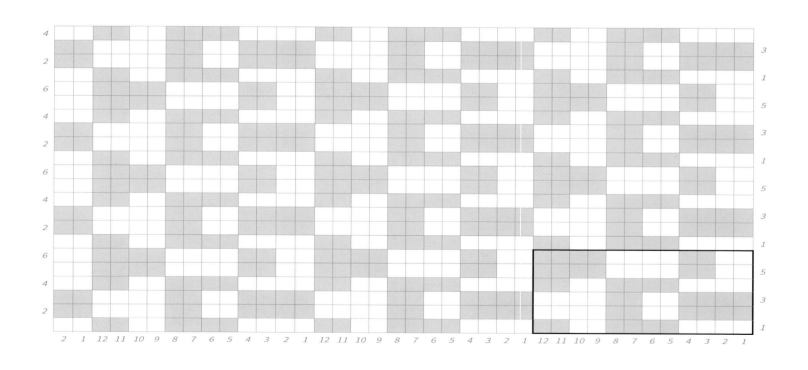

A SERIES OF SERPENTINE PATTERNS: RIB AND SEED DIAMONDS

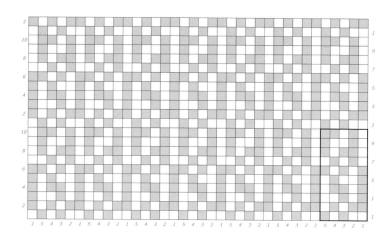
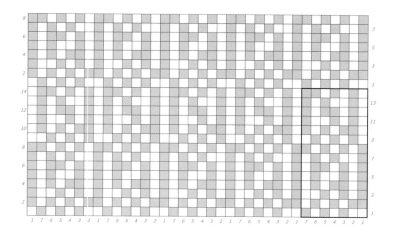

Going from left to right, this progression of charts and swatches shows the sequences [K1, 2(K1, P1)] on 5+1, [K1, 3(K1, P1)] on 7+1, [K1, 4(K1, P1)] on 9+1, and [K1, 5(K1, P1)] on 11+1. The fabric is comprised of diamonds of 1x1 ribbing and seed stitch, which become more and more distinct as the sequence length increases. The Woolston pattern on the next page uses [K1, 4(K1, P1)] on 9+1.

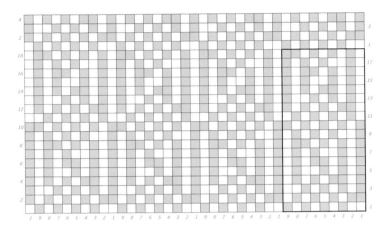
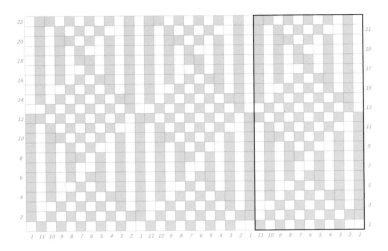

WOOLSTON

Woolston uses the same sequence demonstrated in the left swatch on page 109, except the permutation has been changed so the seed diamonds begin and end at the top and bottom edges. The sample is made with Brooklyn Tweed's Shelter in Woodsmoke.

Materials and supplies

200 g of worsted weight yarn

Size 7 (4.5 mm) needles

Gauge

5 stitches/inch in stockinette

Dimensions

8 x 70 inches (20.5 x 178 cm)

Pattern notes

1. The scarf is created with a permutation of the sequence [K1, 4(K1, P1)] on a pattern multiple of 9+1 using the serpentine method.
2. The pattern repeat is 9 stitches and 18 rows.
3. This pattern can be hard to read, so use lifelines and check it frequently.

Directions

Cast on 46 (multiple of 9+1) stitches and work the sequence [2(K1, P1), K1, 2(K1, P1)] in the serpentine method until the piece measures approximately 70 inches (178 cm), ending on row 18 of the chart.

Bind off. Wash, block and weave in ends.

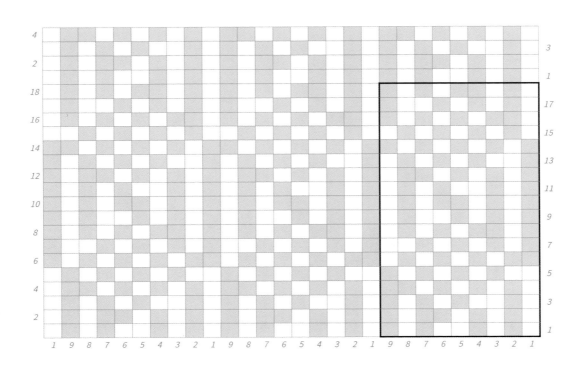

BACH

Bach is a generous, reversible, and incredibly soft scarf in pure cashmere. The sample is done in Karabella Supercashmere in Gray.

Materials and supplies

250 g of bulky weight cashmere

Size 10 (6.5 mm) needles

Gauge

3.5 stitches/inch in stockinette

Dimensions

8.5 x 70 inches (22 x 178 cm)

Pattern Note

The sequence is [K8, P4] and the pattern multiple is 12+8, however the pattern begins with P2. This centers the pattern with 2-stitch columns at each side edge.

Directions

Cast on 32 (multiple of 12+8) stitches.

P2, then work the sequence [K8, P4] using the serpentine method until the scarf measures 70 inches. Bind off.

Wash, block and weave in ends.

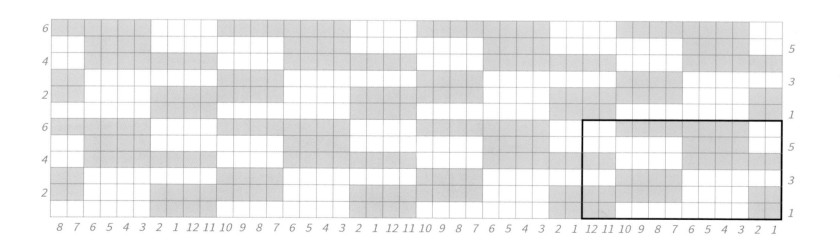

ANDRUS

Andrus is a luxurious wrap for a chilly night based on the same pattern as the Andrus scarf on page 9. The fabric is vertically very stretchy and has a thick, spongy feel. The sample is knit with Lisa Souza's BFL Worsted in Gold.

Go to page 9 to see a variation in solid cream, and page 345 to see another variation where a panel-dyed merino is worked with a strand of silk mohair.

Materials

300 g of worsted weight yarn

Size 7 (4.5 mm) needles

Gauge in stockinette

5 stitches / inch

Dimensions

10 x 60 inches (25.5 x 152 cm)

Pattern notes

1. This fabric has a lot of vertical elasticity and will elongate when worn. The dimensions given are for the piece when laid flat.
2. This pattern works well for both solid and variegated yarns.

Directions

Cast on 50 (multiple of 12+2) stitches. Work the sequence [K3, P6, K3] using the serpentine method until the scarf measures 60 inches (152 cm) when laid flat. Bind off. Wash, block and weave in ends.

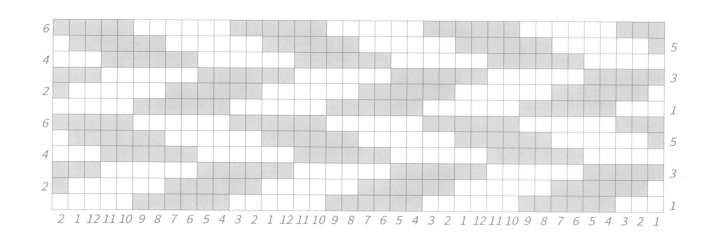

NORTHFIRST

Northfirst is a shift-reversible scarf is made with yarn from the Östergötlands Ullspinneri in Sweden where Ulla-Karin Hellsten and her husband Börje Norberg make lovely yarn from Swedish lambswool. The scarf is knit in Mole and Lime-green using the serpentine method with the sequence [P3, K1, P1, K3] on 8+2. Kaiden on page 118 uses the same sequence with a different permutation.

Materials

200 g of fingering weight yarn in color A

100 g of fingering weight yarn in color B

Size 3 (3.25 mm) needles

Gauge

7.5 stitches/inch in pattern stitch

Dimensions

10 x 70 inches (25.5 x 178 cm)

Pattern Notes

1. The sequence continues uninterrupted from row to row, even when changing colors.
2. When changing color, take care to always bring the new yarn in front of the working yarn.
3. The diagram below shows the layout of colors A and B.

Directions

Cast on 74 (multiple of 8+2) stitches in color A. Work the sequence [P3, K1, P1, K3] using the serpentine method for 4 rows. Continuing the sequence, change to color B and work 2 rows, then change to color A and work 2 rows. Continue alternating colors every 2 rows until the scarf measures 35 inches (89 cm). Continue knitting in color A only until the scarf measures 68 inches (173 cm), ending on the fourth row of the pattern (the row ending with the complete sequence P3, K1, P1, K3). Work 2 rows in color B, then 6 rows in color A. Bind off. Wash, block and weave in ends.

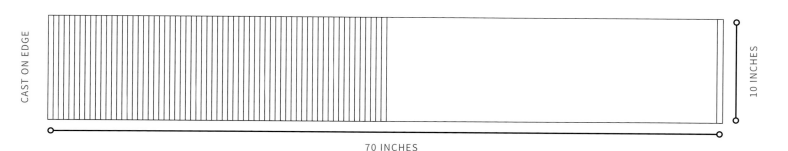

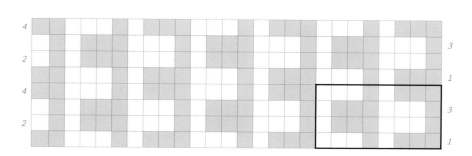

KAIDAN

Kaidan uses the sequence [K3, P3, K1, P1] on 8+2 to create a texture reminiscent of staircases. It is technically aesthetically-reversible in 1 or 2 colors, but it looks shift-flip reversible at first glance. The sample is knit with 2 colors of fingering merino that I panel dyed. Northfirst on page 116 uses the same sequence with a different permutation.

Materials

150 g of fingering weight yarn in color A

150 g of fingering weight yarn in color B

Size 3 (3.25 mm) needles

Gauge

6.5 stitches / inch in stockinette

Dimensions

10 x 70 inches (25 x 78 cm)

Pattern Notes

1. Row 4 will end with a complete sequence.
2. When changing color, take care to always bring the new yarn in front of the working yarn.
3. When switching yarns, do not restart the pattern. Continue working the piece in the serpentine method.

Directions

Cast on 82 (multiple of 8+2) stitches with Color A and work 2 rows of the sequence using the serpentine method:

[K3, P3, K1, P1]

Continuing in sequence, change to color B and work 2 rows. Continue alternating colors A and B every 2 rows until the piece is 70 inches long, ending with 2 rows in color A.

Bind off in A. Wash, block and weave in ends.

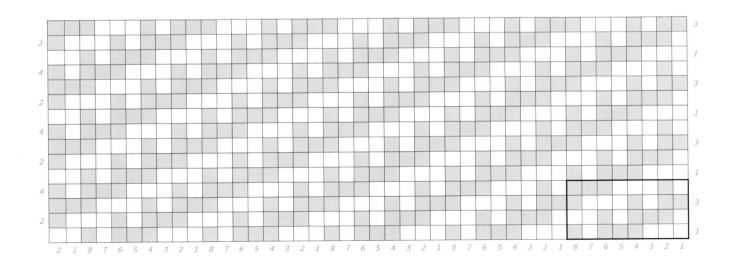

WEGNER

Wegner is knit as a rectangle using the serpentine method, then joined with a 3-needle bind-off. The sample used 2 hanks of Aslan Trends Royal Alpaca in Bone.

Materials

200 g of dk weight yarn

Size 4 (3.5 mm) needles

Size 3 (3.25 mm) needle for 3 needle bind-off

Gauge

6.5 stitches / inch in pattern. Note: the gauge is not critical, but the pattern uses smaller needles than recommended for the yarn weight for a firmer fabric.

Dimensions

9.5 inches wide with a 40 inch circumference (24 x 101.5 cm)

Pattern Notes

1. The chart is provided for reference. It shows that the pattern repeat is 10 x 10.
2. Go down a needle size for a neat 3-needle bind-off.

Instructions

Cast on 62 stitches (multiple of 10+2) using a provisional cast on and larger needles. Work the sequence [K8, P2] using the serpentine method until the piece measures 40 inches. Remove the provisional cast on and carefully place the stitches on a needle. Twist one edge 180° to create a Möbius and with a smaller needle join the edges with a 3-needle bind-off.

Wash, block and weave in ends.

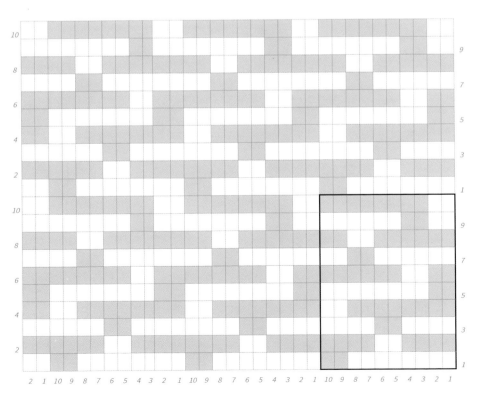

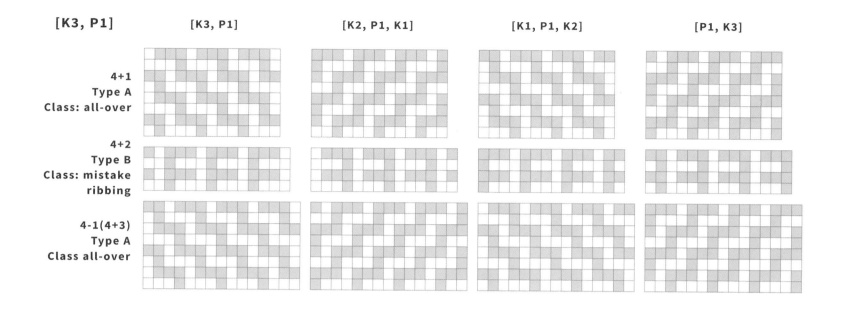

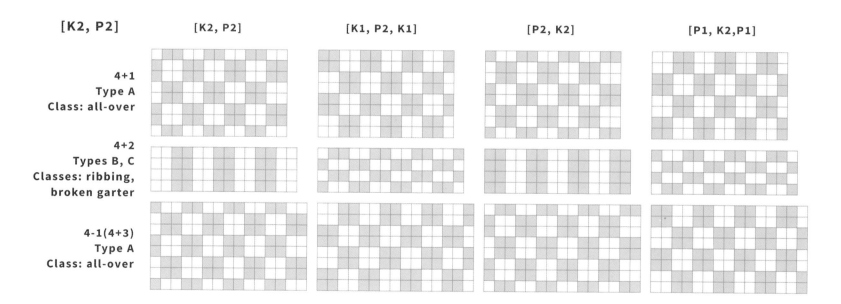

Serpentine fabrics from [K3, P1] and [K2, P2]

These charts show the serpentine fabrics from the sequence [K3, P1] and [K2, P2] worked on 4+1 through 4+3.

FABRIC TYPES AND THE SERPENTINE METHOD

A given sequence worked in the serpentine method can be used to create multiple types of fabrics depending on the pattern multiple and the permutation. When 2 fabrics are related by shifting, shift-flipping, mirroring, or are frontsides/backsides, they are the same *type of fabric*, denoted A, B, C, D... to identify the different types.

Consider the simple examples of [K3, P1] and [K2, P2] charted on the facing page. In each case the charts for all possible pattern multiples and permutations are shown, 12 charts for each sequence.

For [K3, P1] (top set of charts) worked on pattern multiples of 4+/-1, the resulting fabrics are a diagonal rib. Even though the charts look different, the left- and right-leaning diagonals are the frontsides or backsides of the same fabric so all 8 of these charts represent 1 type of fabric. When [K3, P1] is worked on 4+2 (center row of the top set of charts), permutations of the sequence result in 2 mistake ribbings. They are mirror images of each other, and thus are 1 type of fabric.

The [K2, P2] serpentine fabrics (lower set of charts) created with the pattern multiples of 4+/-1 are all 2x2 squares and are 1 type. However, if the pattern multiple is 4+2 there are now 2 dramatically different fabrics, a ribbing and a broken garter.

These behaviors are summarized in the table at right.

	[K3, P1]	**[K2, P2]**
4+/-1	diagonal-rib	blocks
4+2	mistake ribbing	ribbing broken garter
# classes	2	3
# types	2	3
# fabrics	3	3

PERMUTATION EFFECTS

There are several possible effects of permuting a sequence when using the serpentine method:

- The pattern can shift—which is just another way to say that only the selvedges are affected.
- The pattern can flip, and/or go back and forth between what is the frontside or the backside.
- It can change into a completely different type or class of fabric.

The latter behavior is only possible when the pattern-multiple remainder is a factor of the sequence length.

The table below lists the sequence lengths and pattern multiples where these effects can happen.

Sequence Length	Pattern multiples where permutations change the fabric	Pattern multiples where permutations only shift the fabric
2		2+1
3		3+/-1
4	4+2	4+/-1
5		5+/-1, 5+/-2
6	6+3	6+/-1, 6+/-2
7		7+/-1, 7+/- 2, 7+/-3
8	8+/-2, 8+4	8+/-1, 8+/-3
9	9+/-3	9+/-1, 9+/-2, 9+/-4
10	10+5	10+/-1, 10+/-2, 10+/- 3, 10+/- 4
11		11+/-1, 11+/-2, 11+/-3, 11+/-4, 11+/-5
12	12+/-2, 12+/-3, 12+/-4, 12+6	12+/-1, 12+/-5

AESTHETICALLY REVERSIBLE SERPENTINE FABRICS

You might think that all serpentine fabrics would be shift- or shift-flip reversible, and most are. However, some are only aesthetically reversible. An example is shown in the charts below. The sequence is [K3, P3, K1, P1] on a pattern multiple of 8+1. The left chart is the frontside and the right chart is the backside. The row-repeat is 8, so there are 4 frontside rows per repeat. These 4 frontside rows begin differently:

Row 1: K3, P3, K1, P1…

Row 3: K1, P3, K1, P1, K2…

Row 5: P2, K1, P1, K3, P1…

Row 7: K1, P1, K3, P3…

And the backside rows begin:

Row 2: K2, P3, K1, P1, K1…

Row 4: P3, K1, P1, K3…

Row 6: P1, K1, P1, K3, P2…

Row 8: P1, K3, P3, K1….

These 8 beginnings represent all of the possible permutations of the sequence, but those worked on the frontside are *never* repeated on the backside and *vice versa*. Hence the frontside and backside are inherently different.

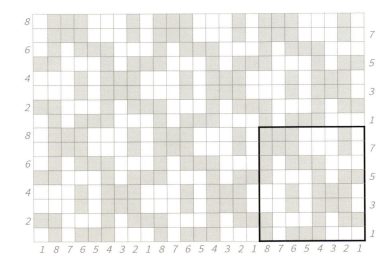

FRONTSIDE

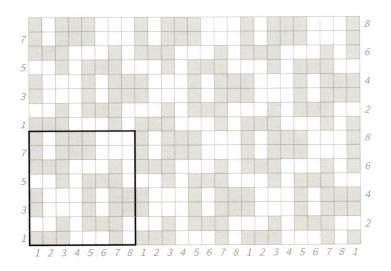

BACKSIDE

A SUMMARY OF SERPENTINE FABRIC PROPERTIES

Understanding how serpentine fabrics vary with different pattern multiples and permutations can be very helpful if you are designing your own pieces. For example, you might want to design a cardigan where the cuffs and pockets use a serpentine pattern. If the stitch count for the cuffs and the pockets are the same, or if they can vary by the sequence length, then it is easy. But if you need more flexibility in stitch count, especially for longer sequences, you could follow a chart or you could use the table on the facing page to figure out how to make the same fabric with a different pattern multiple.

You can also invent your own serpentine fabric. The table will help you know the lowest level of reversibility, the repeat, and whether permutations matter. It summarizes the behaviors of serpentine fabrics for the sequence lengths from 2 to 12 presuming only knits and purls are used.

As an example of how to use the table, imagine you wanted to create fabrics from a sequence of 8 stitches like [K4, P4]. You can predict the following:

- There can be up to 7 types of fabrics: 1 from 8+/-1 and 8+/-3, 2 from 8+/-2 and 4 from 8+4.
- The stitch repeat is always 8, and the row repeats will be 8, 4 or 2 depending on the pattern multiple.
- The fabrics may be aesthetically reversible if the multiple is 8+/-1, 8+/-2, or 8+/-3.
- If the multiple is 8+4 the resulting fabric will be shift reversible.

Some generalizations can be made from the table:

- For prime sequence lengths:
    - Permutations do not affect the number of fabric types.
    - The row repeats for prime sequences are twice the sequence length.
- If the sequence length is not a prime number:
    - Permutations of the sequence may increase the number of fabric types for the pattern multiples where the remainder is a factor of the sequence length.
- If the sequence length is an even number:
    - The middle pattern multiple will behave a lot like a 1-row pattern. The row repeat is 2 and it is always shift-reversible.

The sequence length of 2 is a curiosity. The only possible serpentine fabric is 1x1 ribbing so it does not follow the rules for the other prime numbers, which always have row repeats of twice the sequence length.

Sequence Length	Pattern Multiples	Stitch repeat	Row repeat	Potential Fabric Types	Lowest Level of Reversibility	Max Number of Fabric Types
2	2+/-1	2	2	1	Shift	1
3	3+/-1	3	6	1	Shift	1
4	4+/-1	4	4	1	Aesthetic	3
4	4+2	4	2	2	Shift	3
5	5+/-1	5	10	1	Shift	2
5	5+/-2	5	10	1	Shift	2
6	6+/-1, 6+/-2	6	6	1	Shift	4
6	6+3	6	2	3	Shift	4
7	7+/-1	7	14	1	Shift	3
7	7+/-2	7	14	1	Shift	3
7	7+/-3	7	14	1	Shift	3
8	8+/-1, 8+/-3	8	8	1	Aesthetic	7
8	8+/-2	8	4	2	Aesthetic	7
8	8+4	8	2	4	Shift	7
9	9+/-1	9	18	1	Shift	6
9	9+/-2	9	18	1	Shift	6
9	9+/-3	9	6	3	Shift	6
9	9+/-4	9	18	1	Shift	6
10	10+/-1, 10+/-4	10	10	1	Shift	7
10	10+/-2, 10+/-3	10	10	1	Shift	7
10	10+5	10	2	5	Shift	7
11	11+/-1	11	22	1	Shift	5
11	11+/-2	11	22	1	Shift	5
11	11+/-3	11	22	1	Shift	5
11	11+/-4	11	22	1	Shift	5
11	11+/-5	11	22	1	Shift	5
12	12+/-1, 12+/-5	12	12	1	Aesthetic	12
12	12+/-2, 12+/-4	12	6	2	Shift	12
12	12+/-3	12	4	3	Aesthetic	12
12	12+6	12	2	6	Shift	12

Table summarizing the behaviors of serpentine fabrics for given sequence lengths.

This shift reversible example is based on [K2, P1] on 3+1 worked with the serpentine method. The swatches appear the same on both sides, but the pattern is shifted by 3 rows.

THE SERPENTINE STITCH DICTIONARY

The table on the facing page lists all the fabrics in the serpentine method stitch dictionary, 64 in total. For the sequences with lengths 3 through 5, all the fabric types are included. From sequence lengths of 6 and up, this is a sampling of the many possibilities.

In cases where permutations are included, the fabrics resulting from the 2 permutations are completely different.

I found the fabrics from the sequences [K1, 2(K1, P1)], [K1, 3(K1, P1)], [K1, 4(K1, P1)], and [K1, 5(K1, P1)] particularly interesting. These include the Rib and Seed Diamond patterns and several other complex fabrics. For these sequences, all the types are included.

Unlike the 1-row method, most of these fabrics are aesthetically reversible in 2 colors, so only 1 color is shown.

SERPENTINE STITCHES IN THIS DICTIONARY

Sequence Length (n)	Pattern multiple	Sequence	Start (then continue with sequence)	Reversibility
3	3+1	K2, P1		Shift
4	4+1	K3, P1		Aesthetically
4	4+1	K2, P2		Shift
5	5+1	K4, P1		Shift
5	5+2	K4, P1		Shift
5	5+1	K3, P2	P1	Shift
5	5+2	K3, P2		Shift
5	5+1	K2, P1, K1, P1		Shift
5	5+2	K2, P1, K1, P1		Shift
6	6+1	K5, P1		Shift
6	6+2	K4, P2		Shift
6	6+1	K3, P3		Shift
6	6+2	K2, P2, K1, P1		Shift
7	7+1	K6, P1		Shift
7	7+1	K1, 3(K1, P1)		Shift
7	7+2	K1, 3(K1, P1)		Shift
7	7+3	K1, 3(K1, P1)		Shift
8	8+1	K7, P1		Aesthetically
8	8+1	K5, P3		Aesthetically
8	8+2	K5, P3		Aesthetically
8	8+1	K3, P3, K1, P1		Aesthetically
8	8+2	K3, P3, K1, P1		Aesthetically
8	8+2	K3, P3, K1, P1	P3, K1, P1	Shift
9	9+1	K8, P1		Shift
9	9+1	K6, P3		Shift
9	9+2	K6, P3		Shift
9	9+3	K6, P3		Shift
9	9+3	K6, P3	K5, P3	Shift
9	9+4	K6, P3		Shift
9	9+1	K1, 4(K1, P1)		Shift
9	9+2	K1, 4(K1, P1)		Shift
9	9+3	K1, 4(K1, P1)		Shift
9	9+3	K1, 4(K1, P1)	4(K1, P1)	Shift
9	9+4	K1, 4(K1, P1)		Shift

Sequence Length (n)	Pattern multiple	Sequence	Start (then continue with sequence)	Reversibility
10	10+1	K9, P1		Shift
10	10+2	K8, P2		Shift
10	10+2	K4, P4, K1, P1		Shift
10	10+4	K4, P4, K1, P1		Shift
10	10+2	K3, P3, K2, P2		Shift
10	10+4	K3, P3, K2, P2		Shift
10	10+2	K3, P3, 2(K1, P1)		Shift
10	10+4	K3, P3, 2(K1, P1)		Shift
10	10+2	K2, P2, 3(K1, P1)		Shift
10	10+4	K2, P2, 3(K1, P1)		Shift
10	10+2	2(K2, P2), K1, P1		Shift
10	10+4	2(K2, P2), K1, P1		Shift
11	11+1	K1, 5(K1, P1)		Shift
11	11+2	K1, 5(K1, P1)		Shift
11	11+3	K1, 5(K1, P1)		Shift
11	11+4	K1, 5(K1, P1)		Shift
11	11+5	K1, 5(K1, P1)		Shift
12	12+1	K8, P4		Aesthetically
12	12+3	K8, P4		Aesthetically
12	12+3	K8, P4	K7, P4	Aesthetically
12	12+4	K8, P4		Shift
12	12+4	K8, P4	K7, P4	Shift
12	12+1	K4, P4, K2, P2		Aesthetically
12	12+2	K4, P4, K2, P2		Shift
12	12+2	K4, P4, K2, P2	K3, P4, K2, P2	Shift
12	12+1	K3, P3, 3(K1, P1)		Aesthetically
12	12+3	K3, P3, 3(K1, P1)		Shift
12	12+3	K3, P3, 3(K1, P1)	K2, P3, 3(K1, P1)	Aesthetically
12	12+4	K3, P3, 3(K1, P1)		Shift
12	12+4	K3, P3, 3(K1, P1)	K2, P3, 3(K1, P1)	Shift

SERPENTINE STITCH PATTERN
[K2, P1] ON 3+1

Shift Reversible

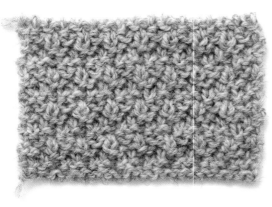

FRONTSIDE

BACKSIDE

SERPENTINE STITCH PATTERN
[K3, P1] ON 4+1

Aesthetically Reversible

FRONTSIDE

BACKSIDE

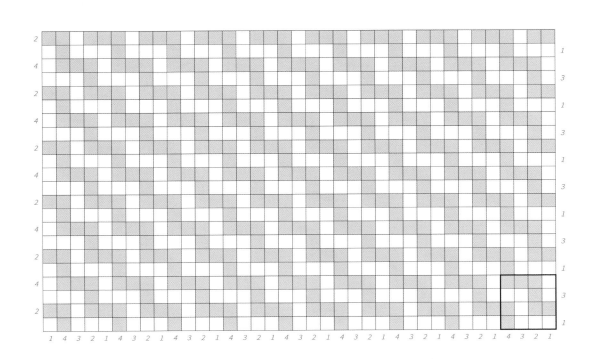

SERPENTINE STITCH PATTERN
[K2, P2] ON 4+1

Shift Reversible 2x2 Squares

This very simple pattern has asymmetric selvedges when worked with the serpentine method.

FRONTSIDE

BACKSIDE

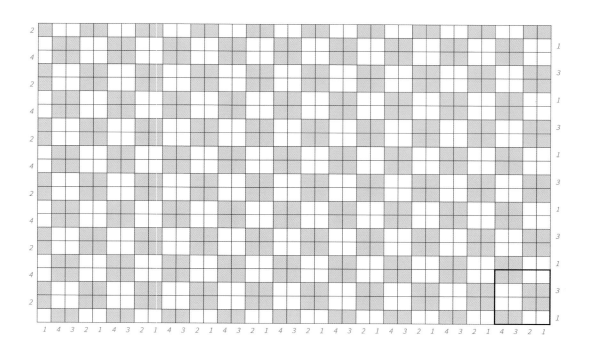

SERPENTINE STITCH PATTERN
[K4, P1] ON 5+1

Shift Reversible

FRONTSIDE

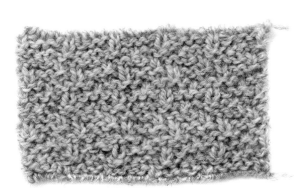

BACKSIDE

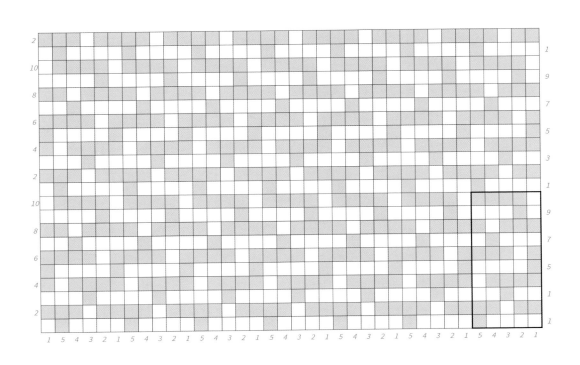

SERPENTINE STITCH PATTERN
[K4, P1] ON 5+2

Shift Reversible

FRONTSIDE

BACKSIDE

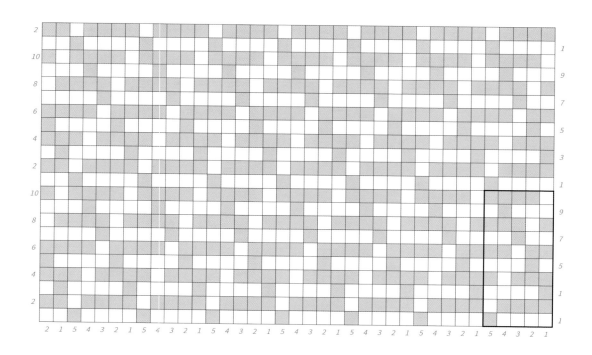

SERPENTINE STITCH PATTERN
[K3, P2] ON 5+1 (START P1)

Shift Reversible Zig Zag

FRONTSIDE

BACKSIDE

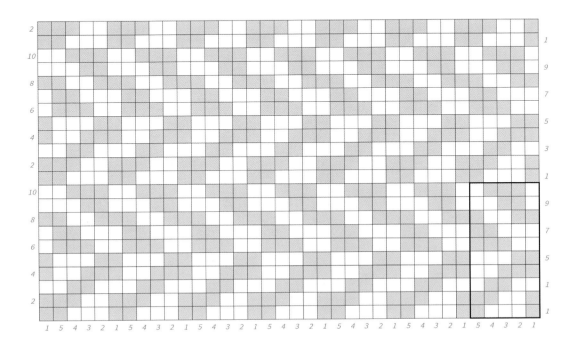

SERPENTINE STITCH PATTERN
[K3, P2] ON 5+2

Shift Reversible

FRONTSIDE

BACKSIDE

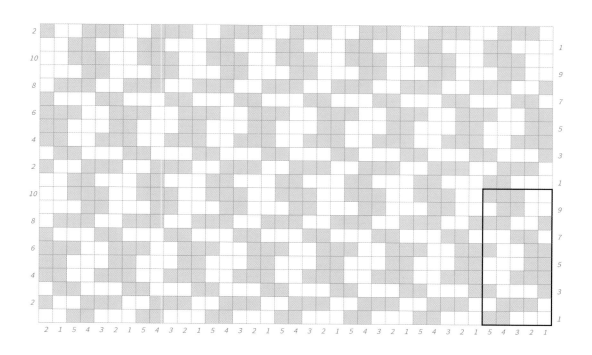

SERPENTINE STITCH PATTERN
[K2, P1, K1, P1] ON 5+1

Shift Reversible

FRONTSIDE

BACKSIDE

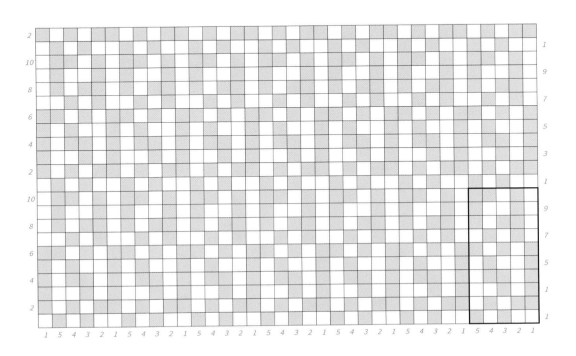

SERPENTINE STITCH PATTERN
[K2, P1, K1, P1] ON 5+2

Shift Reversible

FRONTSIDE

BACKSIDE

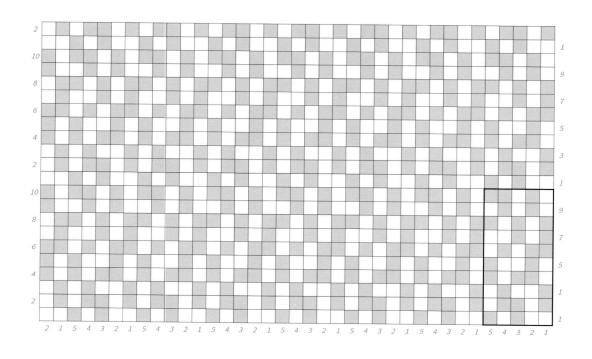

SERPENTINE STITCH PATTERN
[K5, P1] ON 6+1

Shift Reversible

FRONTSIDE

BACKSIDE

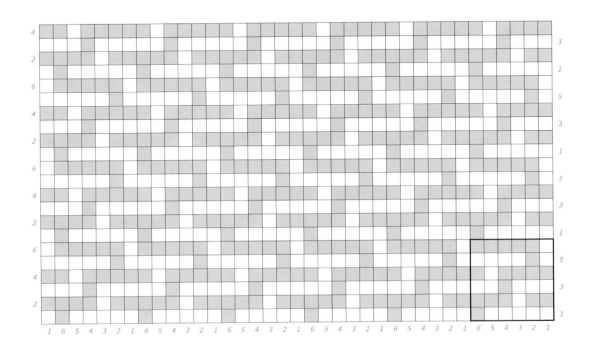

PAGE 139

SERPENTINE STITCH PATTERN
[K4, P2] ON 6+2

Shift Reversible

FRONTSIDE

BACKSIDE

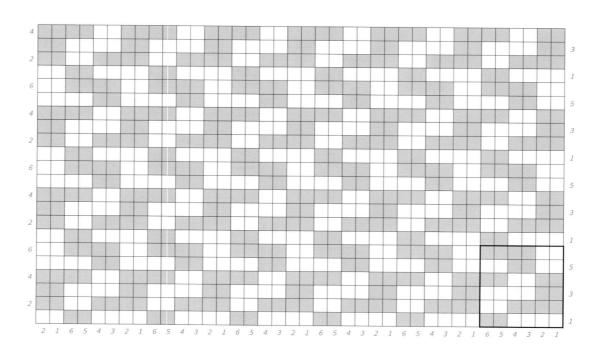

SERPENTINE STITCH PATTERN
[K3, P3] ON 6+1

Shift Reversible

FRONTSIDE

BACKSIDE

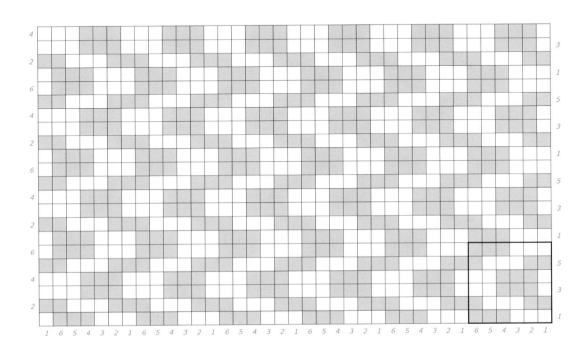

SERPENTINE STITCH PATTERN
[K2, P2, K1, P1] ON 6+2

Shift Reversible

FRONTSIDE

BACKSIDE

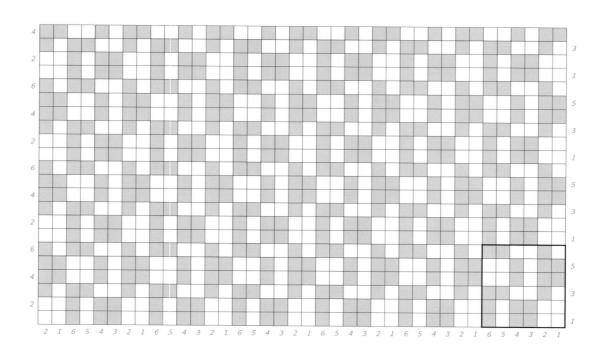

SERPENTINE STITCH PATTERN
[K6, P1] ON 7+1

Shift Reversible

FRONTSIDE

BACKSIDE

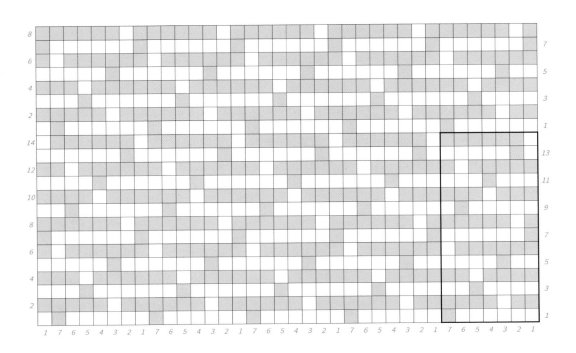

SERPENTINE STITCH PATTERN
[K1, 3(K1, P1)] ON 7+1

Shift Reversible Rib and Seed Diamonds

FRONTSIDE

BACKSIDE

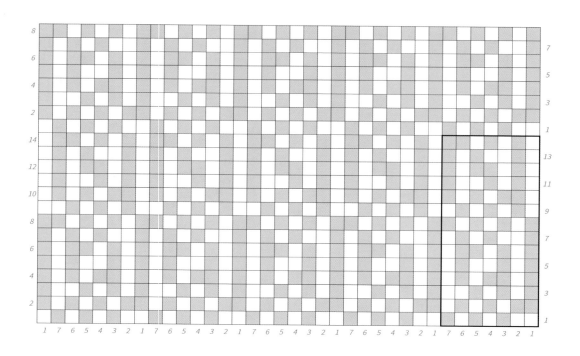

SERPENTINE STITCH PATTERN
[K1, 3(K1, P1)] ON 7+2

Shift Reversible

FRONTSIDE

BACKSIDE

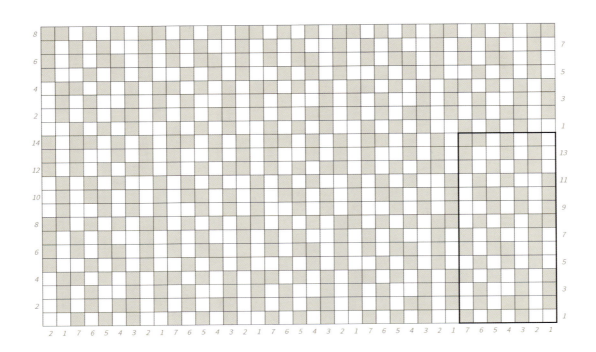

SERPENTINE STITCH PATTERN
[K1, 3(K1, P1)] ON 7+3

Shift Reversible

This pattern has the look and feel of a bouclé.

FRONTSIDE

BACKSIDE

SERPENTINE STITCH PATTERN
[K7, P1] ON 8+1

Aesthetically Reversible

FRONTSIDE

BACKSIDE

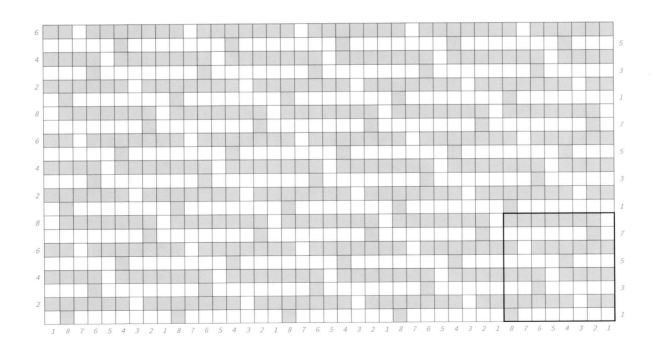

SERPENTINE STITCH PATTERN
[K5, P3] ON 8+1

Aesthetically Reversible

FRONTSIDE

BACKSIDE

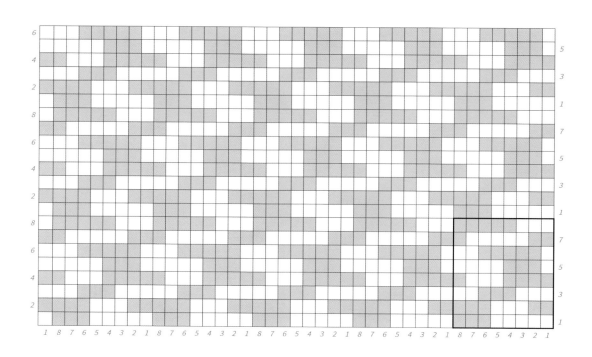

PAGE 148

SERPENTINE STITCH PATTERN
[K5, P3] ON 8+2

Aesthetically Reversible

FRONTSIDE

BACKSIDE

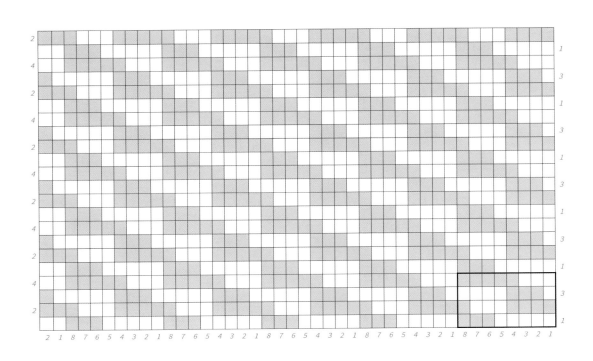

SERPENTINE STITCH PATTERN
[K3, P3, K1, P1] ON 8+1

Aesthetically Reversible

FRONTSIDE

BACKSIDE

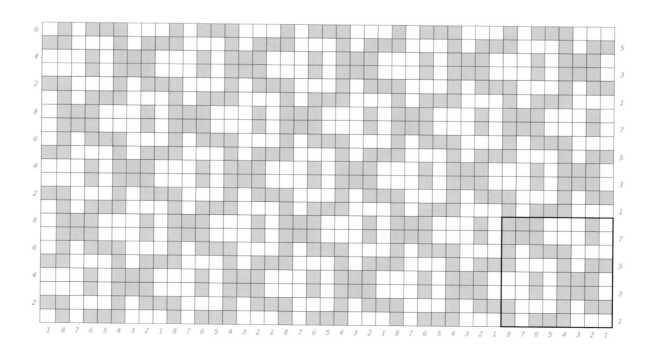

SERPENTINE STITCH PATTERN
[K3, P3, K1, P1] ON 8+2

Aesthetically Reversible

This is the pattern for Kaidan. Even though it is technically aesthetically reversible, the frontside and backsides are visually very similar and could be easily mistaken for being shift-flip reversible.

FRONTSIDE

BACKSIDE

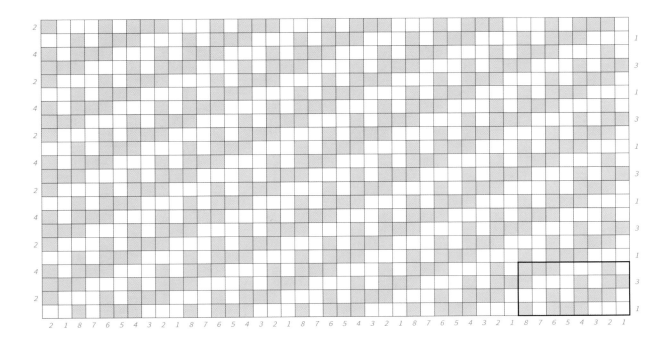

SERPENTINE STITCH PATTERN
[K3, P3, K1, P1] ON 8+2 (START P3, K1, P1)

Shift Reversible Mistake Ribbing

FRONTSIDE

BACKSIDE

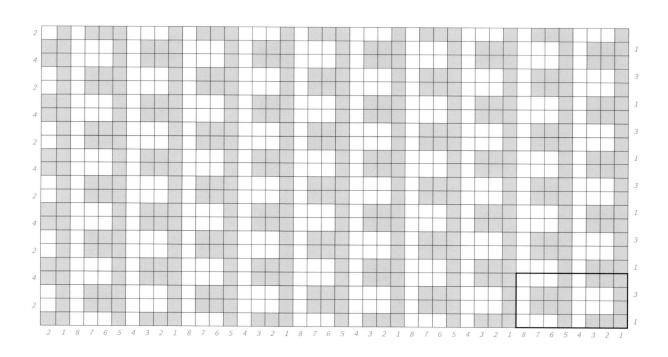

SERPENTINE STITCH PATTERN
[K8, P1] ON 9+1

Shift Reversible

FRONTSIDE

BACKSIDE

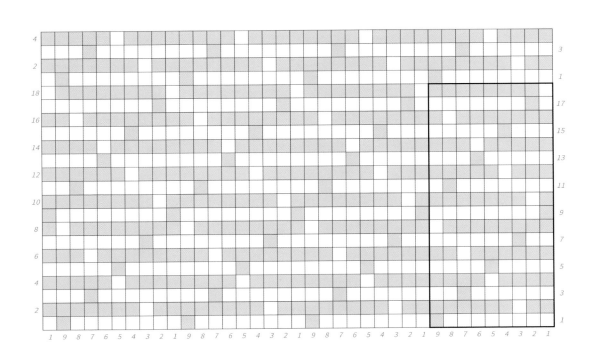

SERPENTINE STITCH PATTERN
[K6, P3] ON 9+1

Shift Reversible

FRONTSIDE

BACKSIDE

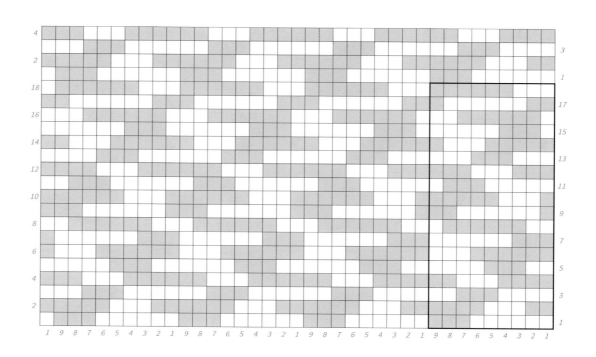

SERPENTINE STITCH PATTERN
[K6, P3] ON 9+2

Shift Reversible Zig Zag

FRONTSIDE

BACKSIDE

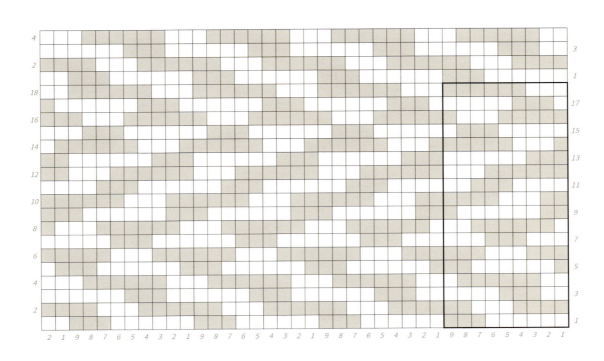

SERPENTINE STITCH PATTERN
[K6, P3] ON 9+3

Shift Reversible

FRONTSIDE

BACKSIDE

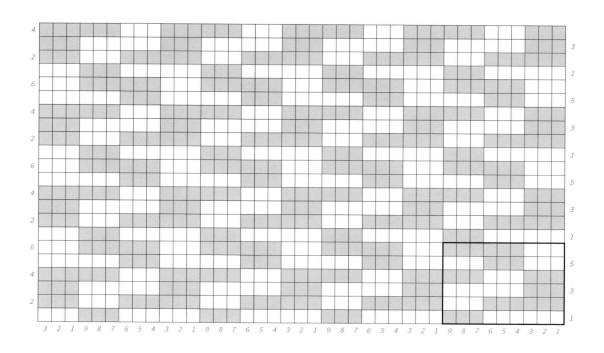

SERPENTINE STITCH PATTERN
[K6, P3] ON 9+3 (START K5, P3)

Shift Reversible

FRONTSIDE

BACKSIDE

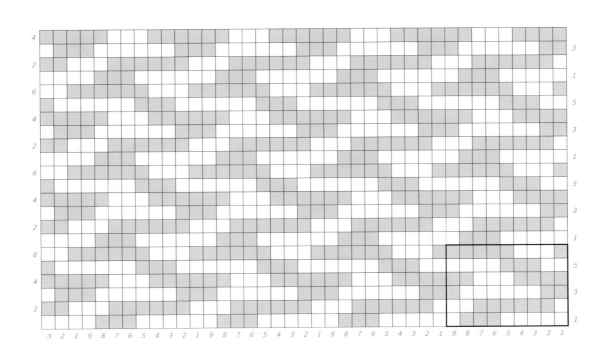

SERPENTINE STITCH PATTERN
[K6, P3] ON 9+4

Shift Reversible

FRONTSIDE

BACKSIDE

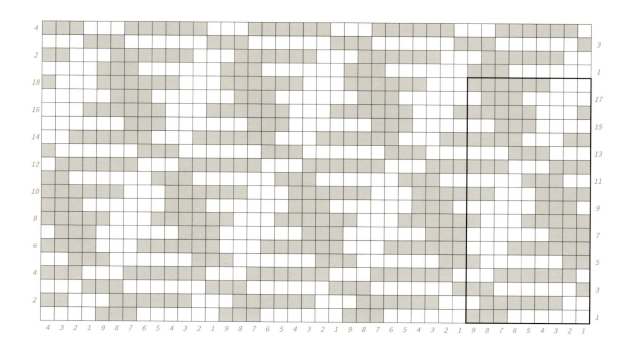

SERPENTINE STITCH PATTERN
[K1, 4(K1, P1)] ON 9+1

Shift Reversible Rib and Seed Diamonds

This pattern is the basis for the Woolston scarf.

FRONTSIDE

BACKSIDE

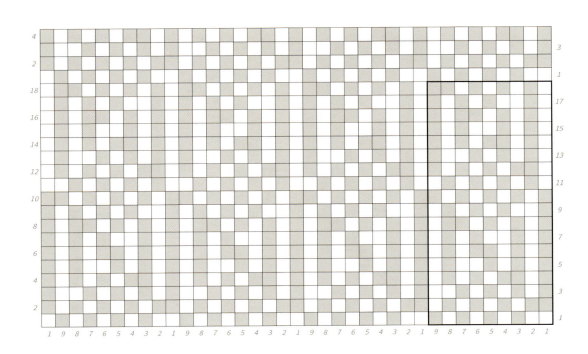

SERPENTINE STITCH PATTERN
[K1, 4(K1, P1)] ON 9+2

Shift Reversible

FRONTSIDE

BACKSIDE

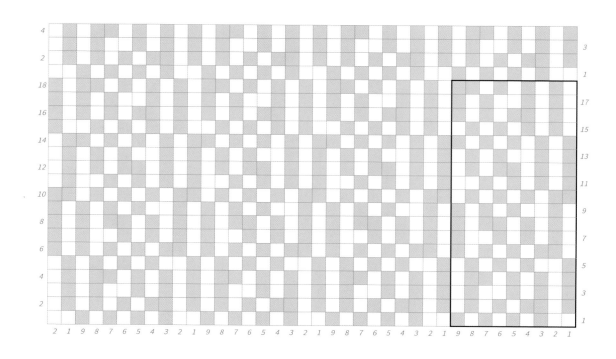

SERPENTINE STITCH PATTERN
[K1, 4(K1, P1)] ON 9+3

Shift Reversible

FRONTSIDE

BACKSIDE

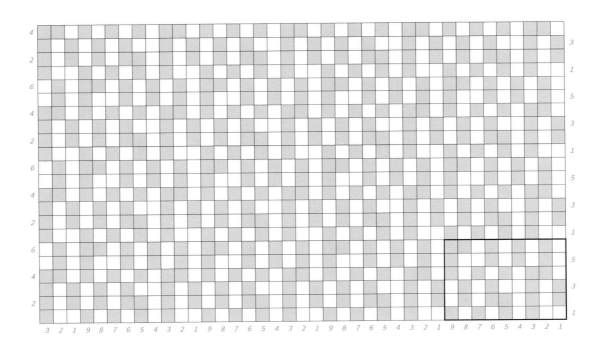

PAGE 161

SERPENTINE STITCH PATTERN
[K1, 4(K1, P1)] ON 9+3 (START 4(K1, P1))

Shift Reversible

This pattern has the look and feel of a bouclé.

FRONTSIDE

BACKSIDE

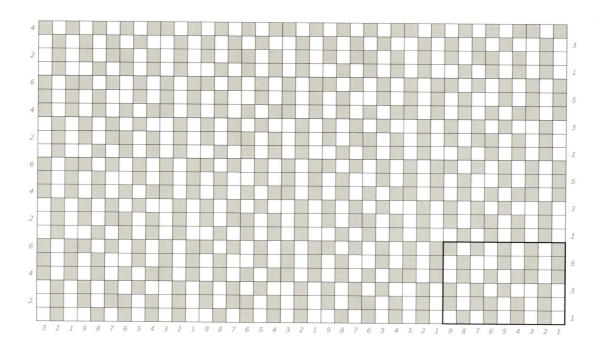

SERPENTINE STITCH PATTERN
[K1, 4(K1, P1)] ON 9+4

Shift Reversible

This pattern has the look and feel of a bouclé.

FRONTSIDE

BACKSIDE

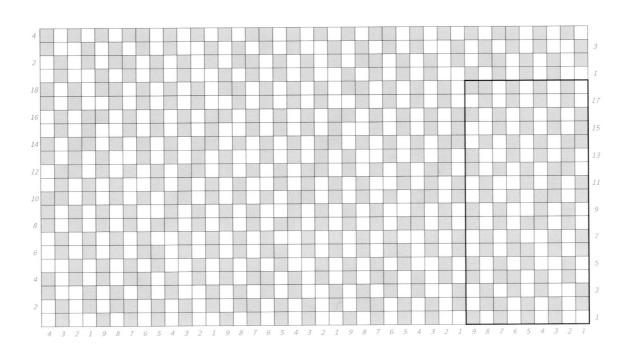

SERPENTINE STITCH PATTERN
[K9, P1] ON 10+1

Shift Reversible

FRONTSIDE

BACKSIDE

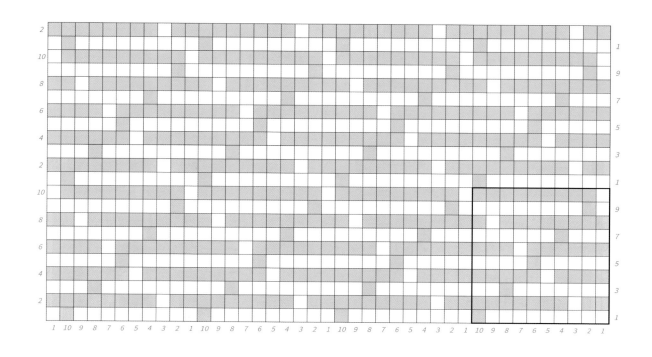

PAGE 164

SERPENTINE STITCH PATTERN
[K8, P2] ON 10+2

Shift Reversible

This pattern is the basis for the Wegner scarf.

FRONTSIDE

BACKSIDE

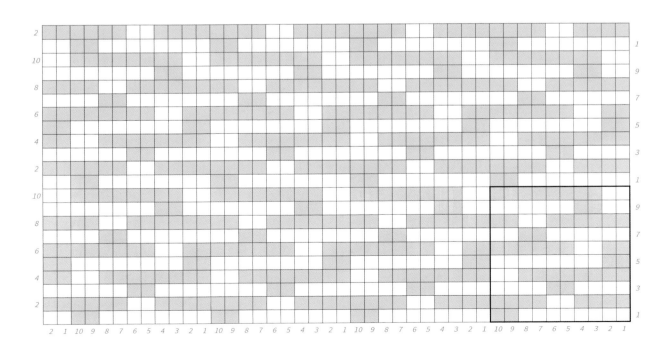

SERPENTINE STITCH PATTERN
[K4, P4, K1, P1] ON 10+2

Shift Reversible

FRONTSIDE

BACKSIDE

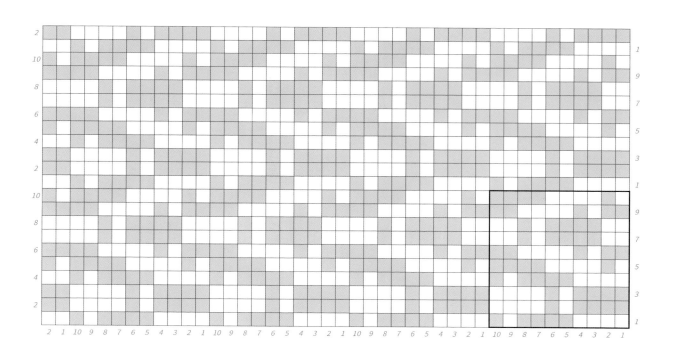

SERPENTINE STITCH PATTERN
[K4, P4, K1, P1] ON 10+4

Shift Reversible

FRONTSIDE

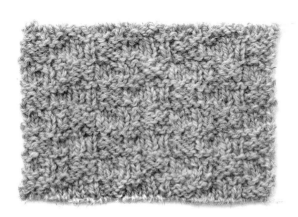

BACKSIDE

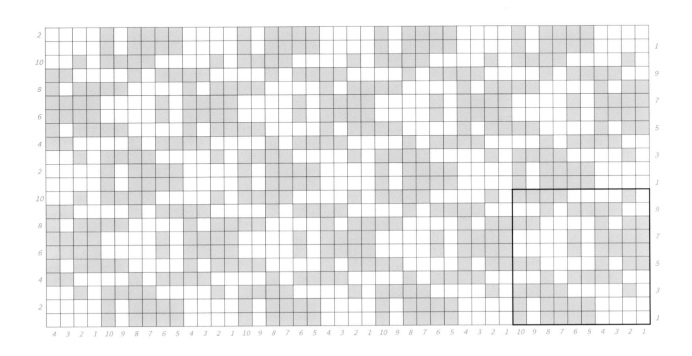

SERPENTINE STITCH PATTERN
[K3, P3, K2, P2] ON 10+2

Shift Reversible

FRONTSIDE

BACKSIDE

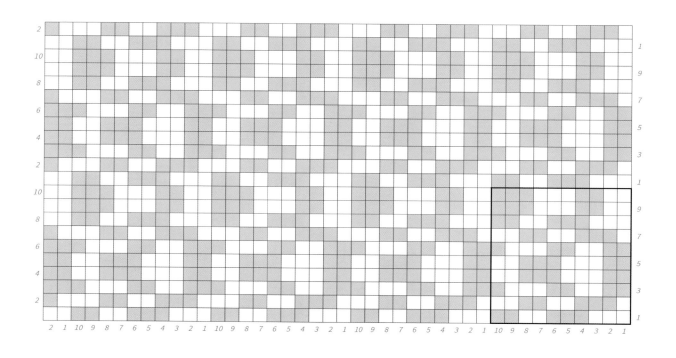

SERPENTINE STITCH PATTERN
[K3, P3, K2, P2] ON 10+4

Shift Reversible Zig Zag

FRONTSIDE

BACKSIDE

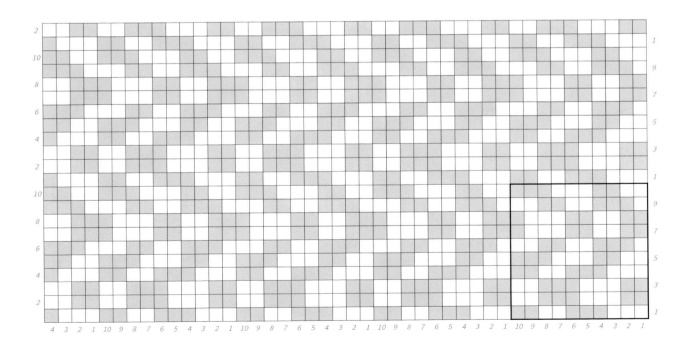

SERPENTINE STITCH PATTERN
[K3, P3, 2(K1, P1)] ON 10+2

Shift Reversible

FRONTSIDE

BACKSIDE

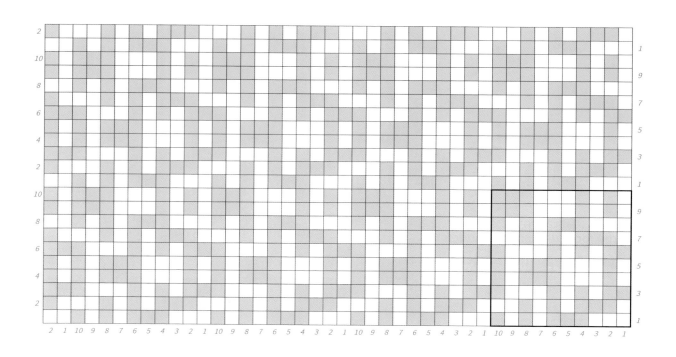

SERPENTINE STITCH PATTERN
[K3, P3, 2(K1, P1)] ON 10+4

Shift Reversible

FRONTSIDE

BACKSIDE

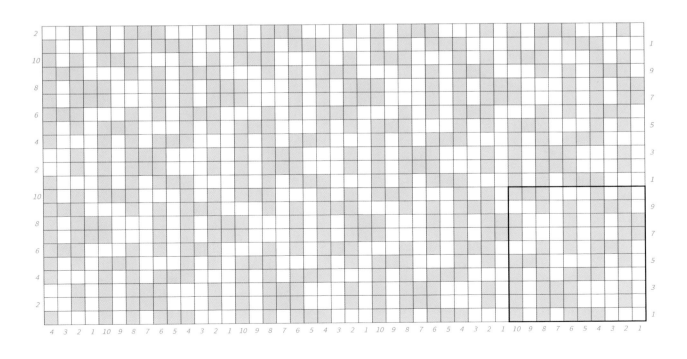

PAGE 171

SERPENTINE STITCH PATTERN
[K2, P2, 3(K1, P1)] ON 10+2

Shift Reversible

FRONTSIDE

BACKSIDE

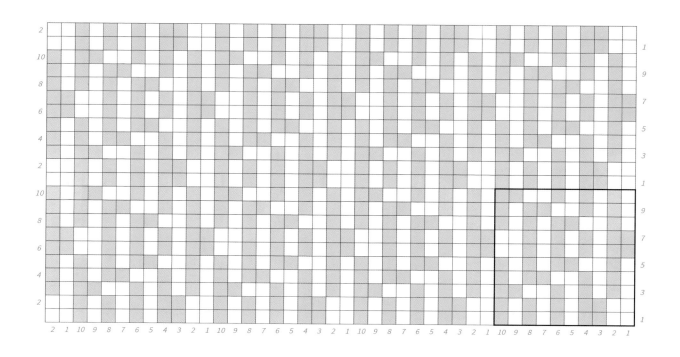

SERPENTINE STITCH PATTERN
[K2, P2, 3(K1, P1)] ON 10+4

Shift Reversible Chain Link

FRONTSIDE

BACKSIDE

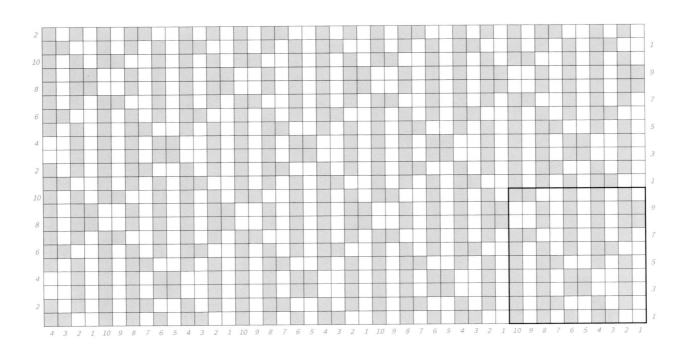

SERPENTINE STITCH PATTERN
[2(K2, P2), K1, P1] ON 10+2

Shift Reversible

FRONTSIDE

BACKSIDE

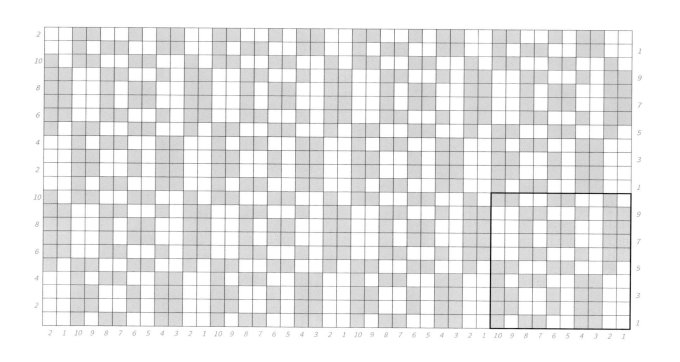

SERPENTINE STITCH PATTERN
[2(K2, P2), K1, P1] ON 10+4

Shift Reversible

FRONTSIDE

BACKSIDE

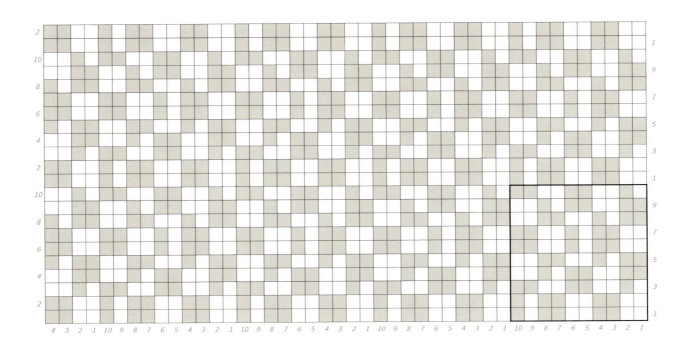

SERPENTINE STITCH PATTERN
[K1, 5(K1, P1)] ON 11+1

Shift Reversible Rib and Seed Diamond

FRONTSIDE

BACKSIDE

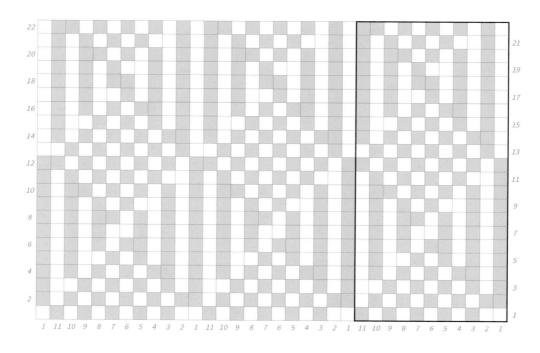

SERPENTINE STITCH PATTERN
[K1, 5(K1, P1)] ON 11+2

Shift Reversible

FRONTSIDE

BACKSIDE

SERPENTINE STITCH PATTERN
[K1, 5(K1, P1)] ON 11+3

Shift Reversible

This pattern has the look and feel of a bouclé.

FRONTSIDE

BACKSIDE

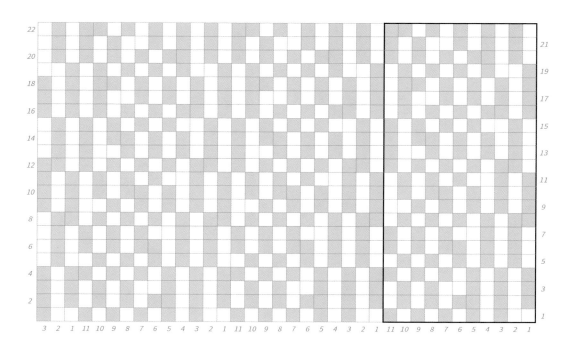

SERPENTINE STITCH PATTERN
[K1, 5(K1, P1)] ON 11+4

Shift Reversible

This pattern has the look and feel of a bouclé.

FRONTSIDE

BACKSIDE

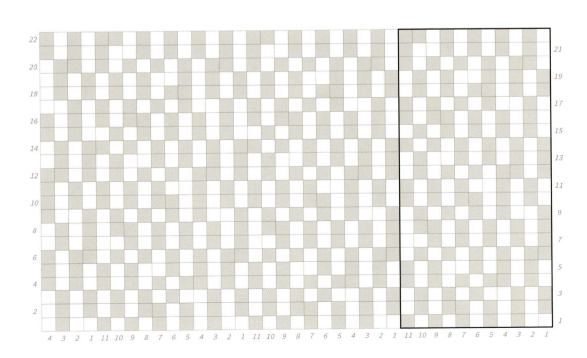

SERPENTINE STITCH PATTERN
[K1, 5(K1, P1)] ON 11+5

Shift Reversible

This pattern has the look and feel of a bouclé.

FRONTSIDE

BACKSIDE

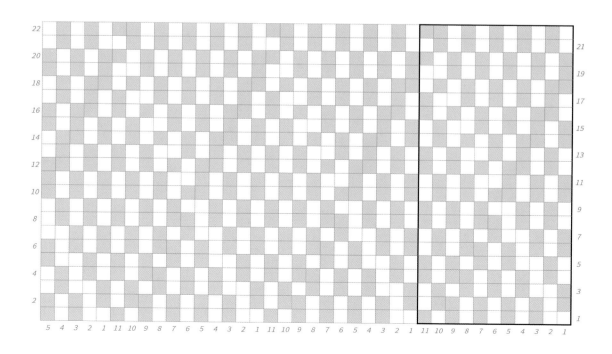

SERPENTINE STITCH PATTERN
[K8, P4] ON 12+1

Aesthetically Reversible

FRONTSIDE

BACKSIDE

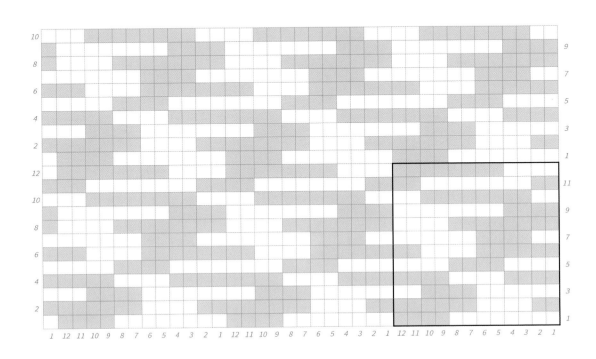

SERPENTINE STITCH PATTERN
[K8, P4] ON 12+3

Aesthetically Reversible

FRONTSIDE

BACKSIDE

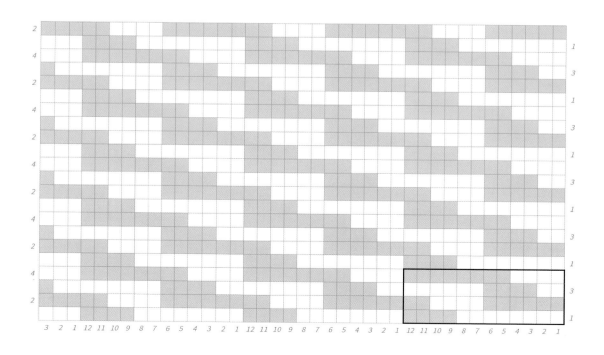

SERPENTINE STITCH PATTERN
[K8, P4] ON 12+3 (START K7, P4)

Aesthetically Reversible

FRONTSIDE

BACKSIDE

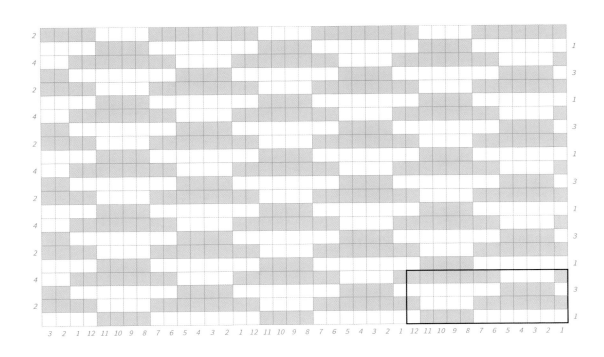

SERPENTINE STITCH PATTERN
[K8, P4] ON 12+4

Shift Reversible

This fabric is the basis for the Bach scarf.

FRONTSIDE

BACKSIDE

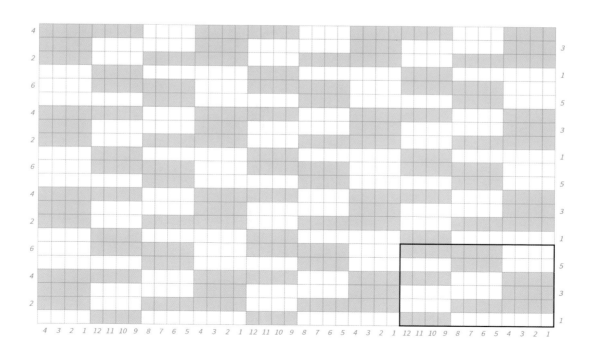

SERPENTINE STITCH PATTERN
[K8, P4] ON 12+4 (START K7, P4)

Shift Reversible

FRONTSIDE

BACKSIDE

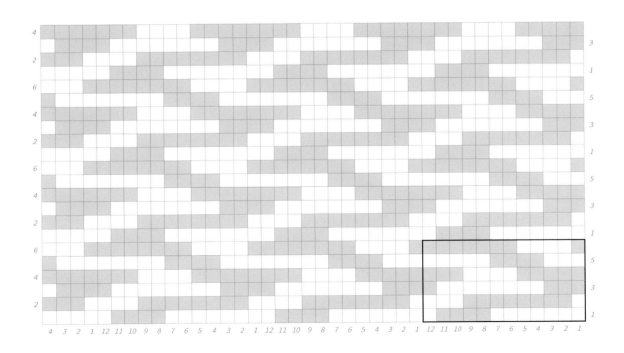

SERPENTINE STITCH PATTERN
[K4, P4, K2, P2] ON 12+1

Aesthetically Reversible

FRONTSIDE

BACKSIDE

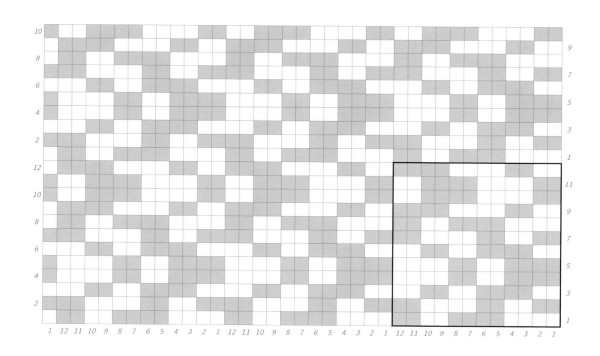

SERPENTINE STITCH PATTERN
[K4, P4, K2, P2] ON 12+2

Shift Reversible

This pattern is the basis for the Hadrians Wall scarf.

FRONTSIDE

BACKSIDE

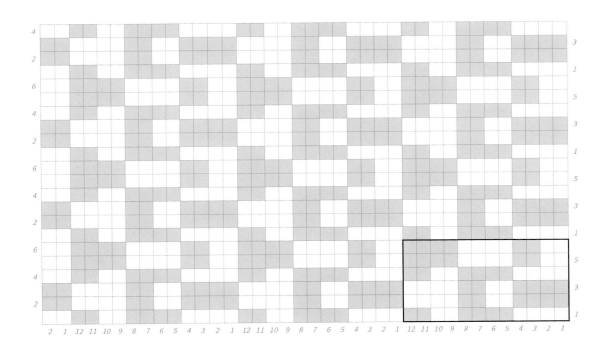

SERPENTINE STITCH PATTERN
[K4, P4, K2, P2] ON 12+2 (START K3, P4, K2, P2)

Shift Reversible

FRONTSIDE

BACKSIDE

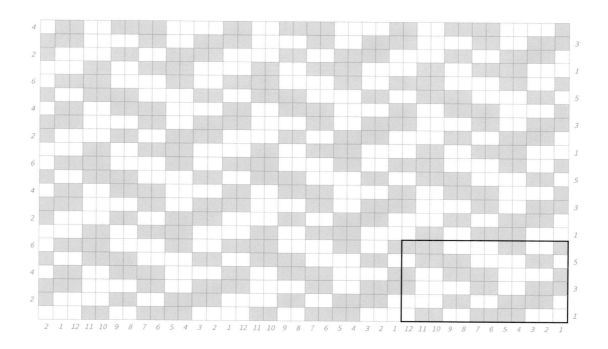

SERPENTINE STITCH PATTERN
[K3, P3, 3(K1, P1)] ON 12+1

Aesthetically Reversible

FRONTSIDE

BACKSIDE

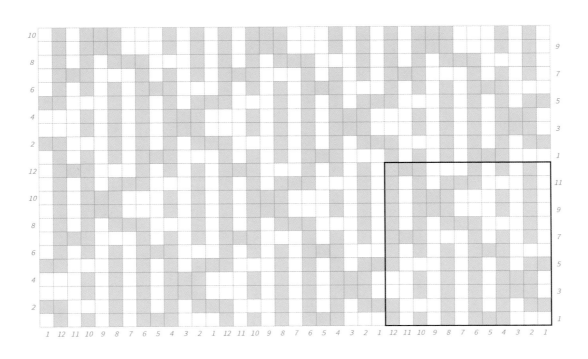

SERPENTINE STITCH PATTERN
[K3, P3, 3(K1, P1)] ON 12+3

Shift Reversible Mistake Ribbing

This mistake ribbing has some characteristics similar to a box pleat, giving it an unusual texture.

FRONTSIDE

BACKSIDE

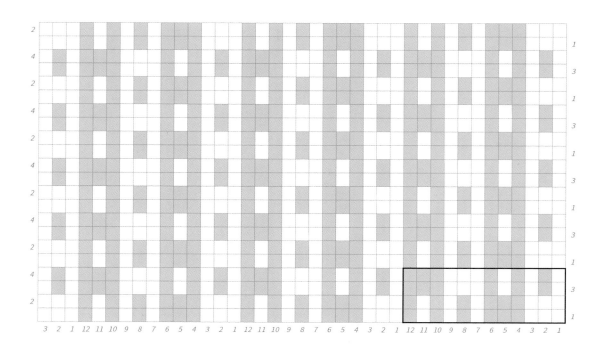

SERPENTINE STITCH PATTERN
[K3, P3, 3(K1, P1)] ON 12+3 (START K2, P3, 3(K1, P1))

Aesthetically Reversible Accordion

This accordion fabric lays flatter than a simpler accordion.

FRONTSIDE

BACKSIDE

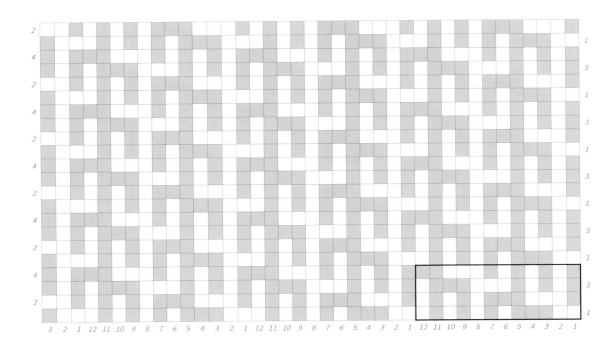

SERPENTINE STITCH PATTERN
[K3, P3, 3(K1, P1)] ON 12+4

Shift Reversible

FRONTSIDE

BACKSIDE

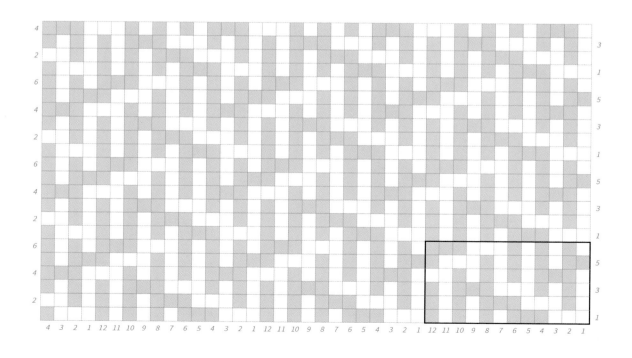

SERPENTINE STITCH PATTERN
[K3, P3, 3(K1, P1)] ON 12+4 (START K2, P3, 3(K1, P1))

Shift Reversible Mistake Ribbing

FRONTSIDE

BACKSIDE

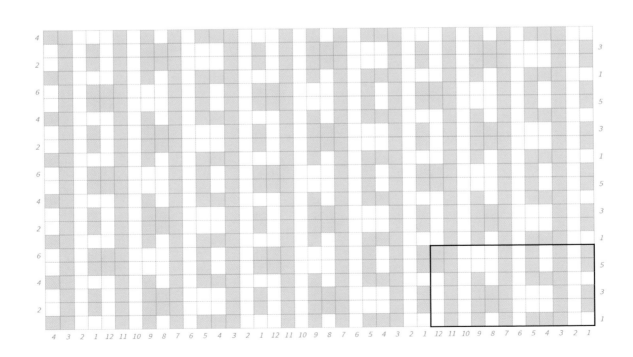

CHAPTER 4

THE SPIRAL METHOD

Sequence Fabrics in the Round

AN INTRODUCTION TO SPIRAL SEQUENCE KNITTING

Spiral Sequence Knitting is simple: choose a sequence and a pattern-multiple, cast on, join in the round, and start working the sequence. When a round is finished, the sequence just continues. The beginning of a round is marked only to keep track of the number of rounds. This method is ideal when the number of stitches per round is constant, for example, the body of hats, the body of sweaters, and the cuffs of gloves, mittens or hand warmers.

The patterns created with spiral knitting are different than 1-row or serpentine patterns because the stitches line up differently. The most common example of this is plain knitting, [K1]. In the 1-row or serpentine methods [K1] results in garter stitch, but in the spiral method, [K1] becomes stockinette.

All the fabric classes found in 1-row knitting and serpentine knitting are possible with spiral knitting, plus a new class called swirls. The most common spiral fabrics are ribbings and swirls.

Ribbing is an easy fabric to create with the spiral method. Working a pattern multiple equal to the sequence length, such as [K2, P2] on a multiple of 4, will always result in ribbing. This rule even works for complex ribbing patterns. For example, the sequence [K4, P4, K3, P3, K2, P2, K1, P1] knit on a multiple of 20 will result in 4x4, 3x3, 2x2, and 1x1 rib pairs. Ribbing can be thought of as a circular version of the 1-row method in that every round is the same.

Things get much more interesting when the pattern multiple is not equal to the sequence length because the stitches do not line up from round to round. And just as

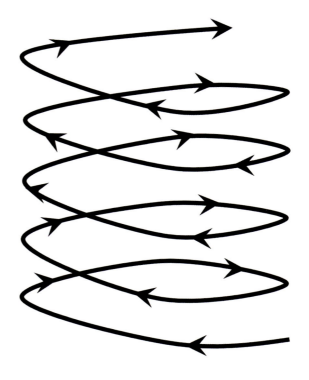

with the serpentine method, wonderful and new fabrics can be created. If the pattern multiple is just 1 stitch greater or less than the sequence length, the resulting fabric will be a swirl. The swirl-type fabrics are found in Dutch Ganseys (Ruhe, 2013) and designer Cathy Carron recently published a sweater pattern based on swirls (Carron, 2014).

The stitch dictionary at the end of this chapter includes all the spiral fabric types with sequence lengths from 1 to 6. A few 12-stitch sequences are also included to provide an introduction to the more complex patterns possible with longer sequences. As with the serpentine method, these fabrics can also be created by following the provided chart. This can be useful if a design needs shaping or to be worked back and forth.

SOME PROPERTIES OF THE SPIRAL METHOD

The facing page shows swatches of some of the possible fabrics that can be created with the spiral method. The simplest fabrics are in the front row: from left to right are stockinette, 1x1 ribbing, 1x1 broken garter (seed), 2x1 ribbing and the simplest swirl, the sequence [K2, P1] on a pattern multiple of 2+1.

The following fabric classes can be created with spiral knitting:

Ribbing
Created when the pattern multiple is equal to the sequence length.

Broken garter
Symmetric broken garter is created with the even sequences ([K1, P1], [K2, P2], [K3, P3], etc.) when the remainder of the pattern multiple is half the sequence length. Other more complex broken garters can also be created with the spiral method.

Swirls
These fabrics are unique to the spiral method. Created when the remainder of the pattern multiple is +/- 1 the sequence length, the resulting fabric will be a right–leaning or left–leaning swirl. For longer sequences pattern multiple remainders of +/-2 or even +/-3 can also result in swirls.

Mistake ribbing
Just as in 1-row knitting, adjoining columns of knit and purl stitches are separated by columns of knit or purl garter. There can be an odd number of rib-columns, for instance 1 knit column and 2 purl columns.

Mock ribbing
Columns of knit ribs are separated by columns of garter. Mock ribbing looks like mistake ribbing, but it is not as stretchy because the columns of knit ribs do not have corresponding purl ribs.

All over
These are patterns where the stitches align in a complex way that is not easy to categorize.

If we consider sequences with just knit and purl stitches, the spiral method has some special qualities that are different from the 1-row or serpentine methods:

- Permutations of the sequence do not change the fabric in spiral knitting, they just change the starting point of the first round.

- If the sequence contains an unequal number of knits and purls, spiral knit fabrics will be aesthetically reversible. If the number of knits and purls are the same, spiral knit fabrics can range from shift reversible to aesthetically reversible.

- Many fabrics are aesthetically reversible based on close analysis of the charts for the frontsides and backsides. In some of these cases, if the number of knit and purl stitches are equal, the actual appearance of the frontside and backside may be close enough to satisfy many as "reversible." An example of this is the pattern used for Welden on page 202.

- Round repeats range from 1 round up to the sequence length. If the pattern multiple is expressed as +/-, the round repeat is the sequence length divided by the remainder. E.g. a sequence length of 8 worked on 8, 8+/-1, 8+/-2, 8+/-3 and 8+4 will have round repeats of 1, 8, 4, 8 and 2.

K2, P1: A SIMPLE EXAMPLE

The charts and swatches below show the same sequence on different pattern multiples. The center chart has a pattern multiple equal to the sequence length, resulting in 2x1 ribbing. Increasing or decreasing the pattern multiple by 1 results in right-leaning or left-leaning swirls. Only right-leaning swirls are shown in the stitch dictionary in this chapter.

[K2, P1] on 3-1

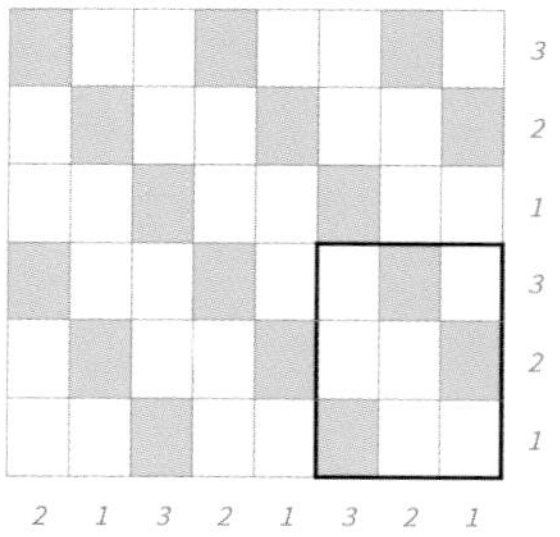

[K2, P1] on 3

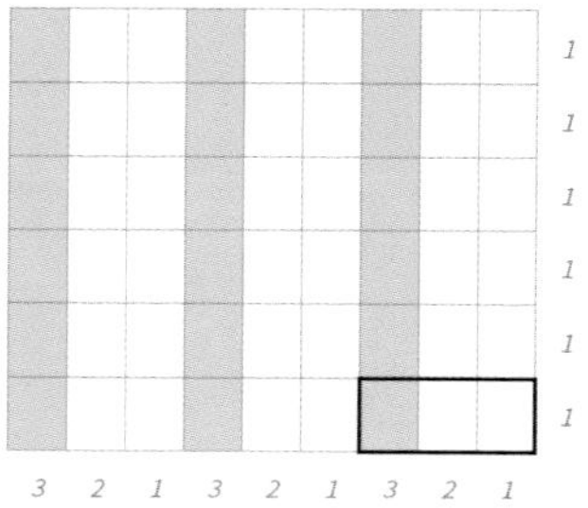

[K2, P1] on 3+1

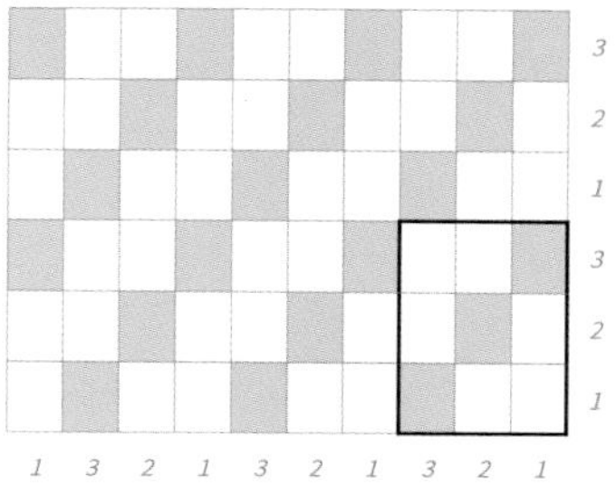

SWIRLS

Swirls are fun and easy to create with the spiral method. The image below shows the following swatches from left to right:

[K1, P1] on 2+1

[K2, P1] on 3+1

[K3, P1] on 4+1

[K4, P1] on 5+1

[K5, P1] on 6+1

[K1, P1] on 2+1 is 1x1 broken garter or seed stitch, but it is helpful to see it in the context of this series, next to [K2, P1] on 3+1, which I consider the simplest swirl.

Moving from left to right the ratio of knits to purls increases and the swirls become more open. As the sequence length grows, so do the stitch and round repeats, opening up the pattern.

WELDEN

To create this textured cowl, just cast on and knit the sequence [K2, P2, K1, P1] until it is time to cast off. Even though this fabric is technically aesthetically reversible, the frontsides and backsides are so similar you might think it is shift-reversible. The sample is made with Madelinetosh Pashmina Worsted in Sugar Plum.

Materials

200 g worsted weight yarn

Size 7 (4.5 mm) 32 inch (80 cm) circular needle

Gauge

5.5 stitches/inch

Dimensions

11 inches wide x 46 inches in circumference (28 x 117 cm)

Pattern notes

1. Reading the pattern as you are knitting can be difficult because of the fine texture. A trick that helps is to check the column of stitches on the first stitch of each round. They will follow the right hand column of the chart: K, P, K, K, P, K.

2. A variation on page 342 uses 2 colors that change every round. Follow the pattern, alternating Color A and Color B every round.

Directions

Cast on 260 stitches, taking care with tension. Join in the round without twisting and place marker at the beginning of round. Work the sequence [K2, P2, K1, P1] with the spiral method until the cowl measures approximately 11 inches (28 cm).

Bind off. Wash, block and weave in ends.

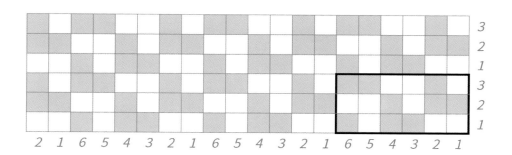

THE ODD SEQUENCES

The spiral fabrics created from odd sequence lengths always have the same behaviors: If the pattern multiple is +/-1 from the sequence length, the fabric is a right- or left-leaning strong spiral. If the pattern multiple is +/-2 from the sequence length, the fabric may also be a spiral, or it may be more complicated depending on the sequence. As the sequence length grows the variations can be more and more complex.

The charts at right illustrate these effects with the sequence [K4, P1] on different pattern multiples. The top and bottom charts represent strong spirals. The middle 2 charts are more nuanced because the 2-stitch shift makes the angle of the swirl lower.

The bigger the remainder on the pattern multiple, the lower the angle of the spiral. If the remainder has a common factor with the sequence length, e.g. sequences of length 9 and pattern multiples of 9+/-3, the stitches may align to create other kinds of patterns like mock or mistake rib.

The 5+/-1 fabrics are clearly the same type, as are the 5+/-2 fabrics. This is generally true for all spiral knitting. For any odd sequence, subtract 1 and then divide by 2 to get the number of fabric types, in this case (5-1)/2 = 2 types.

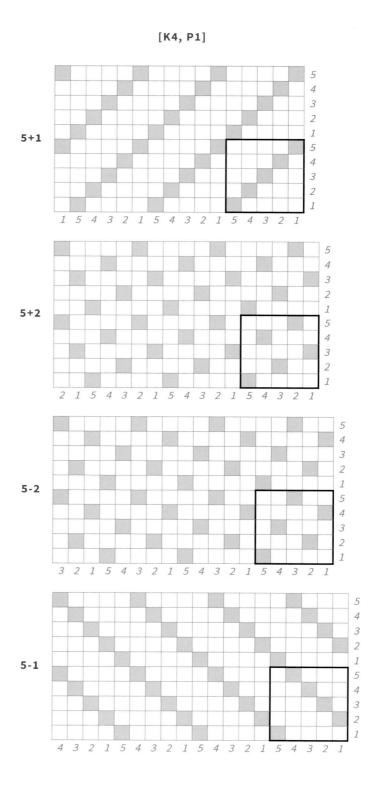

PAGE 204

THE SYMMETRIC EVEN SEQUENCES

The even sequences [K1, P1], [K2, P2], [K3, P3], etc. are interesting illustrations of how spiral knitting is structured. The photographs below and the table at right show how these sequences go from ribbing to a strong swirl, to more nuanced swirls, and finally to broken garter when the remainder on the pattern multiple is exactly half of the sequence length:

Front row: [K1, P1] on a multiple of 2 and 2+1 resulting in 1x1 ribbing and 1x1 broken garter (seed).

Center row: [K2, P2] on a multiple of 4, 4+1, and 4+2 resulting in 2x2 ribbing, a right-leaning swirl and 2x2 broken garter.

Back row: [K3, P3] on a multiple of 6, 6+1, 6+2 and 6+3. Here things get more interesting with 3x3 ribbing, a right-leaning swirl, a medium swirl, and 3x3 broken garter.

Pattern-multiple remainder	K1, P1	K2, P2	K3, P3	K4, P4
0	1x1 Rib	2x2 Rib	3x3 Rib	4x4 Rib
+/- 1	Broken Garter	Steep Swirl	Steep Swirl	Steep Swirl
+/-2		Broken Garter	Medium Swirl	Medium Swirl
+/-3			Broken Garter	Gradual Swirl
+/-4				Broken Garter

THE ASYMMETRIC EVEN SEQUENCES

The even sequences behave a little differently from the odd sequences in the spiral method, just as they do with the serpentine method. The charts on this page show the fabrics created with the sequence [K5, P1] on different pattern multiples. In this example there are 3 fabric types: a swirl, a mock rib with single ribs and a mock rib with double ribs.

The charts show that there is a center fabric for the middle pattern multiple 6+3, and mirror-image fabrics for the 6+/-1 and 6+/-2 pairs of pattern multiples.

The charts also show how the round repeats vary when the remainder is a factor of the sequence length. For the sequence length 6, remainders of 1 result in a 6-round repeat, remainders of 2 result in a round repeat of 3, and remainders of 3 result in a 2-round repeat.

The facing page shows 6 charts for the 12-stitch sequence [2(K2, P2), 2(K1, P1)]. The charts illustrate a behavior similar to the 6-stitch sequence on this page: the fabrics go from swirls, to an all-over pattern, to mistake ribbing at the half-way point of 12+6. These charts are used for the Serra hat patterns on the following page.

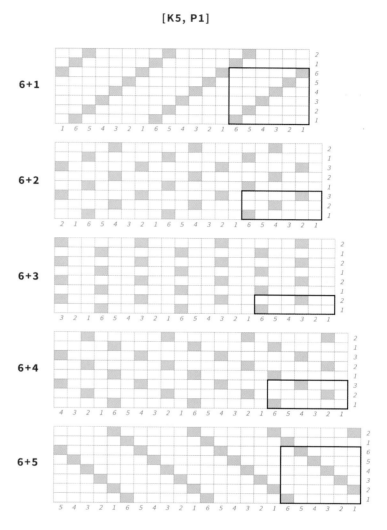

[2(K2, P2), 2(K1, P1)]

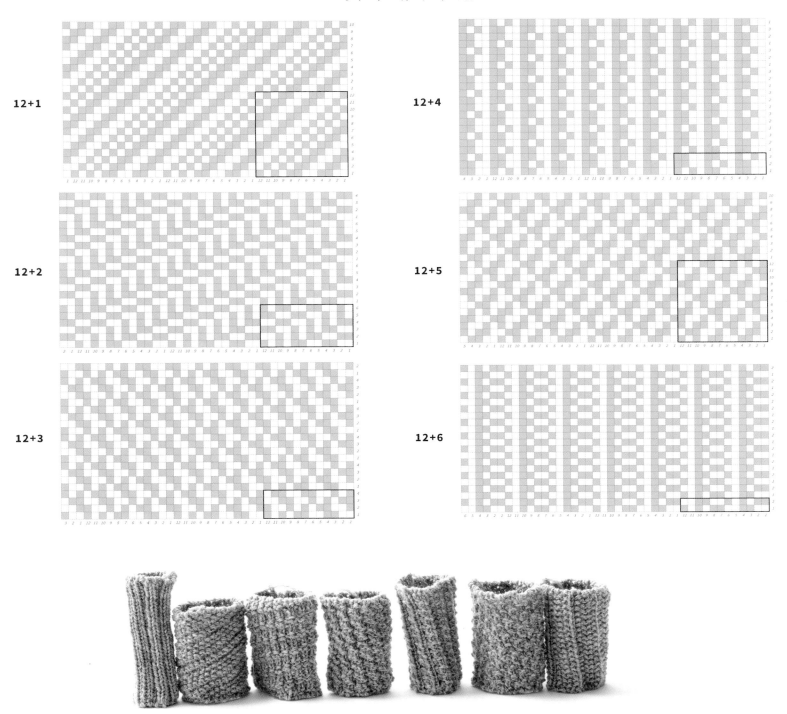

SERRA 1-6

These hats were designed to show how easy it is to create a wide variety of designs using just 1 sequence with the spiral method. Adding 1 stitch changes the fabric completely. The hats are quick and easy to knit and make a perfect last-minute gift. The samples were made with Cascade 128 Superwash Merino Bulky in Silver.

The hats are all worked with the sequence [2(K2, P2), 2(K1, P1)]. Shown from left to right, the pattern multiple is 12+1, 12+2, 12+3, 12+4, 12+5 and 12+6. The charts are on page 207.

The technical reversibility varies from shift to aesthetic, but all patterns are similar on both sides. You can fold up the brim and the reverse side will mirror the pattern.

Materials

100 g bulky yarn

Size 9 (5.5 mm) 16 inch (40 cm) circular needle

Size 9 (5.5 mm) double-pointed needles

Gauge

4 stitches / inch in stockinette

Dimensions

Unstretched brim circumferences are 17, 16, 16, 14, 16.5, and 16 inches (43, 41, 41, 35.5, 42, and 41 cm) for Serra 1-6. All hats are 10.5 inches (26.5 cm) from the top of the crown to the brim.

Pattern notes

1. Any elastic cast-on is suitable. The Alternating Cast-On in Hiatt's Principles of Knitting is a good choice.

2. After casting on and joining in the round, work the sequence [2(K2, P2), 2(K1, P1)] in a spiral. Do not restart the sequence every round, flow the sequence from round to round to create the different patterns.

Directions

For Serra 1 (2, 3, 4, 5, 6), with circular needle, cast on 61 (62, 63, 64, 65, 66) stitches. Place a marker, join to work in the round, and work the sequence [2(K2, P2), 2(K1, P1)] until the hat is 7.5 inches (19 cm) tall. Knit 1 round.

Begin crown shaping:

Serra 1: [K59, K2tog]

Serra 2: [2(K29, K2tog)]

Serra 3: [3(K19, K2tog)]

Serra 4: [4(K14, K2tog)]

Serra 5: [5(K11, K2tog)]

Serra 6: [6(K9, K2tog)]

All hats have 60 stitches. Knit 6 rounds. Switch to double pointed needles.

Decrease round: work 20[K1, K2tog]—40 stitches.

Knit 4 rounds.

Decrease round: work 20[K2tog]—20 stitches.

Knit 3 rounds.

Decrease round: work [K2tog] 10 times—10 stitches.

Pull yarn through remaining stitches, draw up and secure. Weave in ends.

WINTERWORK

These hand warmers are nice to wear when you need your fingertips and the weather is cold. I like to wear them when I am doing outdoor photography. The hand section is 2x2 rib, and the cuff is a spiral knit. The sample is worked in hand-painted fingering merino.

Materials

50 g fingering weight yarn

Size 1 (2.25 mm) double-pointed needles

Size 2 (2.75 mm) double-pointed needles

Gauge

7 stitches / inch in stockinette (28 stitches / 10 cm)

Dimensions

Length 7.5 inches (19 cm) for S/M and M/L

Unstretched circumference for the upper edge is 3.75 (5) inches (9 (12) cm) and the wrist edge is 6 (8.25) inches (15.5 (22) cm)

Pattern notes

1. The cuff is based on the sequence [K3, P1, K2, P2, K1, P3] on a pattern multiple of 12+9. This sequence is easy to remember if you think of it as 3 sets of 4 stitches: 3/1, 2/2, 1/3.
2. A smaller needle is used for the cuff.

Stitch glossary

M1 means to make 1 stitch by knitting into the back and front of the stitch.

Directions

For S/M (M/L) with size 2 (2.75 mm) needles, cast on 44 (56) stitches. Place a marker and join to work in the round. Begin with K2, work in 2x2 ribbing for 1.5 inches (4 cm) ending at marker, then work first 3 stitches of next round (end between 2 purl stitches). Turn and work back and forth in rib as established for thumb opening for 1.5 inches (4 cm). Rejoin and continue in rib in the round for 1.5 inches (4 cm), ending at marker. Change to size 1 (2.25 mm) needles. Next round, M1 (this counts as first 2 stitches of sequence), continue in the sequence [K3, P1, K2, P2, K1, P3] using the spiral method for 3 inches (7.5 cm). Bind off loosely and weave in ends.

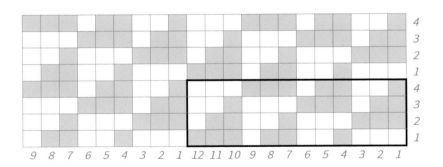

HARLIN

Harlin is a warm winter hat that can be made with any 2 colors of worsted wool. Two skeins of Cascade 220 make a pair of hats with opposite colorways. The sample is worked in the colorways Sapphire Heather and Charcoal Gray.

Materials

50 g worsted weight yarn in color A

50 g worsted weight yarn in color B

Size 7 (4.5 mm) 16 inch (40 cm) circular needle

Size 5 (3.75 mm) 16 inch (40 cm) circular needle

Size 5 (3.75 mm) double pointed needles

Gauge

5 stitches / inch in stockinette

Dimensions

Sized for S/M (M/L) Unstretched brim circumference 16 (17.5) inches / 40.5 (44.5) cm. Both sizes are 8 inches (20 cm) from the top of the crown to the brim.

Pattern notes

1. The pattern multiple is 3 stitches for the band and 6+3 stitches for the body.
2. On the body of the hat the colors are changed at the beginning of every round. When changing colors, always bring new yarn from the front of working yarn to twist.
3. Continue the sequence in the spiral method even when the color changes.

Abbreviations

K1b knit into the back of the stitch.

D2 slip 2 stitches together as if to knit, knit the next stitch through the farside, and then pass the slipped stitches over the knit stitch together—2 stitches decreased.

S1WYIB is to slip 1 purlwise with the yarn in back.

Directions

With color A and size 7 circular needle, cast on 93 (99) stitches. Join in the round without twisting, place marker. Work 4 rounds in stockinette. Change to size 5 circular needle and work the sequence [P1, K1b, P1] in a spiral for 1.5 inches (4 cm). Change back to size 7 circular needle and work the sequence [K3, P1, S1WYIB, P1] for 1 round. Switch to color B and continue in sequence for 1 round. Continue in sequence, alternating between colors A and B each round, until body of hat measures 4 inches (10 cm). Break B and work 2 rounds more in A. Change to size 5 needle. Work the sequence [P1, K1b, P1] for 6 rounds, ending after a P2 at the end of the sixth round.

First decrease round: Work the sequence [K1b, P2tog]—62(66) stitches. Switch to double pointed needles. Work the sequence [K1b, P1] for 3 rounds.

For S/M only

Second decrease round: Work 10[D2, P1, K1b, P1], K1b, P1—42 stitches. Work the sequence [K1b, P1] for 2 rounds. Third decrease round: Work 7[D2, P1, K1b, P1]—28 stitches. Work the sequence [K1b, P1] for 2 rounds. Last decrease round: 7[D2, P1]—14 stitches. Work the sequence [K1b, P1] for 1 round.

For M/L only

Second decrease round: Work 11[D2, P1, K1b, P1]—44 stitches. Work the sequence [K1b, P1] for 2 rounds. Third decrease round: Work 7[D2, P1, K1b, P1], K1b, P1—30 stitches. Work the sequence [K1b, P1] for 2 rounds. Fourth decrease round: Work 5[D2, P1, K1b, P1]—20 stitches. Work the sequence [K1b, P1] for 1 round. Last decrease round: Work 5[D2, P1]—10 stitches.

Pull yarn through the remaining stitches, draw up and secure. Weave in ends.

SPIRAL STITCHES IN THIS DICTIONARY

Sequence Length (n)	Pattern multiple	Sequence	Pattern Type	1-color Reversibility
1	1	K1	Stockinette	Aesthetically
2	2	K1, P1	Ribbing	Perfectly
2	2+1	K1, P1	Broken Garter	Shift
3	3	K2, P1	Ribbing	Aesthetically
3	3+1	K2, P1	Swirl	Aesthetically
4	4	K3, P1	Ribbing	Aesthetically
4	4+1	K3, P1	Swirl	Aesthetically
4	4+2	K3, P1	Mock ribbing	Aesthetically
4	4	K2, P2	Ribbing	Perfectly
4	4+1	K2, P2	Swirl	Aesthetically
4	4+2	K2, P2	Broken Garter	Shift
5	5	K4, P1	Ribbing	Aesthetically
5	5+1	K4, P1	Swirl	Aesthetically
5	5+2	K4, P1	Swirl	Aesthetically
5	5	K3, P2	Ribbing	Aesthetically
5	5+1	K3, P2	Swirl	Aesthetically
5	5+2	K3, P2	Swirl	Aesthetically
5	5	K2, P1, K1, P1	Ribbing	Aesthetically
5	5+1	K2, P1, K1, P1	Swirl	Aesthetically
5	5+2	K2, P1, K1, P1	All over	Aesthetically
6	6	K5, P1	Ribbing	Aesthetically
6	6+1	K5, P1	Swirl	Aesthetically
6	6+2	K5, P1	Mock Ribbing	Aesthetically
6	6+3	K5, P1	Mock Ribbing	Aesthetically
6	6	K4, P2	Ribbing	Aesthetically
6	6+1	K4, P2	Swirl	Aesthetically
6	6+2	K4, P2	Swirl	Aesthetically
6	6+3	K4, P2	Mock Ribbing	Aesthetically
6	6	K3, P1, K1, P1	Ribbing	Aesthetically
6	6+1	K3, P1, K1, P1	Swirl	Aesthetically
6	6+2	K3, P1, K1, P1	Mock Ribbing	Aesthetically
6	6+3	K3, P1, K1, P1	Mock Ribbing	Aesthetically
6	6	K3, P3	Ribbing	Perfectly
6	6+1	K3, P3	Swirl	Aesthetically
6	6+2	K3, P3	Swirl	Aesthetically
6	6+3	K3, P3	Broken Garter	Shift
6	6	K2, P1, K1, P2	Ribbing	Perfectly
6	6+1	K2, P1, K1, P2	Swirl	Aesthetically
6	6+2	K2, P1, K1, P2	All Over	Aesthetically
6	6+3	K2, P1, K1, P2	Mistake Ribbing	Shift
6	6	K2, P2, K1, P1	Ribbing	Shift
6	6+1	K2, P2, K1, P1	Swirl	Aesthetically
6	6+2	K2, P2, K1, P1	All Over	Aesthetically
6	6+3	K2, P2, K1, P1	Mistake Ribbing	Shift
12	12	K4, P4, K2, P2	Ribbing	Shift
12	12+1	K4, P4, K2, P2	Swirl	Aesthetically
12	12+2	K4, P4, K2, P2	Swirl	Aesthetically
12	12+3	K4, P4, K2, P2	Swirl	Aesthetically
12	12+4	K4, P4, K2, P2	All Over	Shift
12	12+5	K4, P4, K2, P2	Swirl	Aesthetically
12	12+6	K4, P4, K2, P2	Mistake Ribbing	Shift
12	12	2(K2, P2), 2(K1, P1)	Ribbing	Shift
12	12+1	2(K2, P2), 2(K1, P1)	Swirl	Aesthetically
12	12+2	2(K2, P2), 2(K1, P1)	Swirl	Aesthetically
12	12+3	2(K2, P2), 2(K1, P1)	All Over	Aesthetically
12	12+4	2(K2, P2), 2(K1, P1)	Mistake Ribbing	Shift
12	12+5	2(K2, P2), 2(K1, P1)	All Over	Aesthetically
12	12+6	2(K2, P2), 2(K1, P1)	Mistake Ribbing	Shift
12	12	K1, P3, 4(K1, P1)	Ribbing	Aesthetically
12	12+1	K1, P3, 4(K1, P1)	Swirl	Aesthetically
12	12+2	K1, P3, 4(K1, P1)	Swirl	Aesthetically
12	12+3	K1, P3, 4(K1, P1)	All Over	Aesthetically
12	12+4	K1, P3, 4(K1, P1)	Mistake Ribbing	Aesthetically
12	12+5	K1, P3, 4(K1, P1)	All over	Aesthetically
12	12+6	K1, P3, 4(K1, P1)	Mistake Ribbing	Aesthetically

SPIRAL
K1 ON ANY NUMBER OF STITCHES

Aesthetically Reversible Stockinette Stitch

FRONTSIDE

BACKSIDE

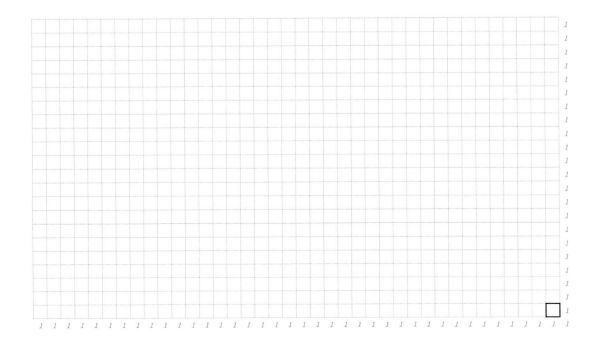

SPIRAL
K1, P1 ON 2

Perfectly Reversible Ribbing

FRONTSIDE

BACKSIDE

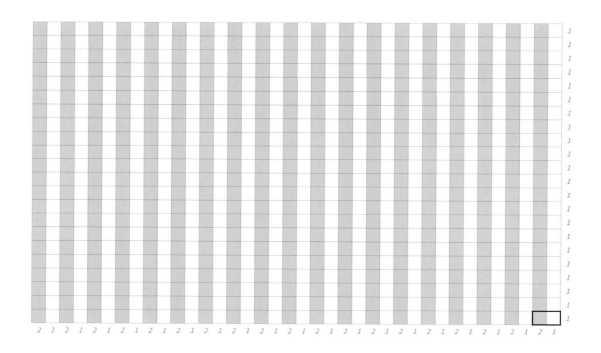

SPIRAL
K1, P1 ON 2+1

Shift Reversible Broken Garter (Seed Stitch)

FRONTSIDE

BACKSIDE

SPIRAL
K2, P1 ON 3

Aesthetically Reversible Ribbing

FRONTSIDE

BACKSIDE

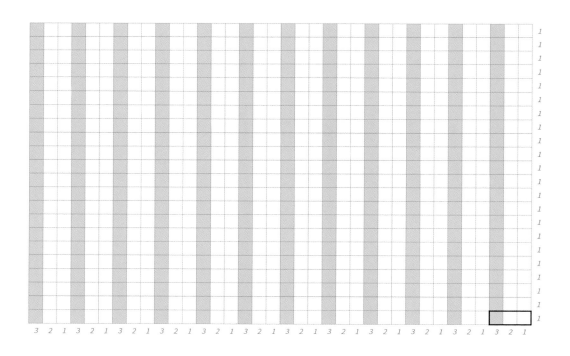

SPIRAL
K2, P1 ON 3+1

Aesthetically Reversible Swirl

FRONTSIDE

BACKSIDE

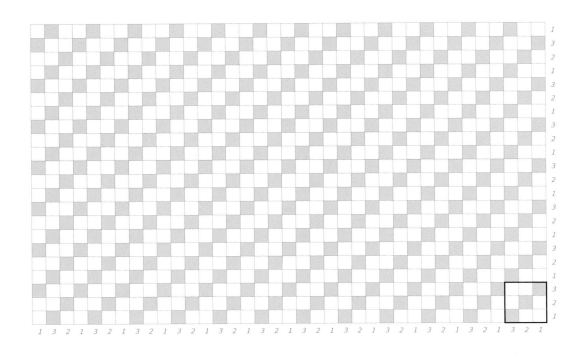

SPIRAL
K3, P1 ON 4

Aesthetically Reversible Ribbing

FRONTSIDE

BACKSIDE

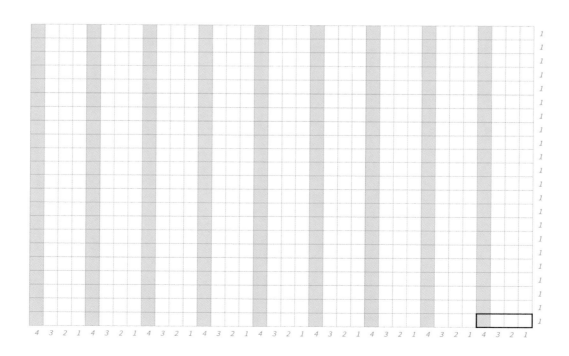

SPIRAL
K3, P1 ON 4+1

Aesthetically Reversible Swirl

FRONTSIDE

BACKSIDE

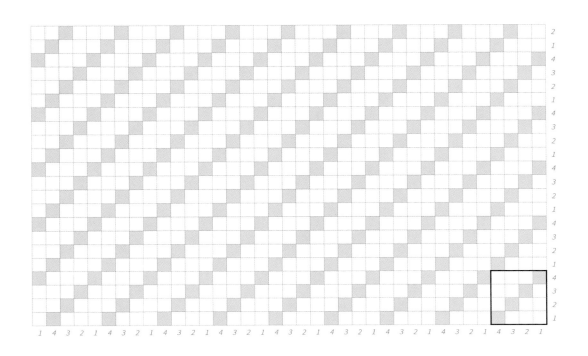

SPIRAL
K3, P1 ON 4+2

Aesthetically Reversible Mock Ribbing

FRONTSIDE

BACKSIDE

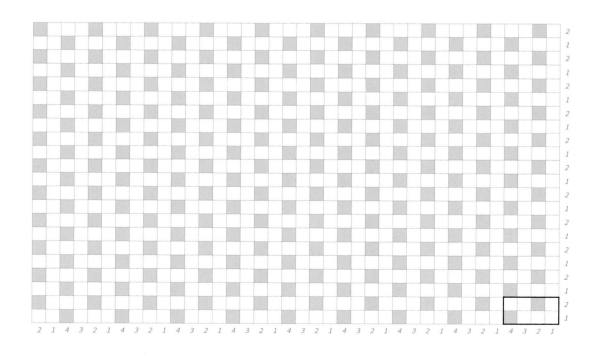

SPIRAL
K2, P2 ON 4

Perfectly Reversible Ribbing

FRONTSIDE

BACKSIDE

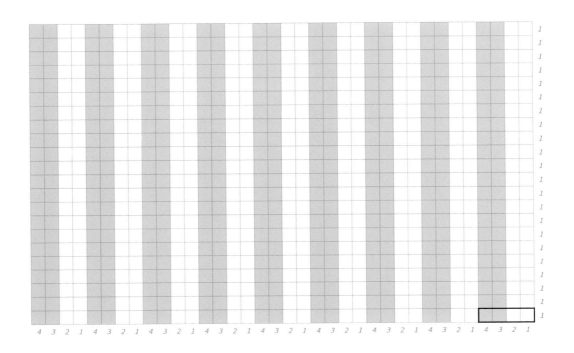

SPIRAL
K2, P2 ON 4+1

Aesthetically Reversible Swirl

FRONTSIDE

BACKSIDE

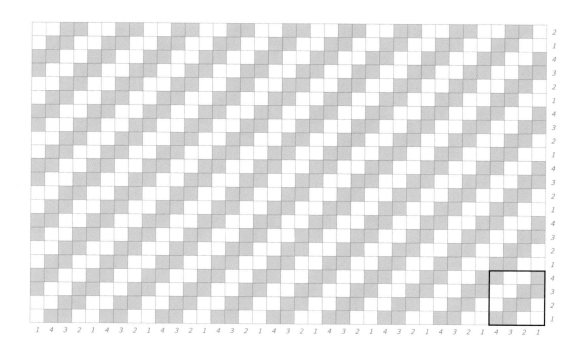

SPIRAL
K2, P2 ON 4+2

Shift Reversible Broken Garter

FRONTSIDE

BACKSIDE

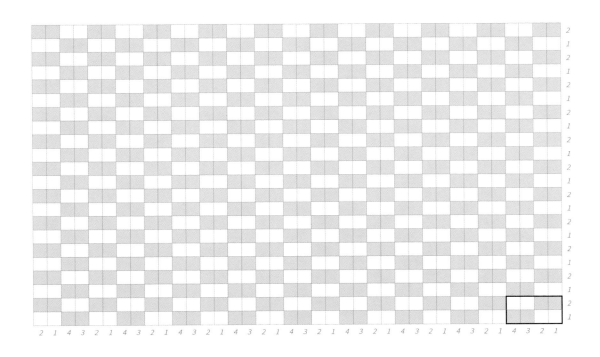

SPIRAL
K4, P1 ON 5

Aesthetically Reversible Ribbing

FRONTSIDE

BACKSIDE

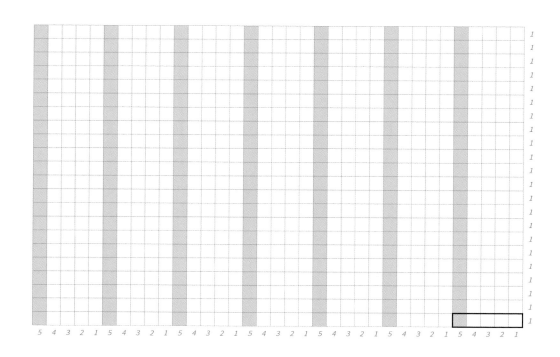

SPIRAL
K4, P1 ON 5+1

Aesthetically Reversible Swirl

FRONTSIDE

BACKSIDE

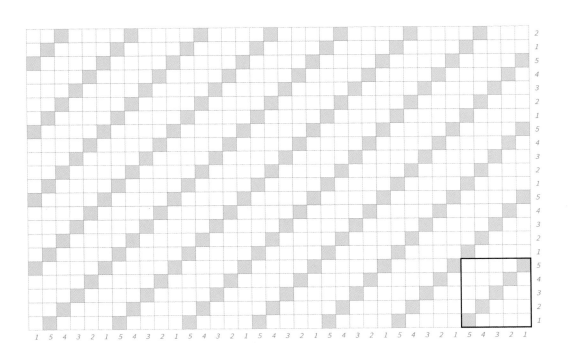

PAGE 227

SPIRAL
K4, P1 ON 5+2

Aesthetically Reversible Swirl

FRONTSIDE

BACKSIDE

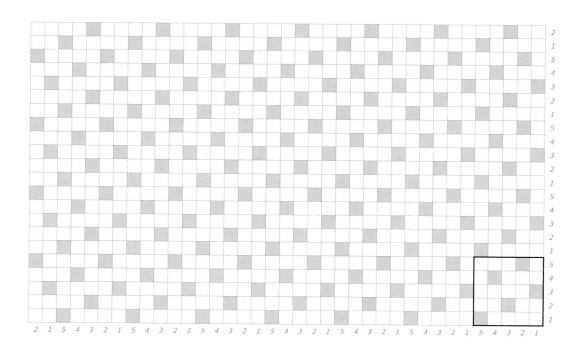

SPIRAL
K3, P2 ON 5

Aesthetically Reversible Ribbing

FRONTSIDE

BACKSIDE

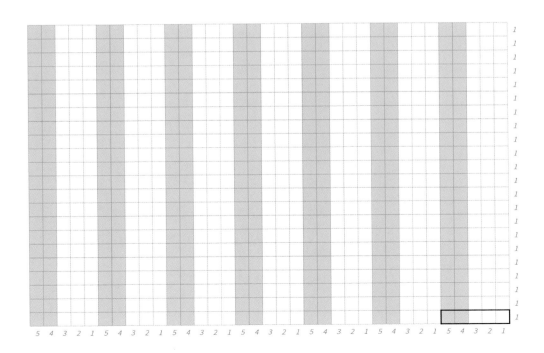

SPIRAL
K3, P2 ON 5+1

Aesthetically Reversible Swirl

FRONTSIDE

BACKSIDE

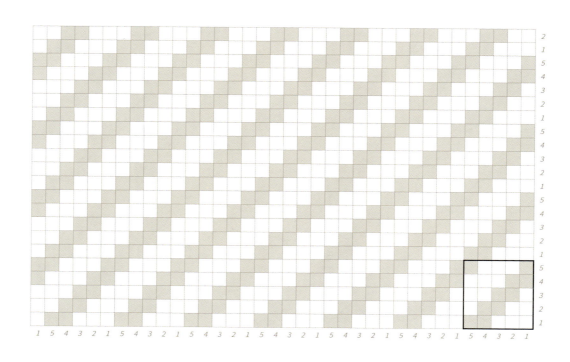

SPIRAL
K3, P2 ON 5+2

Aesthetically Reversible Swirl

FRONTSIDE

BACKSIDE

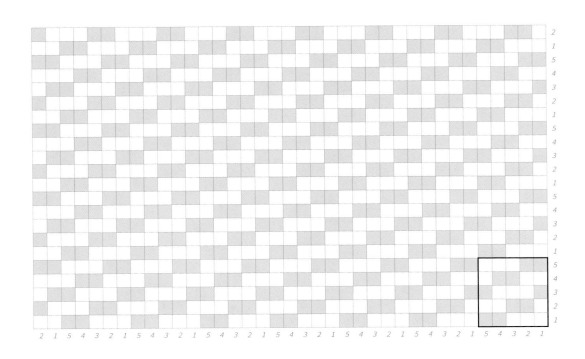

SPIRAL
K2, P1, K1, P1 ON 5

Aesthetically Reversible Ribbing

FRONTSIDE

BACKSIDE

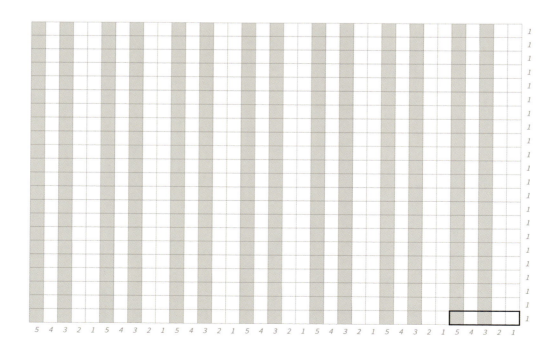

SPIRAL
K2, P1, K1, P1 ON 5+1

Aesthetically Reversible Swirl

FRONTSIDE

BACKSIDE

SPIRAL
K2, P1, K1, P1 ON 5+2

Aesthetically Reversible All Over Pattern

FRONTSIDE

BACKSIDE

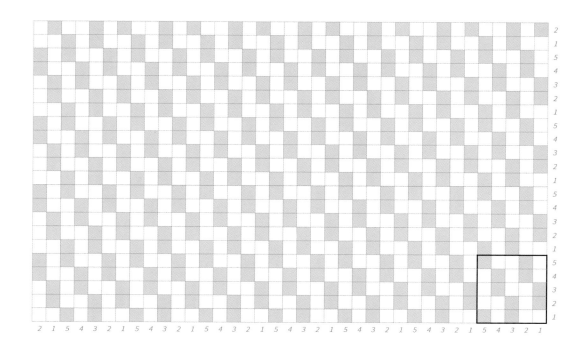

SPIRAL
K5, P1 ON 6

Aesthetically Reversible Ribbing

FRONTSIDE

BACKSIDE

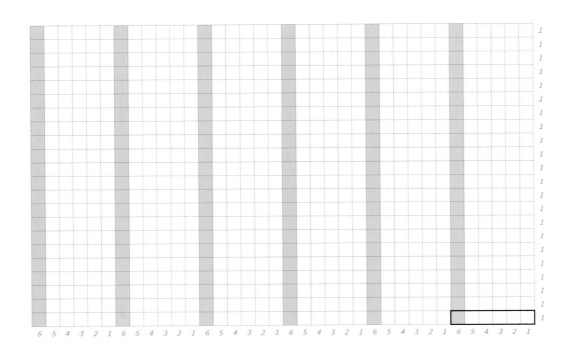

SPIRAL
K5, P1 ON 6+1

Aesthetically Reversible Swirl

FRONTSIDE

BACKSIDE

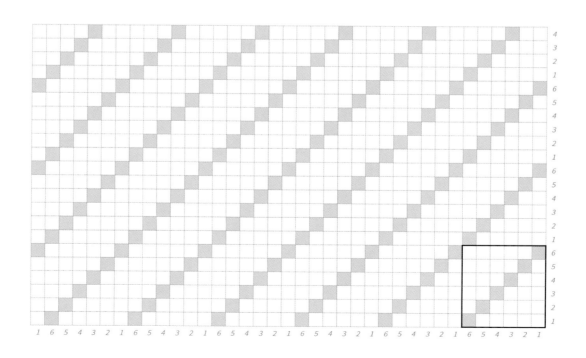

SPIRAL
K5, P1 ON 6+2

Aesthetically Reversible Mock Ribbing

FRONTSIDE

BACKSIDE

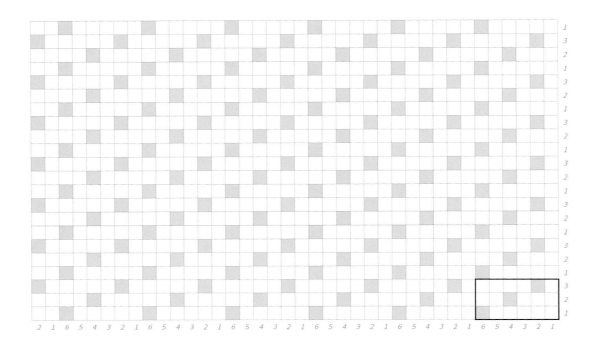

SPIRAL
K5, P1 ON 6+3

Aesthetically Reversible Mock Ribbing

FRONTSIDE

BACKSIDE

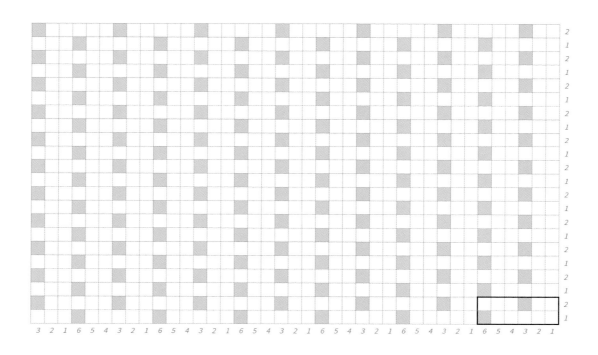

SPIRAL
K4, P2 ON 6

Aesthetically Reversible Ribbing

FRONTSIDE

BACKSIDE

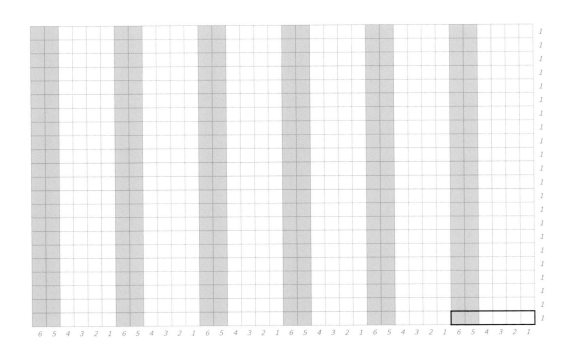

SPIRAL
K4, P2 ON 6+1

Aesthetically Reversible Swirl

FRONTSIDE

BACKSIDE

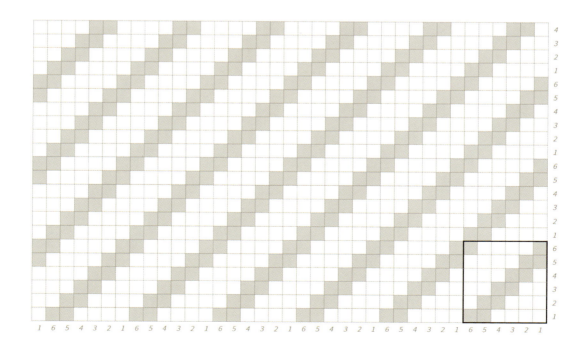

SPIRAL
K4, P2 ON 6+2

Aesthetically Reversible Swirl

FRONTSIDE

BACKSIDE

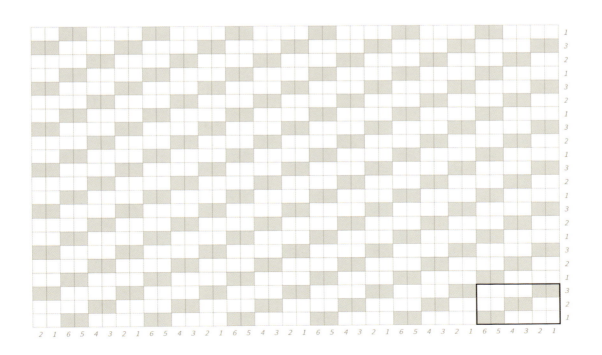

SPIRAL
K4, P2 ON 6+3

Aesthetically Reversible Mock Ribbing

FRONTSIDE

BACKSIDE

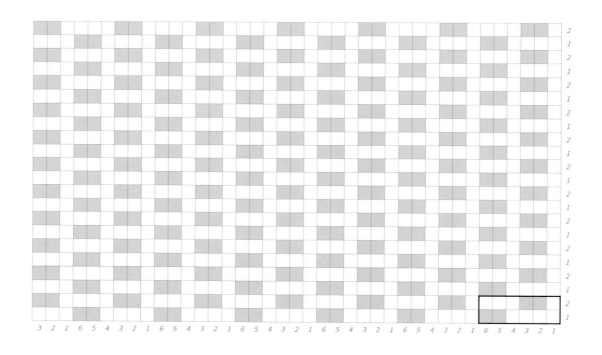

SPIRAL
K3, P1, K1, P1 ON 6

Aesthetically Reversible Ribbing

FRONTSIDE

BACKSIDE

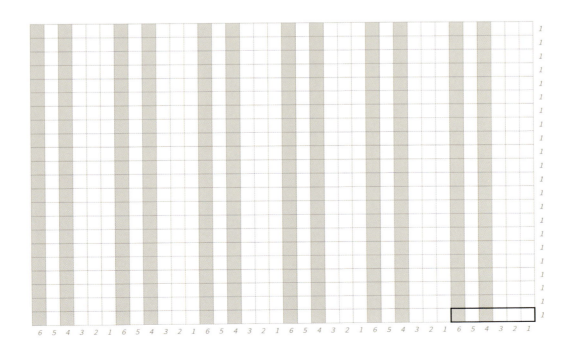

SPIRAL
K3, P1, K1, P1 ON 6+1

Aesthetically Reversible Swirl

FRONTSIDE

BACKSIDE

SPIRAL
K3, P1, K1, P1 ON 6+2

Aesthetically Reversible Mock Ribbing

FRONTSIDE

BACKSIDE

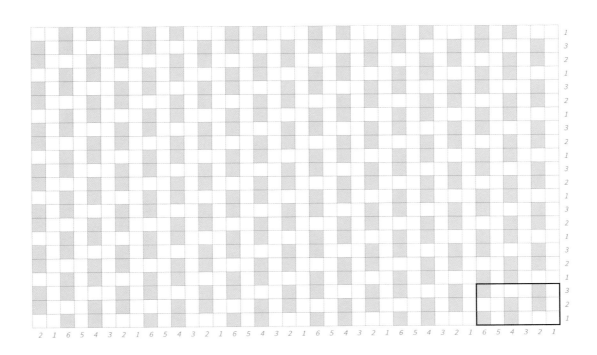

PAGE 245

SPIRAL
K3, P1, K1, P1 ON 6+3

Aesthetically Reversible Mock Ribbing

FRONTSIDE

BACKSIDE

SPIRAL
K3, P3 ON 6

Perfectly Reversible Ribbing

FRONTSIDE

BACKSIDE

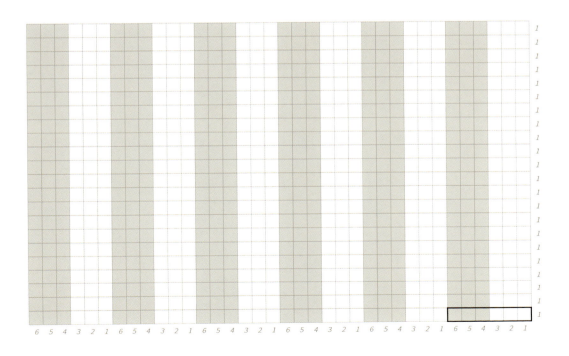

PAGE 247

SPIRAL
K3, P3 ON 6+1

Aesthetically Reversible Swirl

FRONTSIDE

BACKSIDE

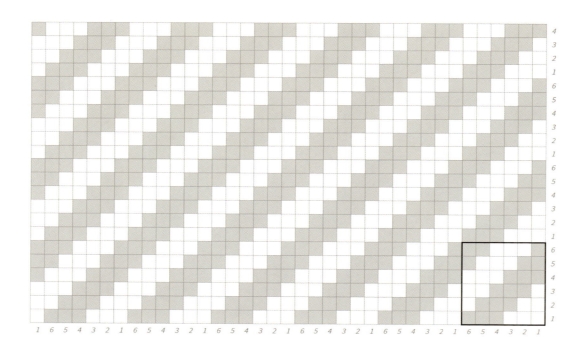

SPIRAL
K3, P3 ON 6+2

Aesthetically Reversible Swirl

FRONTSIDE

BACKSIDE

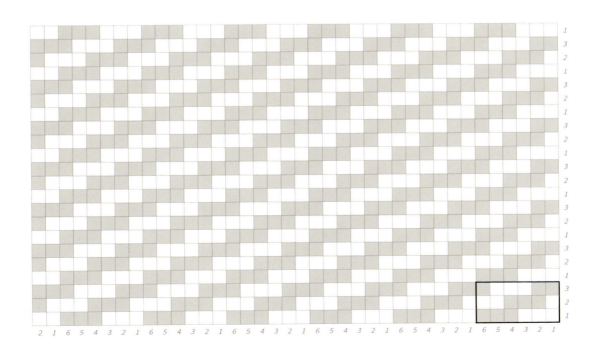

SPIRAL
K3, P3 ON 6+3

Shift Reversible Broken Garter

FRONTSIDE

BACKSIDE

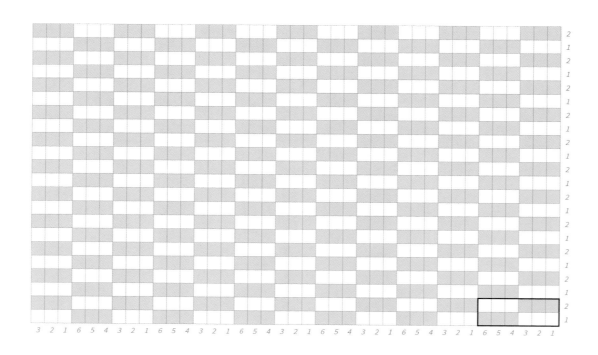

SPIRAL
K2, P1, K1, P2 ON 6

Perfectly Reversible Ribbing

FRONTSIDE

BACKSIDE

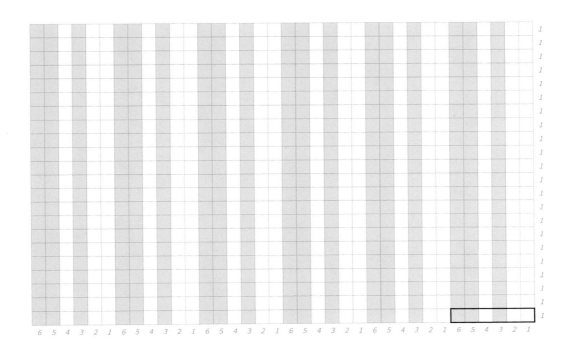

SPIRAL
K2, P1, K1, P2 ON 6+1

Aesthetically Reversible Swirl

FRONTSIDE

BACKSIDE

SPIRAL
K2, P1, K1, P2 ON 6+2

Aesthetically Reversible All Over Pattern

FRONTSIDE

BACKSIDE

SPIRAL
K2, P1, K1, P2 ON 6+3

Shift Reversible Mistake Ribbing

FRONTSIDE

BACKSIDE

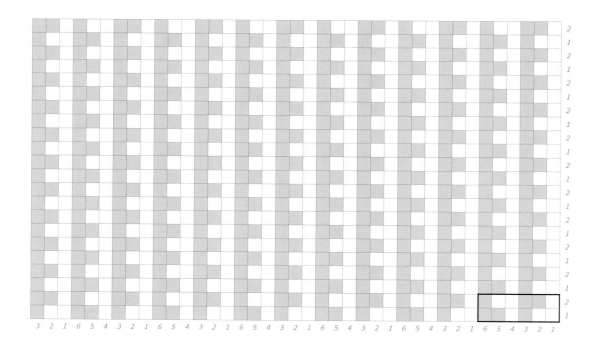

SPIRAL
K2, P2, K1, P1 ON 6

Shift Reversible Ribbing

FRONTSIDE

BACKSIDE

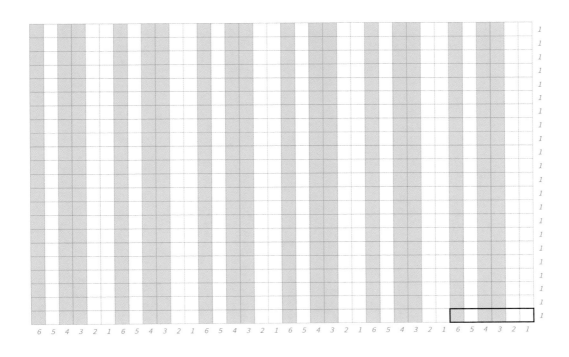

SPIRAL
K2, P2, K1, P1 ON 6+1

Aesthetically Reversible Swirl

FRONTSIDE

FRONTSIDE

BACKSIDE

SPIRAL
K2, P2, K1, P1 ON 6+2

Aesthetically Reversible All Over Pattern

FRONTSIDE

BACKSIDE

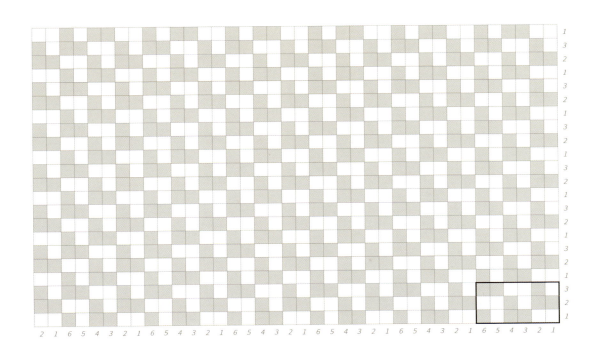

PAGE 257

SPIRAL
K2, P2, K1, P1 ON 6+3

Shift Reversible Mistake Ribbing

FRONTSIDE

BACKSIDE

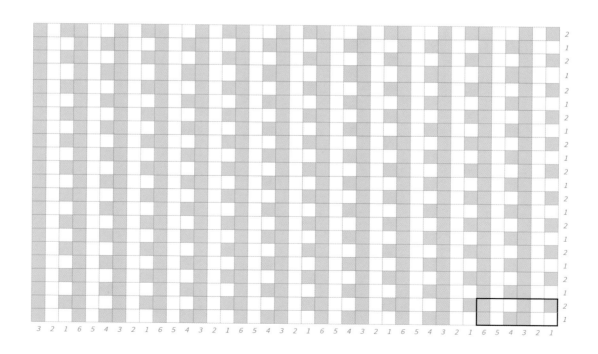

PAGE 258

SPIRAL
K4, P4, K2, P2 ON 12

Shift Reversible Ribbing

FRONTSIDE

BACKSIDE

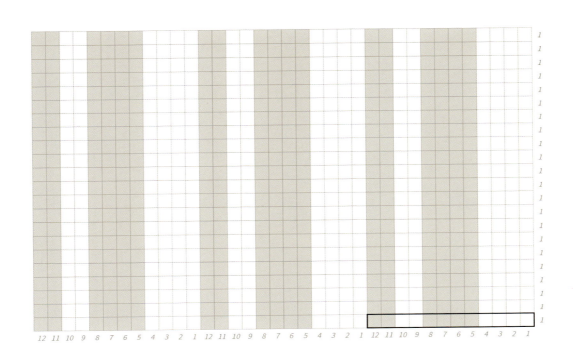

SPIRAL
K4, P4, K2, P2 ON 12+1

Aesthetically Reversible Swirl

FRONTSIDE

BACKSIDE

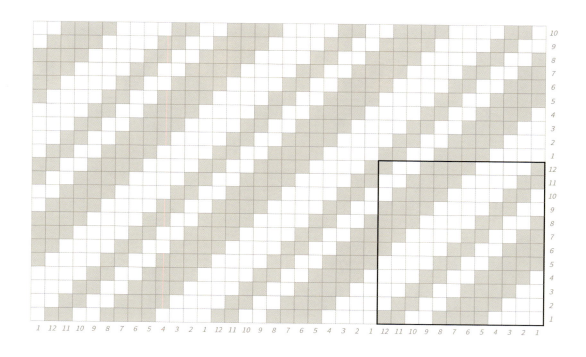

SPIRAL
K4, P4, K2, P2 ON 12+2

Aesthetically Reversible Swirl

FRONTSIDE

BACKSIDE

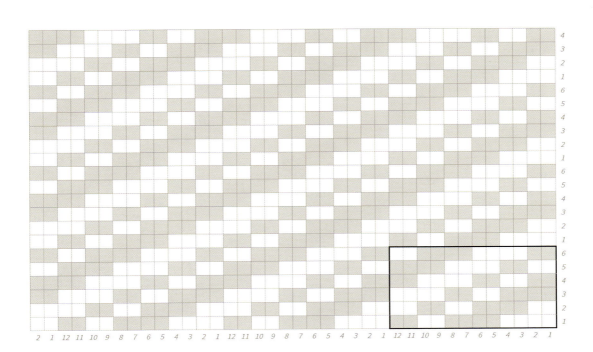

SPIRAL
K4, P4, K2, P2 ON 12+3

Aesthetically Reversible Swirl

FRONTSIDE

BACKSIDE

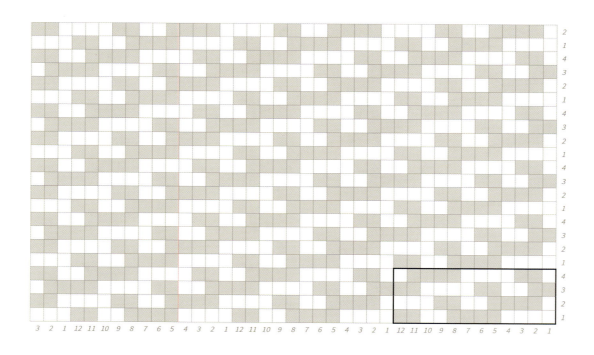

SPIRAL
K4, P4, K2, P2 ON 12+4

Shift Reversible All Over Pattern

FRONTSIDE

BACKSIDE

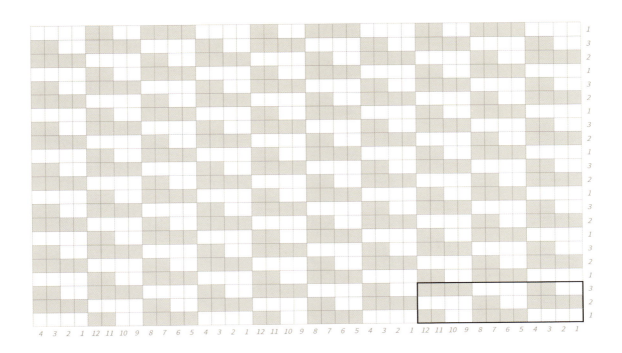

SPIRAL
K4, P4, K2, P2 ON 12+5

Aesthetically Reversible Swirl

FRONTSIDE

BACKSIDE

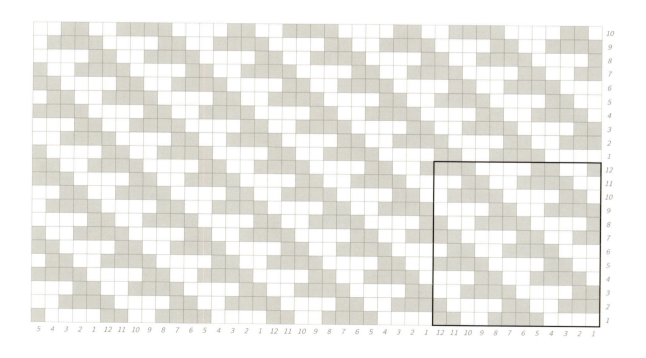

SPIRAL
K4, P4, K2, P2 ON 12+6

Shift Reversible Mistake Ribbing

FRONTSIDE

BACKSIDE

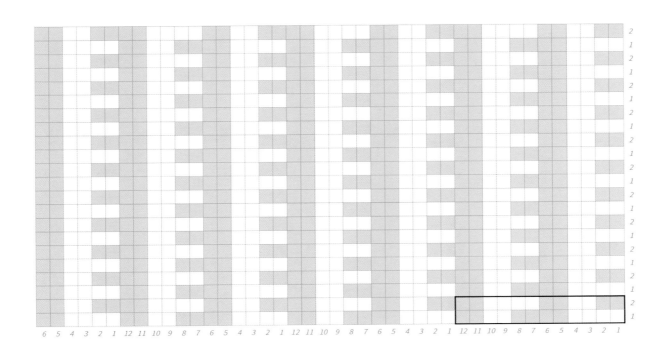

SPIRAL
[2(K2, P2), 2(K1, P1)] ON 12

Shift Reversible Ribbing

FRONTSIDE

BACKSIDE

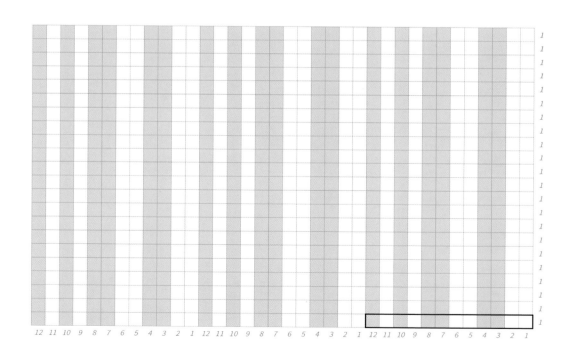

SPIRAL
[2(K2, P2), 2(K1, P1)] ON 12+1

Aesthetically Reversible Swirl

FRONTSIDE

BACKSIDE

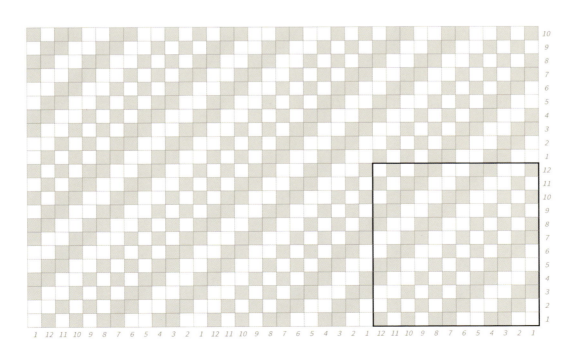

SPIRAL
[2(K2, P2), 2(K1, P1)] ON 12+2

Aesthetically Reversible Swirl

FRONTSIDE

BACKSIDE

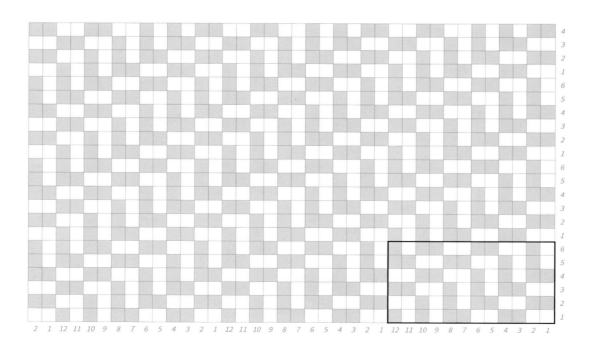

SPIRAL
[2(K2, P2), 2(K1, P1)] ON 12+3

Aesthetically Reversible All Over Pattern

FRONTSIDE

BACKSIDE

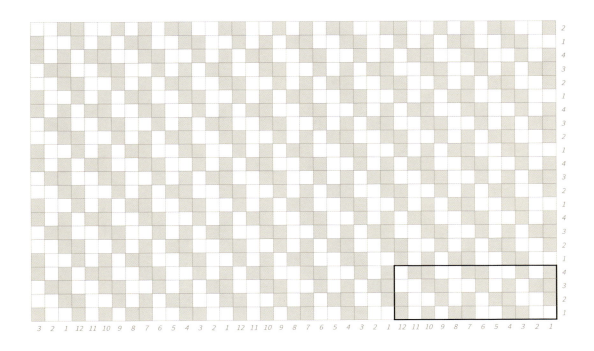

SPIRAL
[2(K2, P2), 2(K1, P1)] ON 12+4

Shift Reversible Mistake Ribbing

FRONTSIDE

BACKSIDE

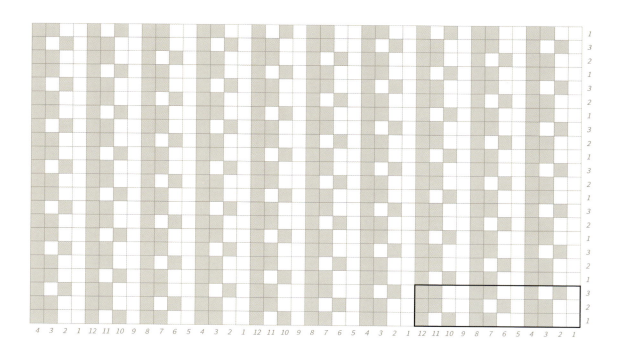

SPIRAL
[2(K2, P2), 2(K1, P1)] ON 12+5

Aesthetically Reversible All Over Pattern

FRONTSIDE

BACKSIDE

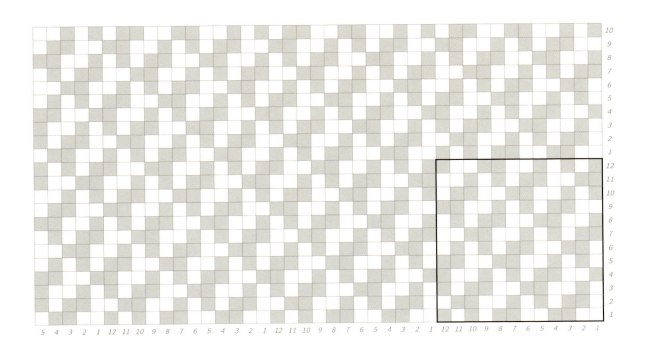

SPIRAL
[2(K2, P2), 2(K1, P1)] ON 12+6

Shift Reversible Mistake Ribbing

FRONTSIDE

BACKSIDE

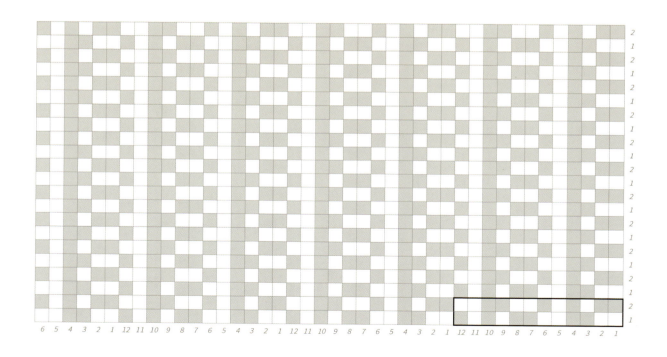

SPIRAL
[K1, P3, 4(K1, P1)] ON 12

Aesthetically Reversible Ribbing

FRONTSIDE

BACKSIDE

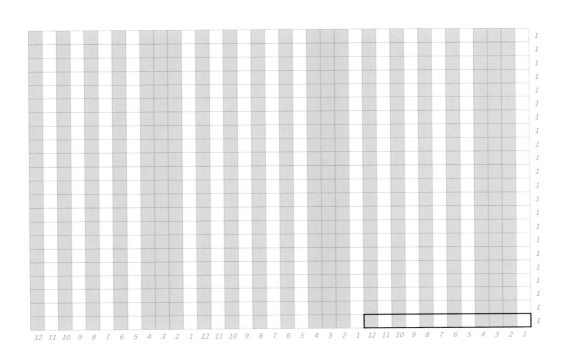

PAGE 273

SPIRAL
[K1, P3, 4(K1, P1)] ON 12+1

Aesthetically Reversible Swirl

FRONTSIDE

BACKSIDE

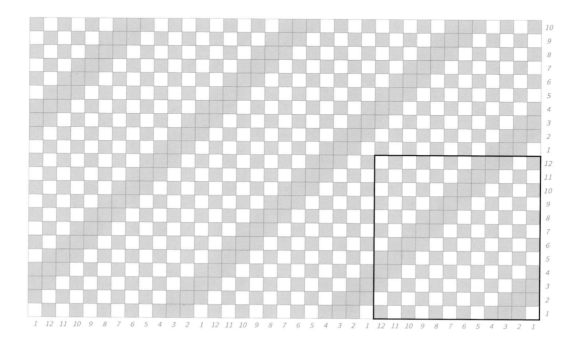

SPIRAL
[K1, P3, 4(K1, P1)] ON 12+2

Aesthetically Reversible Swirl. This complex fabric is also a mock ribbing.

FRONTSIDE

BACKSIDE

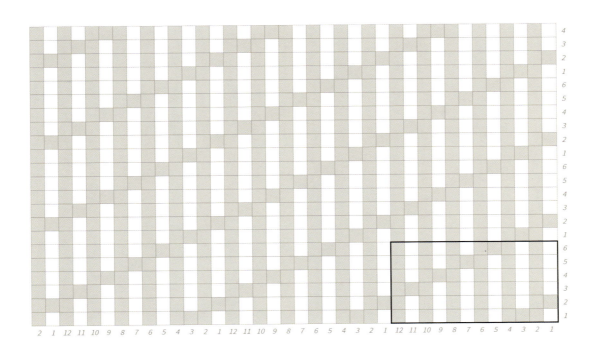

SPIRAL
[K1, P3, 4(K1, P1)] ON 12+3

Aesthetically Reversible All Over Pattern

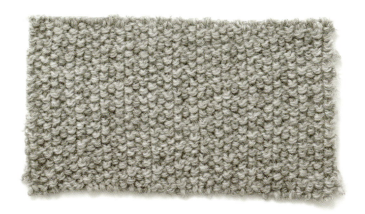

FRONTSIDE

BACKSIDE

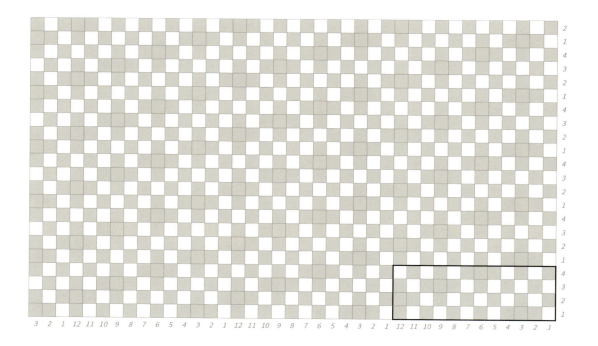

SPIRAL
[K1, P3, 4(K1, P1)] ON 12+4

Aesthetically Reversible Mistake Ribbing

FRONTSIDE

BACKSIDE

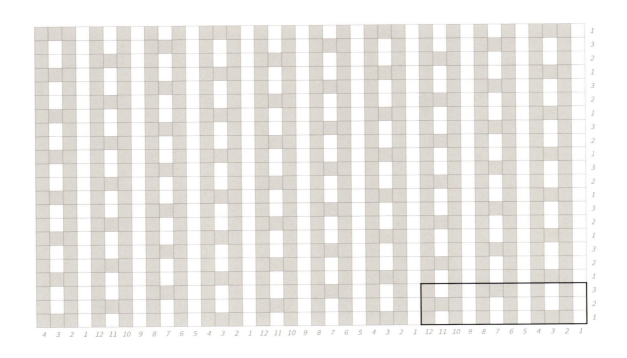

SPIRAL
[K1, P3, 4(K1, P1)] ON 12+5

Aesthetically Reversible All Over Pattern

FRONTSIDE

BACKSIDE

SPIRAL
[K1, P3, 4(K1, P1)] ON 12+6

Aesthetically Reversible Mistake Ribbing

FRONTSIDE

BACKSIDE

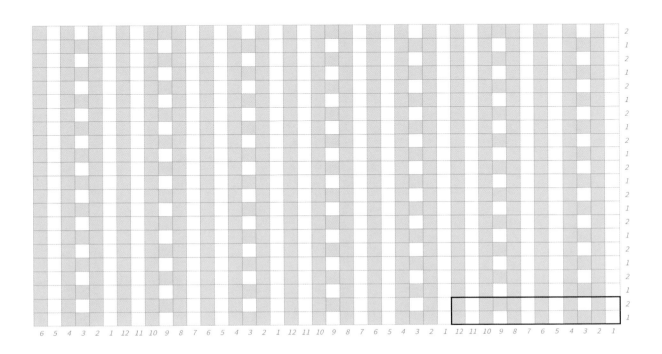

PAGE 279

CHAPTER 5

THE SHAPED 1-ROW METHOD

Triangles and Parallelograms

INTRODUCTION TO THE SHAPED 1-ROW METHOD

If you throw in an increase or a decrease at the edge of a 1-row pattern, the change in stitch count from row to row shifts the stitches back and forth. Just as in the serpentine or spiral methods, surprisingly complex fabrics can be created with this simple shift.

An example of a shaped 1-row pattern might look like this:

[K2, P2] until 3 stitches remain, then knit 3 together.

or

Knit into the front and back of the first stitch, then [K2, P2] for the remainder of the row.

In both examples each row will end differently, depending on the number of stitches in the row.

In this chapter we will look at how to create triangles and parallelograms using the shaped 1-row method. These 2 basic shapes are wonderful for shawls and scarves. Several patterns are included to illustrate the concepts. Finally, there is a stitch dictionary to explore more of the possibilities.

THE 3 TYPES OF TRIANGLES

Triangles are created by decreasing (or increasing) stitches each row. There are 3 basic triangles included in this chapter: 1x1, 2x2 and 1x2. 2x2 is my favorite because it knits up quickly.

You can start at either end of a triangle, but I prefer to start at the wide end so that the knitting is like walking downhill with fewer and fewer stitches each row.

The charts do not specify the method of increasing or decreasing, and can be used as a guide for shaping either from the wide end, or from the tip.

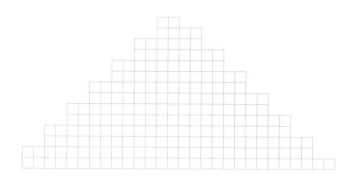

2x2 Triangle
Stitch count changes by 2 stitches every row.

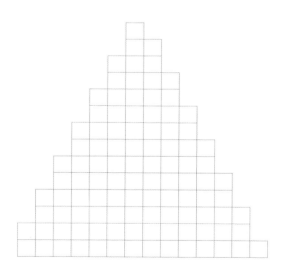

1x1 Triangle
Stitch count changes by 1 stitch every row.

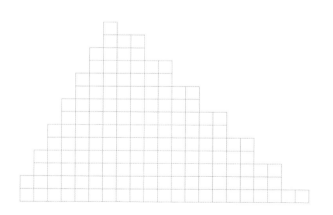

1x2 Triangle
Stitch count changes by 1 stitch at one edge and 2 stitches at the other edge.

HOW PATTERN MULTIPLES AFFECT TRIANGLES

In the 1-row, serpentine and spiral methods, varying the pattern multiple often has a big effect on the final fabric. The behavior is a little bit different with triangles using the shaped 1-row method.

For a 1x1 triangle, the stitch count changes by 1 stitch on every row. Imagine a sequence length of 5. If you cast on 25 stitches and decreased every row, the subsequent stitch count per row would be 24, 23, 22, 21, 20, etc. The pattern multiple for each row is 5, 5-1, 5-2, 5-3, 5-4, 5... This means that for any 1x1 triangle made with the shaped 1-row method, the cast-on can be any number of stitches.

This is also true of the 1x2 triangles. Imagine the same scenario as above: the sequence length is 5 and the cast on is 25. The subsequent stitch counts per row will be 24, 22, 21, 19, 18, 16, 15... the stitch count eventually gets back to the original pattern multiple.

2x2 triangles are different. Because the rows decrease by two stitches, the stitch count per row is always even or odd and this affects the pattern.

The charts below illustrate how the fabrics of the 2x2 triangles can vary. They are the charts for the Twigs and Gravel shawls on the following page. These richly textured pieces are shaped 1-row patterns where each rows ends with a K3tog. The sequence to create them is [K2, 4(P1 , K1), P2], which contains 4 knit-purl pairs. These knit-purl pairs become diamonds of 1x1 ribbing or seed stitch depending on whether the cast-on is even or odd.

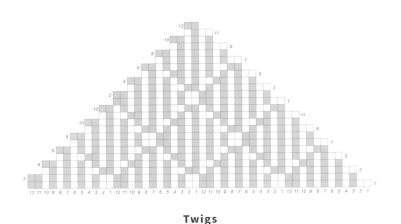

Twigs

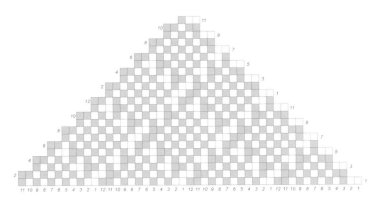

Gravel

TWIGS AND GRAVEL

These shawls are 2x2 triangles. If an even number of stitches are cast on, the result is Twigs, if an odd number of stitches are cast on the result is Gravel. Both samples are knit in Catherine Lowe's beautiful Merino Bespoke 5 yarn. Twigs (left) is in Smoke and Gravel (right) is in Black-violet. Solid colors are best for showing off the textures.

The fabrics are technically aesthetically reversible, but in practice the frontsides and backsides are quite similar.

Materials and supplies

300 g of dk weight yarn for 1 shawl

Size 6 (4 mm) 47 inch (100 cm) circular needle

Gauge

5.5 stitches / inch in stockinette

Dimensions

Twigs: 22 x 70 (56 x 178 cm)

Gravel: 18 x 92 (46 x 234 cm)

Pattern notes

1. The tension of the cast-on is important. See the Appendix.
2. Take care with the tension from row to row, and check the work frequently as the patterns are hard to see or "read." Life-lines are recommended.
3. The pattern multiple is 2 for Twigs and 2+1 for Gravel.

Directions for Twigs

Cast on 396 stitches. Work every row as follows:

[K2, 4(P1 , K1), P2] until 3 stitches remain, K3tog.

Continue until the stitch count is 2. Bind off. Wash, block and weave in ends.

Directions for Gravel

Cast on 395 stitches. Work as for Twigs until stitch count is 3. Bind off. Wash, block and weave in ends.

DELTA WING

Delta Wing is an asymmetric, shift-reversible shawl. It looks complicated, but it is just a 1-row pattern with a single or double decrease on every other row. The sample is worked in Brooklyn Tweed Shelter in Fauna (A), Soot (B), and Sweatshirt (C).

Materials

20 g of worsted weight yarn in color A

200 g of worsted weight yarn in color B

100 g of worsted weight yarn in color C

Size 7 (4.5 mm) 40-60 inch (100 - 150 cm) circular needles

3 removable stitch markers

Gauge

5 stitches / inch in stockinette

Dimensions

20 x 71 inches (51 x 180 cm)

Pattern Notes

1. Every row is worked the same except for the decrease at the end. Odd rows end with K3tog, and even rows end with K2tog.

2. Take care with the tension from row to row, especially on rows where the color is changed.

Stitch glossary:

S1WYIF is to slip 1 stitch with the yarn in front.

S1WYIB is to slip 1 stitch with the yarn in back.

Directions

Cast on 300 stitches in color A.

Row 1 (setup row): [K6, P6]

Place 1 marker at beginning of setup row (right edge of work) and 2 markers at end of setup row (left side of work). Do not slip markers, they will indicate the number of decreases worked at each edge. Change to color B.

Row 2: [K5, S1WYIF, P5, S1WYIB] until 3 stitches remain, then K3tog.

Row 3: [K5, S1WYIF, P5, S1WYIB] until 2 stitches remain, then K2tog.

Repeat rows 2 and 3 with color B until 59 rows are completed and the stitch count is 212. The shawl should measure approximately 6 inches (15 cm) from the cast-on edge. With C, work 2 rows, with B work 2 rows. Continue in pattern alternating C and B every 2 rows until 8 stitches remain, ending with 2 rows in B. With B, bind off. Wash, block and weave in ends.

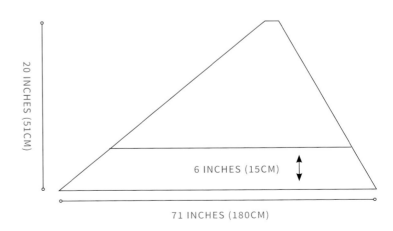

PARALLELOGRAMS

2 kinds of parallelograms are explored in this chapter: 1x1 and 2x2. Like the triangles, the 1x1 parallelogram varies by 1 stitch per row while the 2x2 parallelogram varies by 2 stitches per row.

To create a parallelogram the rows are increased on one edge and decreased on the other; the following example is for a 1x1 parallelogram:

- Odd rows: [K2, P2] to last stitch, then make 1 stitch
- Even rows: [K2, P2] to last 2 stitches, then K2tog

A 2x2 parallelogram is made almost the same way:

- Odd rows: [K2, P2] to last stitch, make 2 stitches
- Even rows: [K2, P2] to last 3 stitches, then K3tog

As with the triangles, the sequence will not always fit within the number of stitches, and the row will often finish with a partial sequence. Parallelograms are easy to knit because every odd row is the same and every even row is the same, so an error is easy to spot.

All parallelograms are sensitive to the number of stitches cast on and the sequence permutation – if the cast-on varies by even 1 stitch the fabric may be completely different.

On the facing page are 2 diagrams of parallelograms. The top diagram is a 1x1 parallelogram and the lower diagram is a 2x2 parallelogram. Both show 15 stitches and 15 rows. The shapes are very different, and the 2x2 parallelogram appears narrower even though the stitch count is the same. It is always a good idea to swatch parallelograms to make sure you get the desired width.

Selvedges are particularly important and tricky for parallelograms. They have the same tension challenges as triangles. If the tension is too tight at the selvedge, the parallelogram will curl to one side, and blocking may not correct the problem.

There are many ways to handle the increases and decreases and each has a different look. The standard decreases K2tog and K3tog are the easiest. For increases, I like to increase by knitting into the back, then the front of a stitch for a single increase, or knit into the back, the front and the back for a double increase. However, any method of increasing or decreasing can be used. Try experimenting with yarn overs, lifted increases, or centered double decreases for different effects.

1x1 Parallelogram

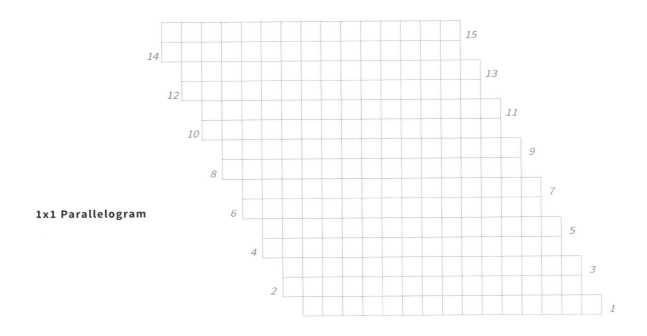

2x2 Parallelogram

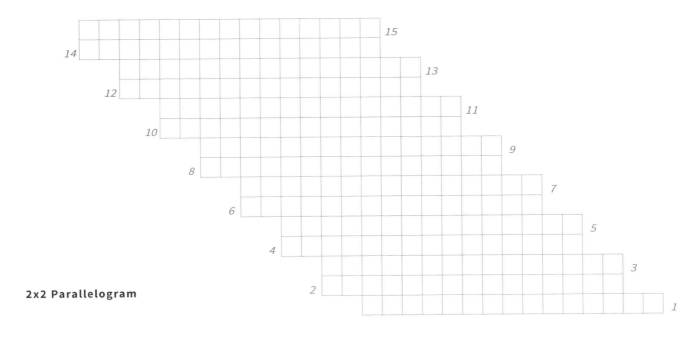

ROBSON

If you want to show off hand painted or variegated yarns, this shift-reversible scarf is an excellent choice. The sample is worked in 2 skeins of my hand-painted fingering merino. Also see the variations on pages 348 and 354.

Materials

100 g of fingering weight yarn in color A

100 g of fingering weight yarn in color B

US 4 (3.5 mm) needles

Gauge

6.5 stitches / inch in stockinette

Dimensions

8 x 80 inches (20 x 203 cm)

Pattern notes

1. The pattern multiple is 12-1 and the row repeat is 12.
2. The color is changed every 2 rows. Take care with the tension when changing colors or the edge of the scarf will pucker.
3. Consider putting 2 coil less pins or locking stitch markers on the increase edge as a guide.

Stitch glossary

M2 means to make 2 stitches by knitting into the back, front and back of the stitch.

Directions

Cast on 119 (12-1) stitches in color A.

Row 1: color A, [K3, P3, 3(K1, P1)], K3, P3, 2(K1, P1), M2

Row 2: color A, [K3, P3, 3(K1, P1)], K3, P3, 2(K1, P1), K3tog

Row 3: color B, [K3, P3, 3(K1, P1)], K3, P3, 2(K1, P1), M2

Row 4: color B, [K3, P3, 3(K1, P1)], K3, P3, 2(K1, P1), K3tog

Repeat rows 1-4, always bringing the new color in front of the working yarn, until the scarf measures 80 inches from tip to tip and ending in 2 rows of color A. Bind off in A.

Wash, block and weave in ends.

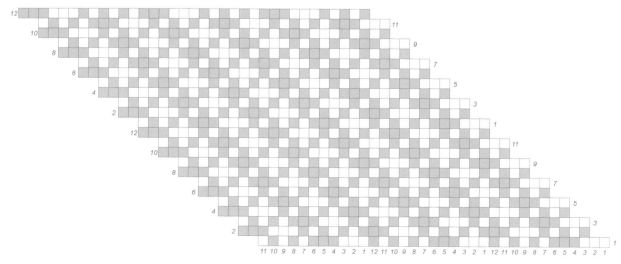

TRIANGLES AND PARALLELOGRAMS IN THIS DICTIONARY

Sequence Length (n)	Pattern Multiple	Sequence	Type	1-color Reversibility	2-color Reversibility
2	Any	K1, P1	1x1 Triangle	Shift	
3	Any	K2, P1	1x1 Triangle	Shift	
4	Any	K2, P2	1x1 Triangle	Shift-flip	
4	Any	K3, P1	1x1 Triangle	Aesthetically	
12	Any	K6, P6	1x1 Triangle	Shift	Shift
12	Any	K6, 3(K1, P1)	1x1 Triangle	Shift	
12	Any	K3, P3, 3(K1, P1)	1x1 Triangle	Shift	
4	Any	K2, P2	1x2 Triangle	Shift-flip	
12	Any	K6, P6	1x2 Triangle	Shift-flip	Shift-flip
12	Any	K5, Slip1, P5, Slip 1	1x2 Triangle	Shift-flip	Shift-flip
4	2	K2, P2	2x2 Triangle	Shift	
4	2+1	K2, P2	2x2 Triangle	Aesthetically	
6	2	K3, P3	2x2 Triangle	Shift	
6	2+1	K3, P3	2x2 Triangle	Shift	
12	2	K2, 4(P1, K1), P2	2x2 Triangle	Aesthetically	
12	2+1	K2, 4(P1, K1), P2	2x2 Triangle	Aesthetically	
12	12	K3, P3, 3(K1,P1)	1x1 Parallelogram	Aesthetically	
12	12	K3, P3, 3(K1,P1)	2x2 Parallelogram	Aesthetically	
12	12-1	K3, P3, 3(K1,P1)	2x2 Parallelogram	Shift-flip	Shift-flip
12	12	K3, P6, K3	1x1 Parallelogram	Shift-flip	Shift-flip
12	12	K3, P6, K3	2x2 Parallelogram	Shift-flip	Shift-flip
12	12-1	K3, P6, K3	2x2 Parallelogram	Shift-flip	Shift-flip
12	12	K3, 3(K1, P1), K3	1x1 Parallelogram	Aesthetically	
12	12	K3, 3(K1, P1), K3	2x2 Parallelogram	Shift-flip	
12	12-1	K3, 3(K1, P1), K3	2x2 Parallelogram	Aesthetically	
12	12	K3, 3(K1, P1), P3	1x1 Parallelogram	Aesthetically	
12	12	K3, 3(K1, P1), P3	2x2 Parallelogram	Aesthetically	
12	12-1	K3, 3(K1, P1), P3	2x2 Parallelogram	Aesthetically	

1-ROW TRIANGLE: SYMMETRIC SINGLE DECREASES [K1, P1] ON ANY NUMBER OF STITCHES

Shift Reversible

K2tog at the end of every row after the setup row. This moss stitch would be perfectly reversible if the edge decreases were reversible.

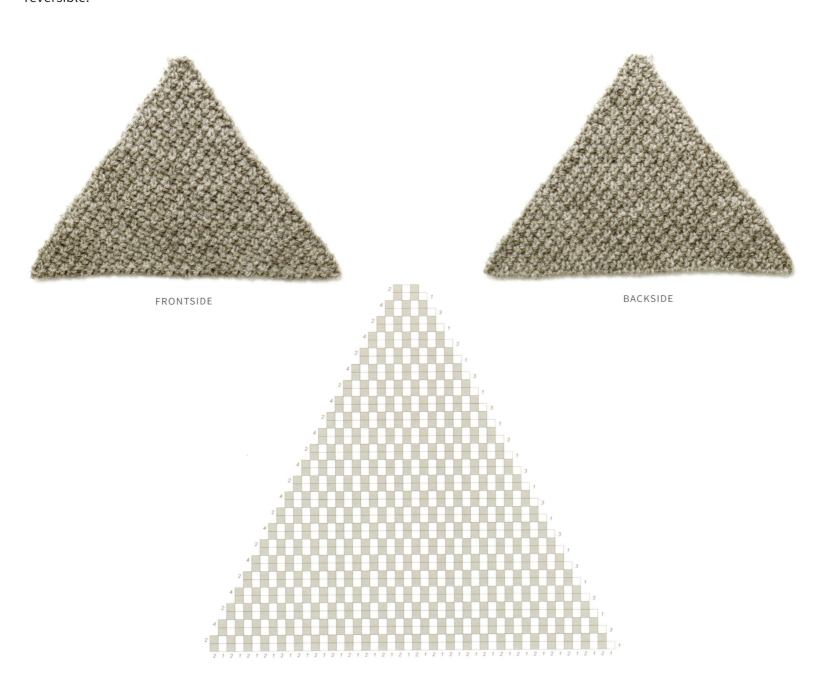

FRONTSIDE

BACKSIDE

1-ROW TRIANGLE: SYMMETRIC SINGLE DECREASES [K2, P1] ON ANY NUMBER OF STITCHES

Shift Reversible

K2tog at the end of every row after the setup row.

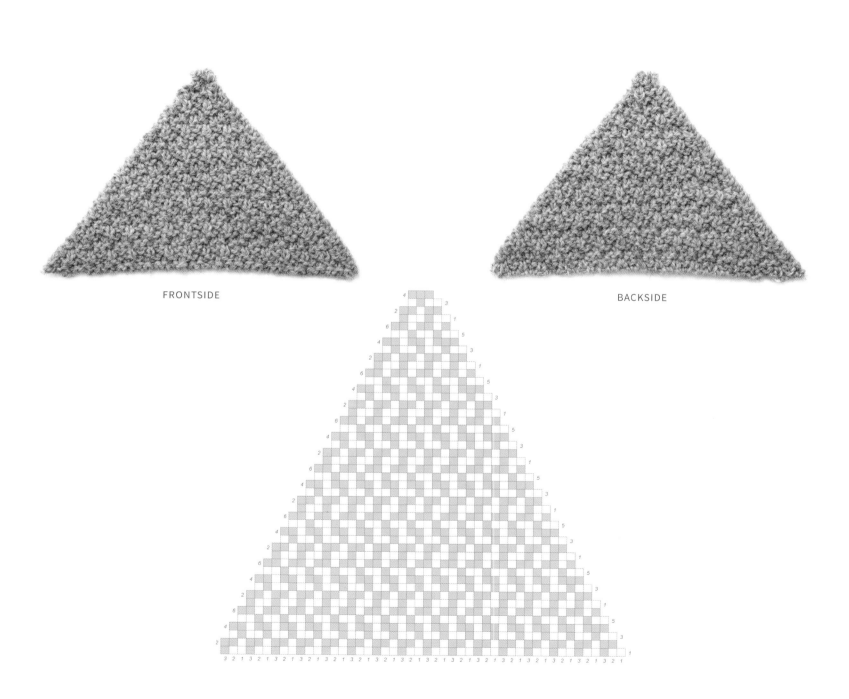

1-ROW TRIANGLE: SYMMETRIC SINGLE DECREASES [K2, P2] ON ANY NUMBER OF STITCHES

Shift-Flip Reversible

K2tog at the end of every row after the setup row.

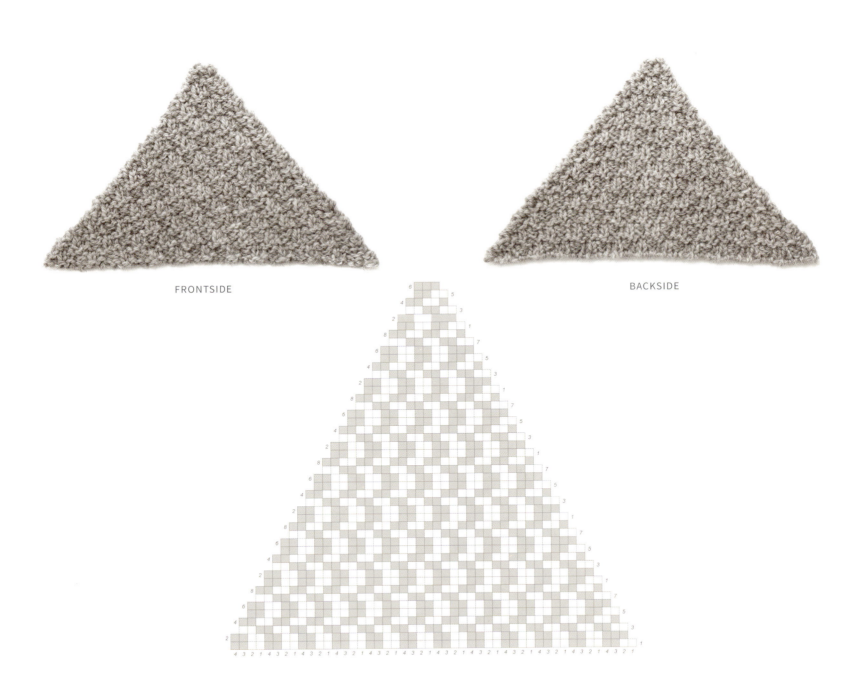

FRONTSIDE

BACKSIDE

1-ROW TRIANGLE: SYMMETRIC SINGLE DECREASES
[K3, P1] ON ANY NUMBER OF STITCHES

Aesthetically Reversible

K2tog at the end of every row after the setup row.

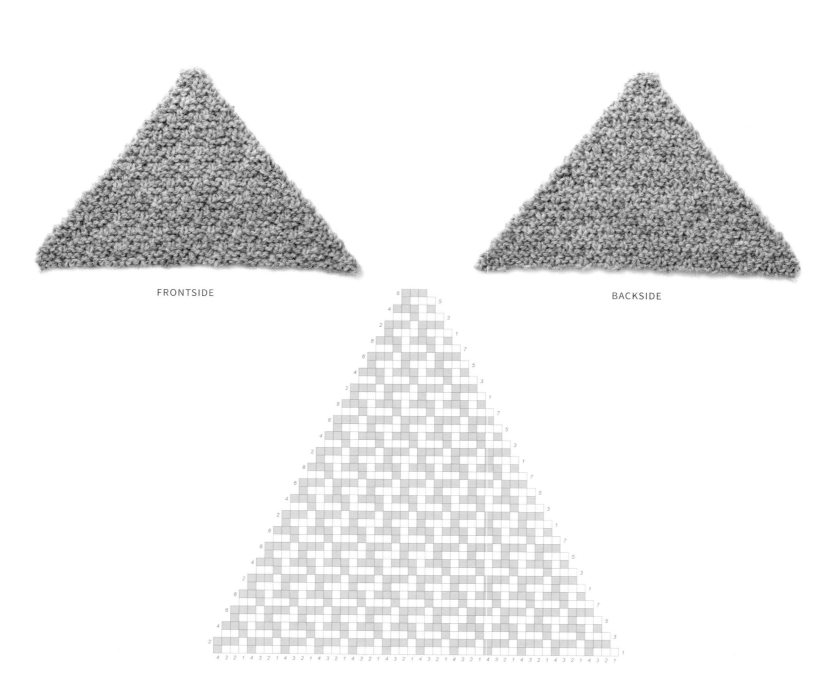

FRONTSIDE

BACKSIDE

1-ROW TRIANGLE: SYMMETRIC SINGLE DECREASES [K6, P6] ON ANY NUMBER OF STITCHES

Shift Reversible

K2tog at the end of every row after the setup row.

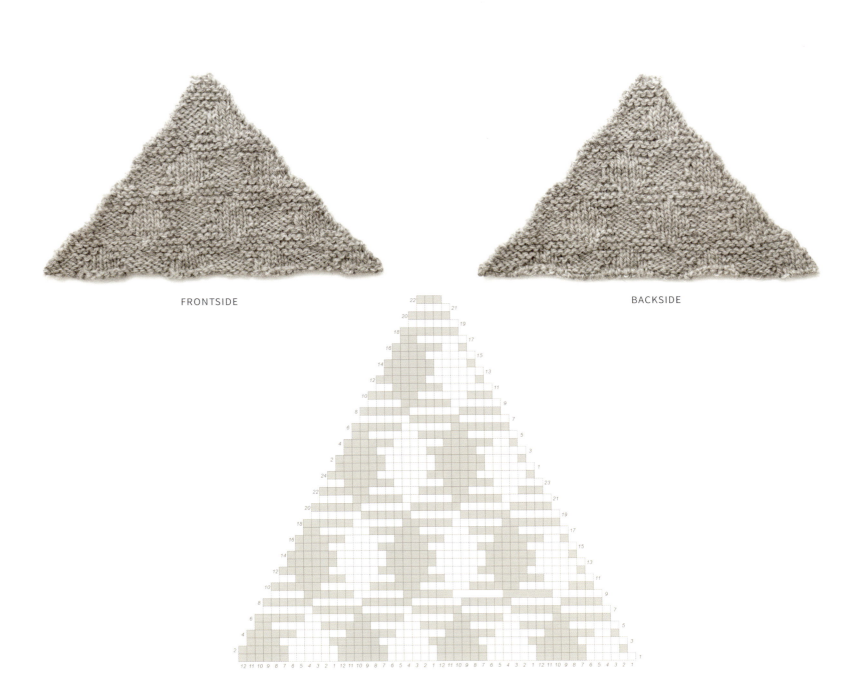

FRONTSIDE

BACKSIDE

1-ROW TRIANGLE: SYMMETRIC SINGLE DECREASES
[K6, P6] IN 2 COLORS ON ANY NUMBER OF STITCHES

Shift Reversible

K2tog at the end of every row after the setup row.

FRONTSIDE

BACKSIDE

1-ROW TRIANGLE: SYMMETRIC SINGLE DECREASES [K6, 3(K1, P1)] ON ANY NUMBER OF STITCHES

Shift Reversible

K2tog at the end of every row after the setup row.

FRONTSIDE

BACKSIDE

1-ROW TRIANGLE: SYMMETRIC SINGLE DECREASES [K3, P3, 3(K1, P1)] ON ANY NUMBER OF STITCHES

Shift Reversible

K2tog at the end of every row after the setup row.

FRONTSIDE

BACKSIDE

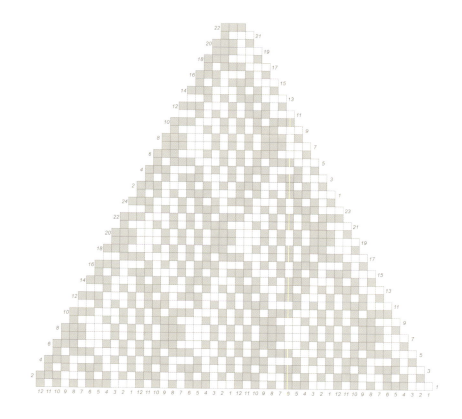

1-ROW TRIANGLE: ASYMMETRIC SINGLE/DOUBLE DECREASES [K2, P2] ON ANY NUMBER OF STITCHES

Shift-Flip Reversible

After the setup row, K3tog at the end of even rows and K2tog at the end of odd rows.

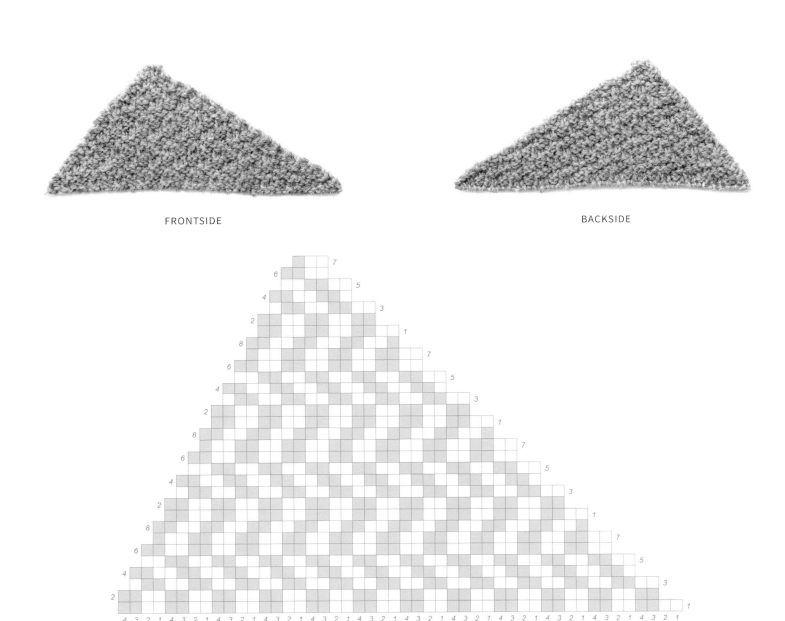

FRONTSIDE

BACKSIDE

1-ROW TRIANGLE: ASYMMETRIC SINGLE/DOUBLE DECREASES [K6, P6] ON AN EVEN NUMBER OF STITCHES

Shift-Flip Reversible

After the setup row, K3tog at the end of even rows and K2tog at the end of odd rows.

FRONTSIDE

BACKSIDE

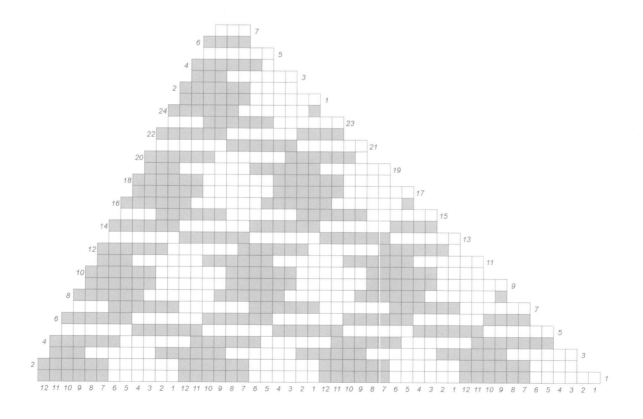

PAGE 304

1-ROW TRIANGLE: ASYMMETRIC SINGLE/DOUBLE DECREASES [K6, P6] IN 2 COLORS ON AN EVEN NUMBER OF STITCHES

Shift-Flip Reversible

After the setup row, K3tog at the end of even rows and K2tog at the end of odd rows.

FRONTSIDE

BACKSIDE

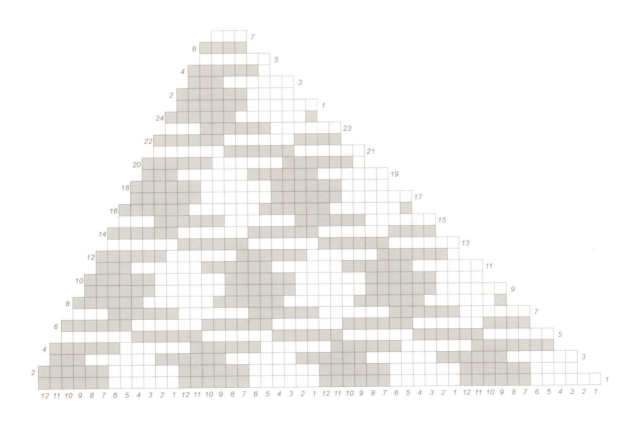

1-ROW TRIANGLE: ASYMMETRIC SINGLE/DOUBLE DECREASES [K5, SL1, P5, SL1] ON AN EVEN NUMBER OF STITCHES

Shift-Flip Reversible

After the setup row, K3tog at the end of even rows and K2tog at the end of odd rows.

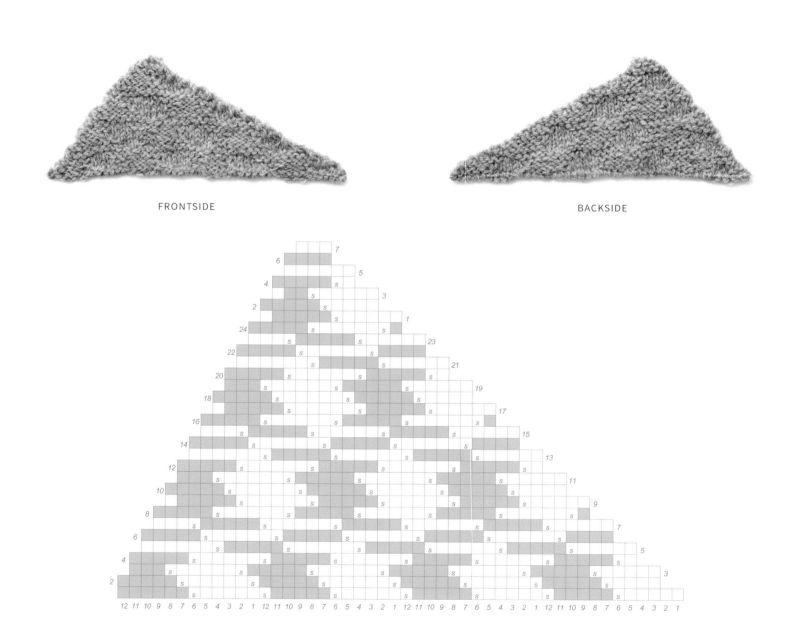

FRONTSIDE

BACKSIDE

1-ROW TRIANGLE: ASYMMETRIC SINGLE/DOUBLE DECREASES [K5, SL1, P5, SL1] IN 2 COLORS ON AN EVEN NUMBER OF STITCHES

Shift-Flip Reversible

After the setup row, K3tog at the end of even rows and K2tog at the end of odd rows.

FRONTSIDE

BACKSIDE

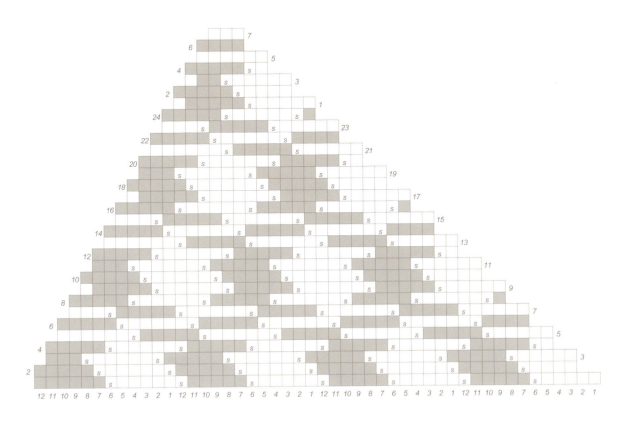

1-ROW TRIANGLE: SYMMETRIC DOUBLE DECREASES [K2, P2] ON 2

Shift Reversible

After the setup row, K3tog at the end of every row. This common 2x2 block pattern is called Double Seed Stitch in Walker's Treasury (1968).

FRONTSIDE

BACKSIDE

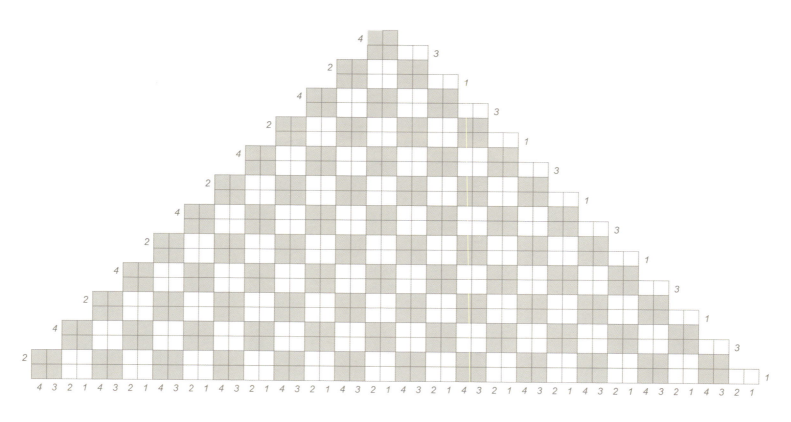

1-ROW TRIANGLE: SYMMETRIC DOUBLE DECREASES [K2, P2] ON 2+1

Aesthetically Reversible

After the setup row, K3tog at the end of every row.

FRONTSIDE

BACKSIDE

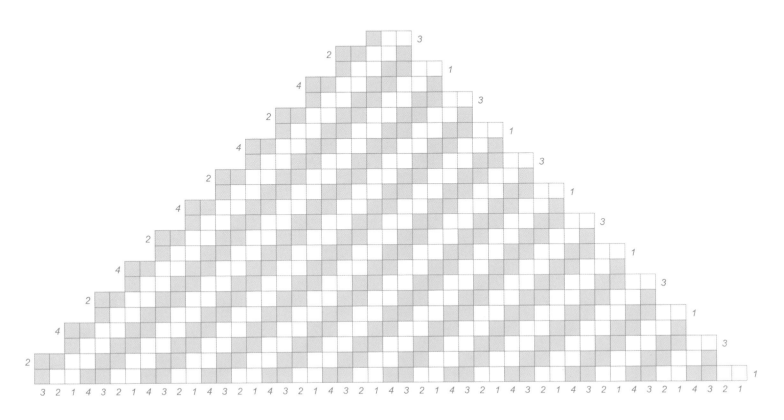

1-ROW TRIANGLE: SYMMETRIC DOUBLE DECREASES [K3, P3] ON 2

Shift Reversible

After the setup row, K3tog at the end of every row.

FRONTSIDE

BACKSIDE

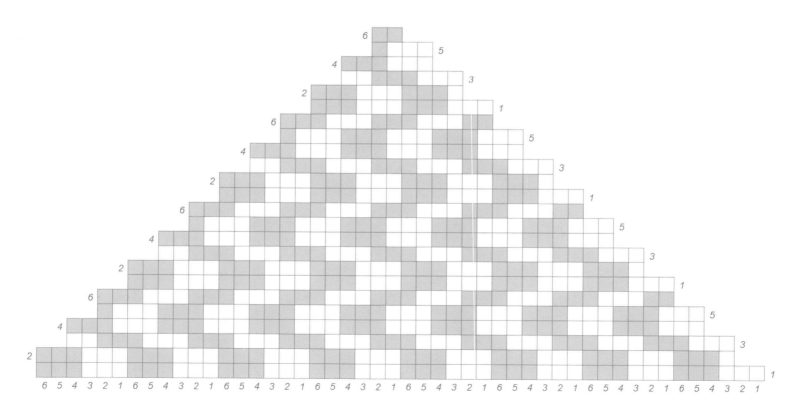

1-ROW TRIANGLE: SYMMETRIC DOUBLE DECREASES [K3, P3] ON 2+1

Shift Reversible

After the setup row, K3tog at the end of every row.

FRONTSIDE

BACKSIDE

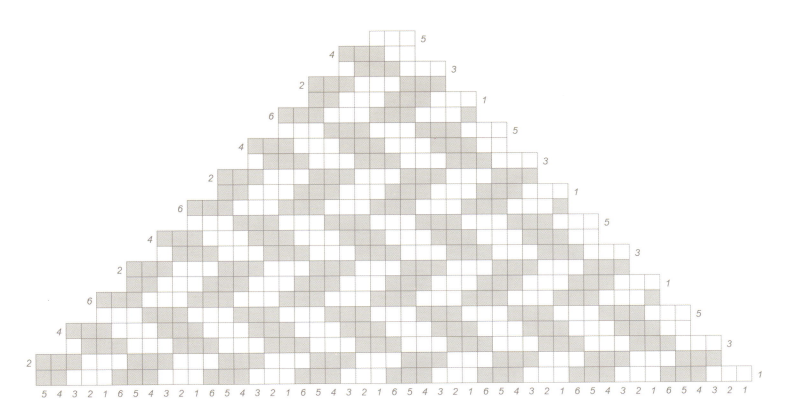

1-ROW TRIANGLE: SYMMETRIC DOUBLE DECREASES [K2, 4(P1, K1), P2] ON 2

Aesthetically Reversible

After the setup row, K3tog at the end of every row.

FRONTSIDE

BACKSIDE

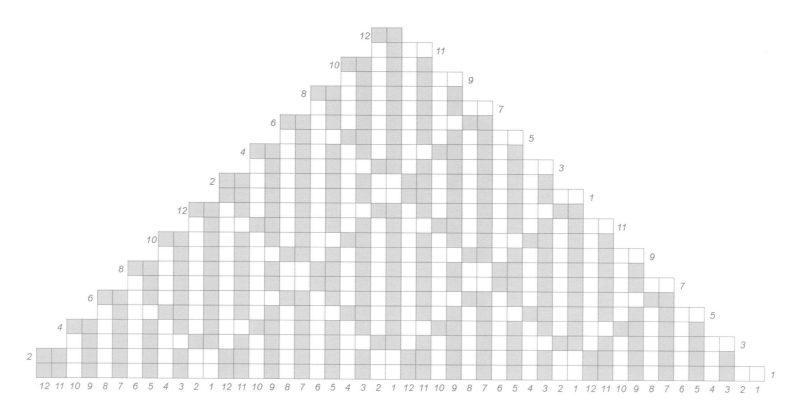

PAGE 312

1-ROW TRIANGLE: SYMMETRIC DOUBLE DECREASES
[K2, 4(P1, K1), P2] ON 2+1

Aesthetically Reversible

After the setup row, K3tog at the end of every row.

FRONTSIDE

BACKSIDE

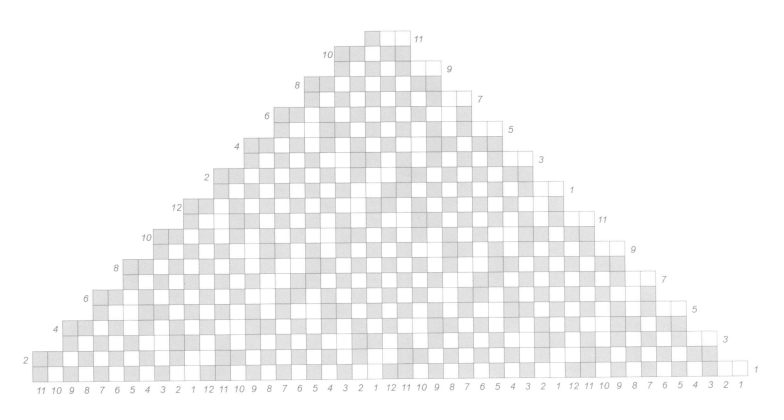

PARALLELOGRAM: SINGLE INCREASES AND DECREASES
[K3, P3, 3(K1, P1)] ON 12

Aesthetically Reversible

Make 1 at the end of every odd row, and K2tog at the end of every even row.

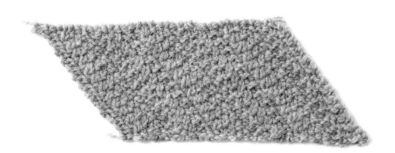

FRONTSIDE

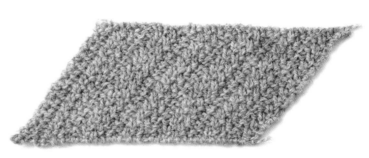

BACKSIDE

PARALLELOGRAM: DOUBLE INCREASES AND DECREASES [K3, P3, 3(K1, P1)] ON 12

Aesthetically Reversible

Make 2 at the end of every odd row, and K3tog at the end of every even row.

FRONTSIDE   BACKSIDE

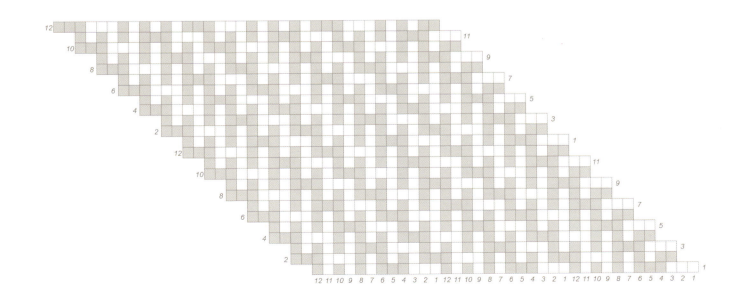

PARALLELOGRAM: DOUBLE INCREASES AND DECREASES [K3, P3, 3(K1, P1)] ON 12-1

Shift-Flip Reversible

Make 2 at the end of every odd row, and K3tog at the end of every even row.

FRONTSIDE   BACKSIDE

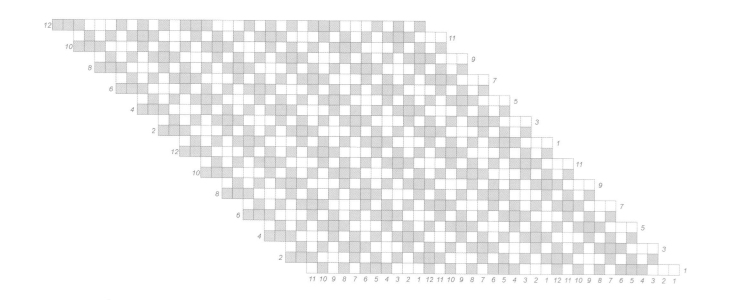

PARALLELOGRAM: DOUBLE INCREASES AND DECREASES [K3, P3, 3(K1, P1)] IN 2 COLORS ON 12-1

Shift-Flip Reversible

Make 2 at the end of every odd row, and K3tog at the end of every even row.

FRONTSIDE

BACKSIDE

PARALLELOGRAM: SINGLE INCREASES AND DECREASES [K3, P6, K3] ON 12

Shift-Flip Reversible

Make 1 at the end of every odd row, and K2tog at the end of every even row.

FRONTSIDE

BACKSIDE

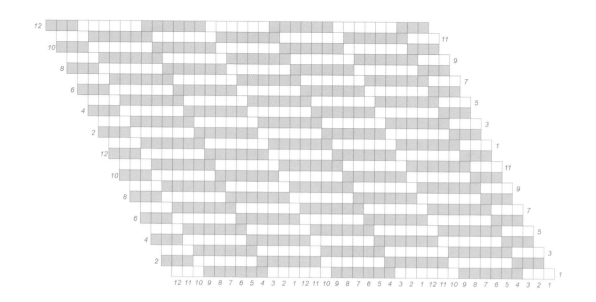

PARALLELOGRAM: SINGLE INCREASES AND DECREASES [K3, P6, K3] IN 2 COLORS ON 12

Shift-Flip Reversible

Make 1 at the end of every odd row, and K2tog at the end of every even row.

FRONTSIDE

BACKSIDE

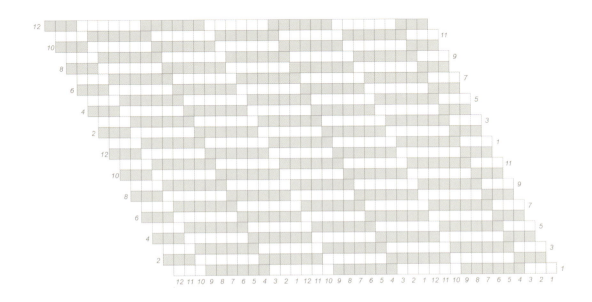

PARALLELOGRAM: DOUBLE INCREASES AND DECREASES [K3, P6, K3] ON 12

Shift-Flip Reversible

Make 2 at the end of every odd row, and K3tog at the end of every even row.

FRONTSIDE						BACKSIDE

PARALLELOGRAM: DOUBLE INCREASES AND DECREASES [K3, P6, K3] IN 2 COLORS ON 12

Shift-Flip Reversible

Make 2 at the end of every odd row, and K3tog at the end of every even row.

FRONTSIDE

BACKSIDE

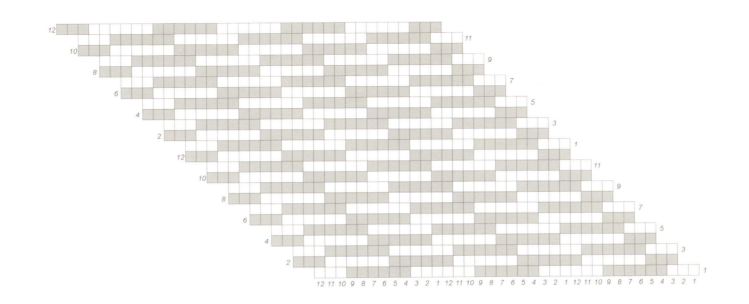

PARALLELOGRAM: DOUBLE INCREASES AND DECREASES [K3, P6, K3] ON 12-1

Shift-Flip Reversible

Make 2 at the end of every odd row, and K3tog at the end of every even row.

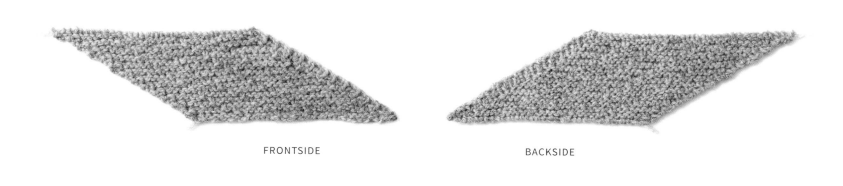

FRONTSIDE BACKSIDE

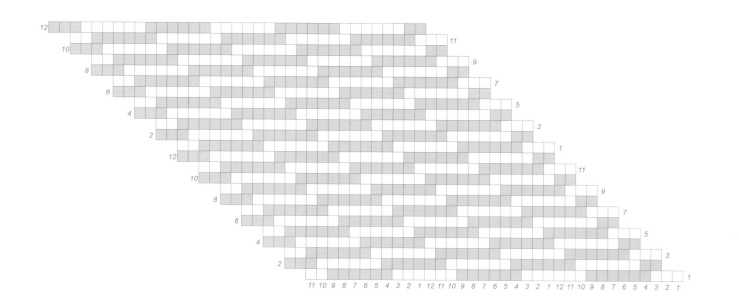

PARALLELOGRAM: DOUBLE INCREASES AND DECREASES [K3, P6, K3] IN 2 COLORS ON 12-1

Shift-Flip Reversible

Make 2 at the end of every odd row, and K3tog at the end of every even row.

FRONTSIDE

BACKSIDE

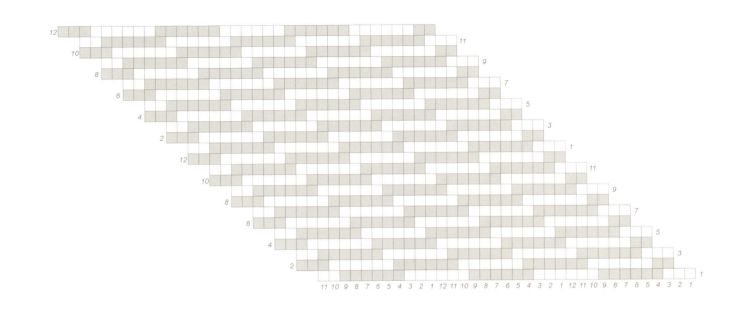

PARALLELOGRAM: SINGLE INCREASES AND DECREASES [K3, 3(K1, P1), K3] ON 12

Aesthetically Reversible

Make 1 at the end of every odd row, and K2tog at the end of every even row.

FRONTSIDE　　　　　　　　　　　BACKSIDE

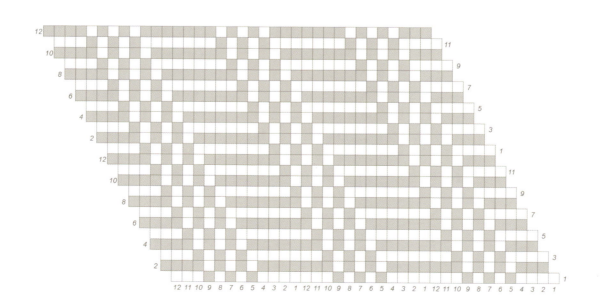

PARALLELOGRAM: DOUBLE INCREASES AND DECREASES
[K3, 3(K1, P1), K3] ON 12

Shift-Flip Reversible

Make 2 at the end of every odd row, and K3tog at the end of every even row.

FRONTSIDE

BACKSIDE

PARALLELOGRAM: DOUBLE INCREASES AND DECREASES [K3, 3(K1, P1), K3] ON 12-1

Aesthetically Reversible

Make 2 at the end of every odd row, and K3tog at the end of every even row.

FRONTSIDE

BACKSIDE

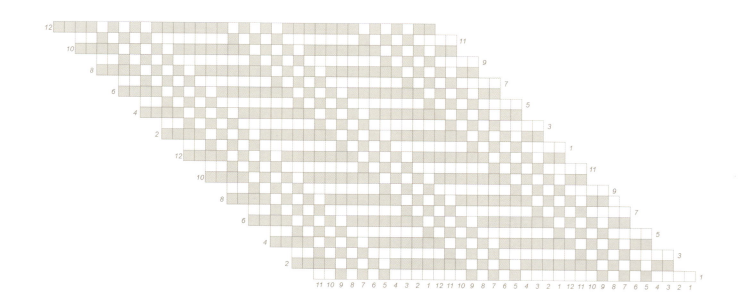

PARALLELOGRAM: SINGLE INCREASES AND DECREASES
[K3, 3(K1, P1), P3] ON 12

Aesthetically Reversible

Make 1 at the end of every odd row, and K2tog at the end of every even row.

FRONTSIDE

BACKSIDE

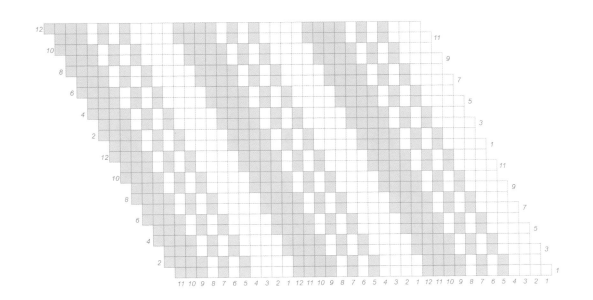

PARALLELOGRAM: DOUBLE INCREASES AND DECREASES
[K3, 3(K1, P1), P3] ON 12

Aesthetically Reversible

Make 2 at the end of every odd row, and K3tog at the end of every even row.

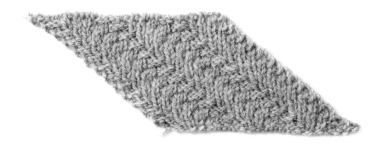

FRONTSIDE

BACKSIDE

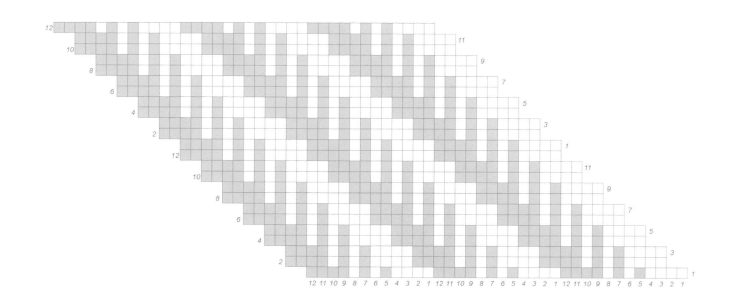

PARALLELOGRAM: DOUBLE INCREASES AND DECREASES [K3, 3(K1, P1), P3] ON 12-1

Aesthetically Reversible

Make 2 at the end of every odd row, and K3tog at the end of every even row.

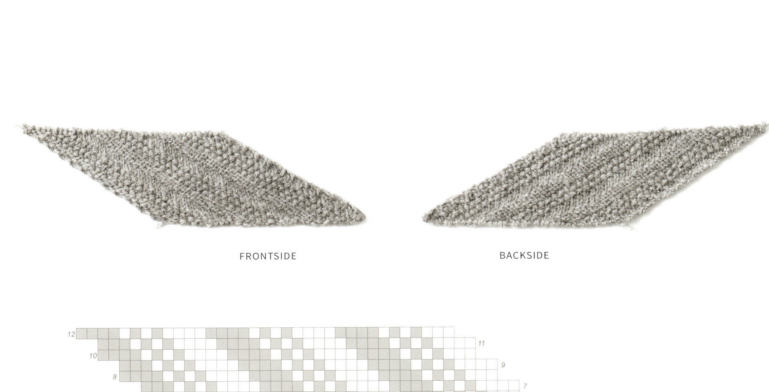

FRONTSIDE   BACKSIDE

CHAPTER 6

DESIGN CONSIDERATIONS

Fiber, Hand, Contrast, and Color

DESIGN DECISIONS

One of the great joys in knitting is choosing the yarn for a new project, but it is also a choice fraught with risk. I know early on if I have made a poor choice, but it is hard to change course once the yarn has been purchased and hours of work are completed. On the other hand, it is also very satisfying when all the elements of a project come together and you know it is going to be exceptional.

Any knitted piece is an integrated combination of the form, the stitch patterns, the fibers, and the colors. While most of this book is about stitch patterns, this chapter focuses on how to choose fibers and colors.

In my experience, disappointing yarn choices usually fall in either one of two categories: the wrong drape or hand, or pooling with variegated yarns. Once I made a sweater out of a bouncy merino, when the pattern was intended for a relaxed alpaca. The sweater was heavy and puffy, just the opposite of the easy and elegant piece I had wanted. Another particularly poor choice was a seamless Elizabeth Zimmerman EPS sweater in a yellow-purple variegated yarn. I did not understanding pooling at the time, and the results were awful.

These were rookie mistakes, but making good decisions before embarking on a project is a complex process. Ravelry has been profoundly helpful in making these decisions, as knitters can view different versions of patterns in different yarns.

Its challenging to give hard and fast rules on choosing fiber and color. However, there are a few factors that I think about when planning a project.

FIBER

Your choice of fiber affects the look, feel, and drape of the final fabric. I gravitate towards animal fibers like fine merino, alpaca, silk or cashmere, as well as the more rustic traditional yarns like those from Shetland or Donegal. The ethereal silk-mohairs are wonderful because of the way they can be mixed with other yarns to lighten the fabric and add a hazy glow.

My go-to fiber is high-twist fingering merino. It feels good against the skin, shows color well, is relatively affordable, does not pill and has enough natural elasticity that it forgives variations in tension. There are many versions of this specific type of yarn available from both larger producers and small independent dyers, including Koigu KPPPM, Louet Gems Fingering, Miss Babs 2-Ply Sock, Blue Mountain Fiber Arts Socks–That–Rock Medium, and Wool2Dye4's Sheila's Sock. Sheila's Sock only comes in undyed skeins or cones and is the base I use for dyeing. The only downside of high-twist merino is that it can be heavy.

The weight of yarn matters, especially for a larger piece. Not only can a garment be physically heavy to wear, but knit fabrics are elastic and a heavy–weight fabric will elongate or sag more than a light–weight fabric. Factors affecting the weight include the fiber itself, the yarn gauge, the way the fiber has been spun into yarn, and the knitting gauge:

- Cotton is usually heavier than wool, which is heavier then cashmere, which is heavier than silk-mohair.
- The larger the yarn gauge, the heavier the fabric, presuming equivalent fiber-content and manufacturing processes.
- A high-twist, worsted-spun wool will be heavier than a woolen-spun wool at the same gauge because the high-twist yarn is denser. As an example, compare the worsted-weight yarns Cascade 220 and Brooklyn Tweed Shelter: Both are intended to be 5 stitches/inch on size 7 needles, but 100 g of Cascade 220 is 220 yards, while 100 g of Shelter is 280 yards. Fabric knit at a similar gauge will be 27% lighter in Shelter vs. Cascade 220.
- Different knitting gauges can dramatically affect the density of a fabric, which impact weight and drape.

Drape also varies with both fiber and gauge. Fingering weight merino knit on Size 0 (2 mm) needles makes a nice firm fabric for socks, but it would be very stiff in a large piece. However, when knit with Size 4 (3.5 mm) needles, the same yarn can be transformed into a light and relaxed fabric well-suited to a shawl.

In fact, any yarn can be made into a more relaxed fabric by increasing the gauge.

Stitch pattern is also integral to drape: a lace pattern will drape more than stockinette, and stockinette will drape more than garter.

WORKING WITH VARIEGATED YARNS

In the past decade the knitting community has seen an explosion in the availability of variegated yarns. To use these yarns, it is essential to know how the color was applied to predict how the yarn will knit up. Depending on the dyeing method, the color changes may be at regular intervals, randomized or very long.

Most hand-dyed yarns are painted systematically as unfurled skeins. The simplest type is when half the loop of the skein is dyed in 1 color and the other half of the loop is dyed in another color. This approach means the different colors change at regular intervals. When you knit, you consume the yarn with some regularity, so the regularity of the knitting combines with the regularity of the dyeing to create interference effects called pooling. If the width of the knitting changes, such as when you go from the body to the shoulders in a sweater, the pooling changes. This pooling effect can be so strong that it drowns out details like texture or shape.

I normally go to great lengths to avoid pooling, but like any strong effect it can be brilliant as a design element. Laura Bryant's book *Artful Color, Mindful Knits* discusses planned pooling where the knitting is carefully engineered to get variegated yarn to make interesting and complex color patterns that can resemble argyles or vertical stripes.

Variegated yarns that are less likely to pool are either dyed randomly, like Koigu KPPPM, or have long repeats like Noro Kureyon. Very short repeats, on the scale of 1-to-3 stitches can also be immune from pooling.

When shopping for hand-dyed yarns, if I unfurl the skein and see that it was dyed as a loop, I know it could pool. If I unfurl the skein and it looks like it was randomly dyed, it is difficult to tell for sure if it will pool because it might have been re-skeined (re-wound) after dyeing into a loop with a different diameter. Ideally the label will explain how the yarn was dyed, but it usually does not. In these cases ask the dyer or the shop owner.

My personal quest to avoid pooling led me to dyeing my own yarn. I have 2 approaches to creating non-pooling yarns: random hand painting or panel dyeing.

Random hand painting is done in skein form by laying the undyed and unfurled skein on a table in an oval and applying the dye in a randomized manner. I paint dots of color here and there, but never across a full segment of the loop. If I need more than 1 skein I lay out multiple skeins side by side and paint them all in exactly the same randomized manner.

Panel dyeing enables many creative options including non-pooling color changes, long-slow repeats and ombres. It can have a tweedy look because the stitches in the panel are touching each other, and this contact creates a shibori effect. It starts with undyed yarn that is made into a panel of stockinette on a knitting machine. The panel is laid out on a table and painted in horizontal stripes. After the dyed panel is washed and dried, the yarn is pulled out onto a swift and steamed to remove the kinks.

For more information about dyeing, I recommend Miser's *The Knitter's Guide to Hand-dyed and Variegated Yarn* and Menz's *Color in Spinning*.

Turn the page to see 4 skeins I dyed with different effects.

VARIEGATED YARNS DYED DIFFERENT WAYS

Four of my hand-dyed yarns, shown unfurled on the left and furled on the right. The top yarn was dyed as a panel, the second and third were painted randomly, and the fourth was painted in loop-sections. The top three yarns will not pool, but the fourth yarn is likely to pool. The second and fourth yarns have not been reskeined. It is easy to see this in the bottom yarn because the color sections are still distinct. You can also see this in the second yarn by looking closely, the dabs of color from the random painting are still intact. The third yarn is a challenge, because it was reskeined. Without unfurling the yarn and studying it, you cannot tell if it was randomly painted or painted in loop-sections. Many dyers like to reskein because it retensions the yarn and makes for a prettier product, so you have to ask how the yarn was dyed to predict how it will knit up.

UNDERSTANDING CONTRAST

There are many important aspects of choosing yarn colors, but the most important are contrast and value. When choosing yarns for a project, I first ask myself whether I want the final piece to be low-contrast or high-contrast, dark or light.

If showing off a complex stitch pattern is the priority, then the shadows created by the stitches need to be the most prominent feature. If the yarn is dark (e.g. has a low value) or has its own inherent contrast (e.g. a tweed or a variegated yarn) it will compete with these shadows. Creamy Aran yarn is optimal for showing off the complex stitch patterns in the eponymous sweaters. Imagine making an Aran sweater in a multi-colored variegated yarn - it would be hard to see the pattern.

- The lighter and lower contrast the yarn, the more the stitch pattern will show.
- The darker and higher contrast the yarn, the more the yarn becomes the focus and the stitch pattern recedes.

To see values and contrast, I like to imagine the yarn in a black and white photograph. In black and white digital photography, an image is translated into shades of gray – and those shades contain the values needed to understand contrast. In black and white images, every pixel has a numerical value that ranges from 0 for black to 255 for white. The contrast of the image is the value of the brightest pixel in the image minus the value of the darkest pixel in the image:

Highest value - lowest value = contrast

The quantity of bright and dark pixels is not part of this equation. A mostly black image with a few white specks will have the same contrast as a mostly gray image with some black and white specks. Only the extrema determine the contrast. This also means that a pure white image has the same contrast as a pure black image, zero.

Applying these concepts to a skein of yarn is easy. Starting within the "solids" there is a range of possible contrasts from those with even color and zero contrast, to the tonal solids which can have high contrast.

The woolen-spun heathers and tweeds also have a wide range depending on the blends of fiber. A light tweed with black flecks is higher contrast than a dark tweed with dark flecks.

Marled yarns where 2 differently colored plies are twisted together can be low or high contrast depending on the values of the 2 colors.

A variegated skein that contains both white and black will have the maximum contrast value. It is crucial to remember that the contrast does not depend on the amount of the yarn within the skein that is bright or dark. A skein can be 99% dark, but if just 1% of the yarn is bright, it will be a high-contrast yarn because those small, bright sections will stand out against the dark background.

It can be hard to understand the relative values of colors. Is a medium red of higher or lower value than a medium green? To see the values of colors within a skein of yarn, take a black and white photograph of the yarn. On the facing page a selection of yarns is arranged from low-contrast on the left to high-contrast on the right. Showing the colored and black and white photographs next to each other makes it easier to see the contrast.

An array of yarns to illustrate contrast

The contrast increases from left to right. Skeins 1–4 have zero contrast, they are pure solids. Skeins 5 and 6 are woolen-spun yarns with low contrast. Skeins 7–9 are tonal solids with medium to high contrast, and the last 3 skeins are variegated yarns with high contrast. From left to right the manufacturers are Quince & Co. (1), Aslan Trends (2), Woolfolk (3), Hifa (4), Brooklyn Tweed (5), Beaverslide (6), Koigu (7-10), Sunshine yarns (11) and Western Sky Knits (12).

MIXING COLORS

Color is a very complicated subject that involves the physics and chemistry of materials, how human eyes work, what real dyes or paints are available and many other factors.

Color wheels are helpful tools to explain how colors mix, but are all approximations of reality. Most books on color knitting and yarn dyeing use the RYB (red, yellow, blue) painter's wheel, but the CMYK printer's wheel (cyan, magenta, yellow, black) better describes how the dyes used for yarns behave (Newhall, 2014). CMYK is a standard in the printing world, and most home ink jet printers have 4 cartridges for C, M, Y and K inks.

Think of an undyed skein like a blank piece of paper with the colors being added to it. White is the result when no color is added. With the RYB color wheel black is a result of using all colors, but in CMYK and in yarn dyeing, black is added as a separate color for 2 reasons: mixing CMY together usually results in a dark brown, not a true black, and using CMY requires more costly dye vs. using a separate black dye.

The diagrams on the facing page are simplified color wheels to explain how the CMYK colors vary in value and how they mix.

Row 1 at the top is composed of 3 wheels. The center wheel shows the 3 primary colors, cyan, magenta and yellow, divided by their secondary colors, blue, red, and green. The wheels on the left and right show the same primary and secondary colors as they transition to white, through dilution, or to black, by adding black pigment.

Row 2 is the same as the first row, rendered in gray scale.

Row 3 shows 3 wheels where the primaries, cyan, magenta, and yellow, are mixed with the other colors in the wheel using a dot pattern.

Row 4 is the same as row 3, but rendered in gray scale. The more pronounced the dot pattern in the bottom row, the higher the contrast between the 2 colors.

Some conclusions can be drawn from the top 2 rows:

- The values of the primaries and secondaries are all different. Value is not a matter of concentration - the pure colors have different values.
- Yellow is nearly white. This means that if you combine yellow with anything other than white or a pastel, the result will be high contrast—and you cannot make yellow any darker by adding black because that changes the color to a greenish-black, as you can see from the top-right wheel.

And also from the bottom 2 rows:

- The mixes of adjacent colors are harmonious.
- The mixes across the wheels, which are complementary colors, make a greenish-brown. You may have to hold the page back and squint to see this effect.
- The contrasts of the mixes are widely variable whether the colors are harmonious or complementary.
- When the mixes are lower contrast, your eyes see a single combined color. But when the mixes are higher contrast, your eyes see a strong dot pattern.

PAGE 341

MIXING COLORS AND MIXING SCALES

So far we have focused on contrast, but two other factors also matter: color and mixing-scale.

Mixing a primary with its opposing secondary results in a green-brown, while mixing adjacent colors results in clear, discernible colors, like yellow and red combining to make orange. Two guidelines I use are:

- For a clear final color, stay within one quadrant of the wheel.
- For an earthy or muddy tone, mix across the wheel.

The scale of how the colors are mixed is crucial. For example, look in the middle wheel of rows 3 and 4 of the diagram on page 341 at the magenta-green mix, which is the wedge opposite pure magenta. Up close you can see both magenta and green squares, but if you hold the page at a distance and squint your eyes, the pattern merges into a muddy green. This effect is well known in art, especially in Impressionism and Pointillism. The scale determines how close you have to be to see the individual colors vs. the combined color.

The mixing-scale also affects how the color-repeats in variegated yarns are perceived. Breaking up the variegated yarn spatially can both reduce pooling and increase visual interest.

In the yarn world, the scales that matter are as follows:

Fiber level

In woolen–spun yarns and many hand-spun yarns, colored fibers are mixed before the yarn is spun. You almost need a magnifying glass to see the individual colors.

Strand level

This category includes marled yarns, hand-spun yarns where 2 strands with different colors are twisted together, and 2 differently–colored yarns held together. You can see the variation up close, but it blends as you move further away from the piece.

Row level

This includes Fair Isle and Bohus knitting, which use different colored yarns within 1 row, Mosiac knitting which mixes colors with slip stitches, and fabrics where the yarn color is changed every 1 or 2 rows. Depending on the contrast and the viewing distance, the colors may stay separate or merge together. I like mixing variegated yarns at the row level.

Large scale

Multi-row stripes, intarsia, long color changes or color blocking keep colors well separated. The colors retain their individuality even at very long viewing distances.

These 4 different scales of color mixing can be used individually or together to create different effects and looks.

The version of Welden (page 202) on the facing page is made with 2 solid colors that are close on the color wheel: red and orange. The overall color is another shade of orange, but the high-contrast between the values and the row-level blend makes for a visually lively effect.

MIXING FIBERS

Combining multiple kinds of yarn in a design lets you create a new fabric with properties of all the fibers. For example, you may have merino in a color you want to use, but to lighten its weight, you may choose to mix it with cashmere or silk mohair.

I mix yarns in 2 ways: Holding the strands together and knitting them as a single composite strand, or knitting 2 rows with 1 strand and then 2 rows with the other strand.

The strands-together approach has been used elegantly and extensively by Setsuko Torii, who combines stainless steel, mohair, paper and other innovative fibers from Habu Textiles to create new mixed fabrics. The looks can range from homogeneous to marled, depending on the relative values of the colors of the individual strands. The gauge is always bigger with strands held together, and swatching is required to find the hand.

Catherine Lowe's Couture Yarns are another example of combining fibers. She combines different plies of merino, alpaca, silk or silk-mohair to optimize the yarn to be exactly what she wants for her couture pieces. The fibers are dyed to match, so the yarns are very low contrast. This allows her to emphasize stitch textures and fine finishing details.

The every-2-rows approach creates fine striping that will be more or less prominent depending on the contrasts of the yarns. The gauge might be the same as for one of the fibers alone, and will depend on the specific choices. Again, swatching is needed to insure the desired result.

Both approaches result in a fabric that blends the properties of the fibers and the colors of the yarns. More importantly, they create a very different look than can be achieved with a single yarn.

The facing page shows 2 examples of a solid silk-mohair combined with panel-dyed merino. On the left is a version of Andrus where the merino and silk mohair are held together, on the right is a scarf-version of Colormill where the same yarns are alternated every 2 rows. In both samples the merino is a hand-painted panel and the silk-mohair is Rowan Kidsilk Haze.

Yarn Mixing Examples

These variations of Andrus on the left and Colormill on the right are combinations of fingering merino and silk mohair. In the Andrus variation, the 2 yarns are held together and worked as 1 strand. In the Colormill variation, they are alternated every 2 rows.

PROXIMITY EFFECTS

The diagram on the facing page illustrates how to think about mixing a variegated yarn with a solid yarn. It shows 6 blocks of colors framed in middle gray. Each block contains stripes of a diagonal pattern and a solid. On the left side there are 3 blocks of a lower-contrast diagonal pattern with grids of light, medium and dark solid shades overlaid from top to bottom. The right is identical except the diagonal pattern is higher contrast.

On the left side, going from top to bottom, the diagonally patterned stripes appear relatively darker, similar, and lighter than the solid stripes because of the proximal effects of the color values. This well-known effect is the subject of Albers' *Interaction of Color*. The situation is different on the right side, where the patterned stripes look more consistent from top to bottom because the contrast within the patterned stripes dominates, rather than the contrast between the patterned and solid stripes. This is another example of how contrast is one of the most important effects in how we perceive patterns.

Some rules of thumb:

- A high-contrast yarn will dominate other yarns when the yarns are combined.
- A yarn can appear darker or lighter, depending on how it is combined with other yarns.

The next few pages show examples where fiber, contrast, color and proximity are all integral to the designs.

Color Proximity Example

Graphic illustration of how a low-contrast variegated yarn looks different than a high-contrast variegated yarn when combined with solids of different values.

ROBSON VARIATION: STUDIES IN COLOR AND TEXTURE

The stitch pattern of the Robson scarf (page 292) is shift-reversible in 2 colors and is especially nice at blending 2 different yarns. When the yarns are mixed this often, they work together to create a new fabric with mechanical, tactile and visual qualities different than either yarn would have alone.

I was pleased with the all-merino Robson scarf, but I wanted to see if I could make it more generous in size, more shawl-like, while also making it lighter and more ephemeral by mixing a panel-dyed merino with a silk-mohair. The result is the piece shown on the facing page.

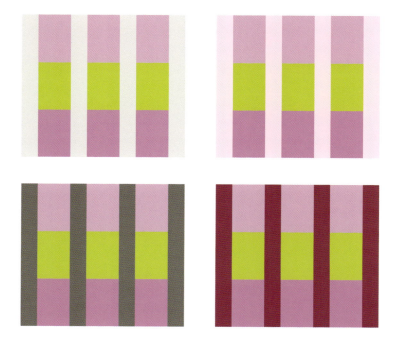

The panel dyed merino is bold and high-contrast, with deep plum, light pink and chartreuse bands. I considered 4 choices for the color of the silk-mohair: light gray, dark gray, light pink and berry. These 4 choices are shown in graphic form above against the colors of the merino. With the 2 lighter shades of silk-mohair, the colors of the merino look darker. With the 2 darker shades, the colors of the merino look lighter. Also, to my eye, the neutral gray picked up a green hue when juxtaposed against the rose colors in the merino. I chose the berry (Rowan Kidsilk Haze in Liqueur) because it is darker than any of the colors in the panel and would be a continuously darker stripe throughout the piece. Most of the colors are harmonious except when the chartreuse comes through.

See page 354 for another variation of Robson using many colors.

NORO SCARVES

The Castro, Dogpatch, and Tenderloin scarves are shown from left to right on the facing page. They illustrate different color and contrast mixing effects possible with Noro Kureyon. The colorways are unknown, but any combinations of Kureyon can work.

Unlike panel-dyed or space-dyed yarns, Kureyon is dyed in the wool. Then the different colored fibers are fed into the carding and spinning machines sequentially to create long repeats. Eisaku Noro set the stage for many of the variegated yarns we have today and especially the variegated woolen-spun yarns.

If you knit with 1 ball of Kureyon, the color changes in a slow and bold way. These colorful fabrics are beautiful, but they do not have the contrast changes that you get when you alternate working with 2 balls.

Jared Flood of Brooklyn Tweed discussed this on his blog and also published a ribbed scarf pattern called "Noro Striped Scarf" (http://brooklyntweed.blogspot.com/2007/04/noro-scarf.html). There are over 13, 000 projects for this scarf on Ravelry as of this writing!

Here simple sequences are used to explore the contrasts in Kureyon colorways using 3 shift-reversible patterns.

Materials

2 balls of Noro Kureyon in color A

2 balls of Noro Kureyon in color B

Size 8 (5 mm) needles

Gauge

4.5 stitches / inch in stockinette

Dimensions

Castro: 7 x 68 inches (18 x 173 cm)

Dogpatch: 6.5 x 68 inches (17 x 173 cm)

Tenderloin: 7.75 x 60 inches (20 x 173 cm)

Pattern Notes

1. To make a longer or wider scarf, use a total of 6 balls, 3 in each colorway.
2. Always bring the new yarn from the front so the edge will look consistent.

Directions

Cast on and work the setup row and 1 main row in color A. Change to color B and work 2 main rows. Continue alternating between A and B every 2 rows, until the piece is the desired length. Bind off. Wash, block and weave in ends.

Castro

Cast on 35 stitches (10+5).

Setup row: K1, [P5, K5], P4

Main row: K1, [P5, K5], P3 , S1WYIF

Dogpatch

Cast on 33 stitches (10+3).

Setup row: [K4, P4, K1, P1], K3

Main row: [K4, P4, K1, P1], K2, S1WYIF

Tenderloin

(see also page 41, this is the same stitch pattern as BG 5)

Cast on 35 (10+5).

Setup row: [K5, P5], K5

Main row: [K5, P5]K4, S1WYIF

IMPROVISATIONAL COLORWORK

The piece shown on the facing page is the prototype for the Colormill shawl on page 44. It is an exercise in color work inspired by Kaffe Fassett and Brandon Mably. In September of 2011, I attended the Vogue Knitting Live workshop in Los Angeles where they gave a talk about their process of working with color. The idea they presented is using a colorwork pattern as a framework for improvisational color studies. The more colors involved, the more interesting the piece.

I have a large stash of fingering weight merino that includes full skeins and small scraps. I divided my collection of fingering merinos into two categories: very dark colors and all the other colors. The lengths of the strands of yarn vary from 10 inches to 10 yards. These two categories became the two colors in the Colormill pattern.

Because the darker yarns are significantly lower value than the lighter yarns, the contrast of the striping pattern is consistent across the piece. This consistency balances the wild color swings within the group of lighter yarns.

The process of choosing the next color is improvisational, and that is the pleasure of working a piece like this. I like the mystery of not knowing where it will go when I start. The rhythm of alternating dark and light provides a framework, but within that framework the knitter has wide latitude for color choices.

ROBSON VALUE STUDY

After creating the Colormill prototype, I was eager to find large sets of colored yarn to explore more multi-color pattern ideas. So in 2012, when I attended the Interweave Knitting Lab in San Mateo I was glad to meet Biggan Ryd-Dups. She was there to promote her lovely Australian merino and she had a kit for sale with 52 tiny balls of her fingering-weight yarn.

Using the Robson pattern as the structure, I began working the colors as a value study from dark to light. I ordered all the balls by their value using black and white photography and began working the pattern from dark to light.

When one color was consumed, I used the next one up in value with no regard to the hue. Sometimes the next color surprised me as it can be challenging to judge values between different colors by eye.

CLOSING WORDS

Sequence Knitting has changed my knitting life. The freedom to create complex fabrics without having to follow charts or detailed instructions led me to a deeper understanding of color, to dyeing my own yarn, and to thinking more deeply about color and texture.

And this is only a beginning. I have many ideas for future projects that build on the simple concepts presented in this book, and I hope you do too.

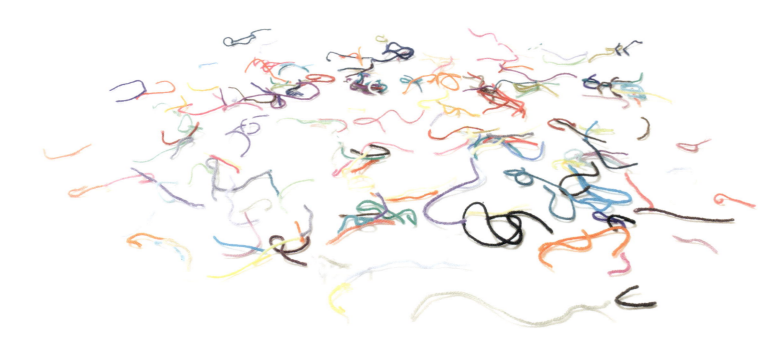

APPENDIX

APPENDIX CONTENTS

- Abbreviations
- Glossary
- Finishing
- References
- Bibliography
- Sources
- Cast-ons for different pattern multiples
- A little math

ABBREVIATIONS

D2	Double decrease: slip 2 stitches together as if to knit, knit the next stitch through the back, and then pass the slipped stitches over the knit stitch together.
K	knit
K1b	knit 1 stitch through the back loop
K2tog	knit 2 stitches together
K3tog	knit 3 stitches together
M1	make 1 by knitting into the back and front of the stitch
M2	make 2 by knitting into the back, front and back of the stitch
P	purl
S1WYIB	slip 1 purl-wise with the working yarn in back
S1WYIF	slip 1 purl-wise with the working yarn in front.
YO	yarn over

GLOSSARY

1-row Method

A method for creating a fabric by working a sequence across a row. If the pattern multiple is different than the sequence, then the row ends with the partial sequence.

Accordion Fabric

A class of fabrics comprised of columns of knit and purl ribs separated by columns of other stitches. The structure is rib-spacer-rib-spacer where the ribs alternate between being knit-ribs or purl-ribs.

All-over Fabric

A class of fabrics with patterns that repeat in row and column, but do not fall into one of the other classes.

Box Pleat Fabric

A fabric comprised of columns of knit and purl ribs separated by columns of other stitches. Unlike the accordion, the ribs do not alternate, but have 2 knit-ribs, then 2 purl-ribs.

Broken Garter Fabric

A fabric comprised of columns of only knit-garter or purl-garter.

Class of Fabric

The classes of fabrics in Sequence Knitting are accordion, all-over, box pleat, broken garter, mistake ribbing, mock ribbing, or ribbing.

Composite Fabric

A fabric created with the 1-row method that can be described as mistake ribbing and an accordion.

Irregular Fabric

A fabric where the spacers between the columns of ribs have varying widths. Typically the class is accordion, mistake ribbing or a box pleat.

Method

Any prescribed or algorithmic way to work a sequence of stitches to create a fabric.

Mistake Ribbing Fabric

A fabric with adjoining columns of knit and purl rib pairs separated by spacers.

Mock Ribbing Fabric

A fabric with knit or purl rib columns separated by spacers.

Pattern multiple or Multiple

The sequence length and remainder, which determine the number of stitches to cast on to create a specific fabric. If the pattern multiple is 5+3, then the cast on can be any multiple of 5, plus 3 more stitches: 8, 13, 18...

Permutation

A permutation of a sequence is a rearrangement of the stitches without changing their order. For example, the permutations of the sequence [K4,P1] are [K3, P1, K1], [K2, P1, K2], [K1, P1, K3], and [P1, K3]. There are always as many permutations as the sequence length.

Remainder

The additional stitches beyond a multiple of the sequence length in a pattern multiple. For the sequence [K4, P1] worked on the pattern multiple of 5+4, 4 is the remainder.

Reversibility, Aesthetic

A property of a knit fabric where the frontside and backside are fundamentally different, but the viewer is pleased by both sides. The interior of the charts of the frontside and the backside cannot be made to be the same by shifting rows or columns, nor are they mirror images. Sometimes the difference between a frontside and a backside is dramatic and sometimes it is subtle.

Reversibility, Perfect

A property of a knit fabric where the frontside and backside are the same including the selvedges. The chart of the backside is identical to the chart of the frontside.

Reversibility, Shift

A property of a knit fabric where the frontside and backside are the same except for the selvedges. The chart of the backside can be shifted left-right or up-down to match the chart of the frontside.

Reversibility, Shift-flip

A property of a knit fabric where the frontside and backside are the right-left mirror images except for the selvedges. The chart of the backside can be shifted left-right or up-down, and mirrored from left to right to match the chart of the frontside.

Ribbing Fabric

A fabric comprised only of columns of knit and purl ribs.

Sequence

Any ordered set of stitches with a fixed length.

Sequence Knitting Chart

A standard knitting chart except for 2 differences:
- The number of columns in the chart is always the pattern multiple
- The highlighted box shows the repeat in columns and rows, not necessarily the pattern multiple

Serpentine Method

A method for creating a fabric by working a sequence continually from row to row. An incomplete sequence at the end of a row is continued on the next row in a serpentine fashion.

Shaped 1-row Method

The same as the 1-row method, except with increases or decreases worked along with the sequences, usually at the beginning or end of each row.

Spiral Method

A method for creating a fabric by working a sequence continually in the round without restarting the sequence at the beginning of the round.

Swirl Fabric

Any knit fabric with a distinct swirl pattern.

Types of Fabrics

A set of related fabrics where the frontsides or backsides are related by shifting, or shift-flipping. A sequence worked over different pattern multiples and/or with different permutations can lead to many fabrics that are the same type.

FINISHING

All the patterns in this book are written in a succinct form, but that does not mean that careful finishing is not important. Finishing neatly matters.

There are many wonderful books and online resources on finishing techniques. I particularly recommend Hiatt's *Principles of Knitting*, Vogue's *Vogue Knitting, the Ultimate Knitting Book*, and Lowe's *The Ravell'd Sleeve*.

Casting on and off

The most important aspect of any cast-on or cast-off is that the gauge is the same as the piece. If the gauge is smaller, it will pucker, and if the gauge is bigger, it will make the edge flare. Getting the gauge right with a cast-on is more difficult than for a cast-off because the gauge of the bulk fabric is yet unknown. Casting off is always easier because you can adjust the tension to suit the fabric.

The safest way to insure a cast-on looks the same as the cast-off and does not distort the fabric is to do a provisional cast-on, and then later go back and "cast off" the first row. To do this without any extra ends to weave in, work the provisional cast-on with scrap yarn. Make a bundle of the working yarn that is long enough for the cast off, tie it in a butterfly, and begin knitting the piece. After working some number of rows, remove the provisional cast-on and put the first row of stitches on a needle, and use the yarn in the butterfly to "cast off" the stitches. This is particularly helpful for less forgiving yarns like cotton, alpaca, silk or cashmere.

If the cast-on needs to be elastic for something like the tops of socks or the bottoms of hats, my favorite is the Alternating Cast-on in Hiatt's *Principles of Knitting*. This cast-on is very quick, but the first row must be a 1x1 rib to "set" the stitches. There are many other nice cast-ons that have similarly beautiful edges like the Tubular

Cast-on or the Channel Island Cast-on.

I usually use a standard cast-off, but I take great care with the tension, especially on the last stitch where I will use a tapestry needle to adjust the tension and avoid a big loop.

Selvedges

For rectangular pieces with the 1-row or serpentine methods, the selvedge can just be the edge of the pattern. However, this will not look as tidy as having a formal selvedge, nor will it be optimized for seaming if the piece needs to be joined to another. As discussed on page 54, a selvedge can always be added, but it needs to be accounted for with the pattern multiple. For example, if a piece is to be knit on a pattern multiple of 8+2 without a selvedge, adding a 1-stitch selvedge would require that the pattern multiple be adjusted to 8+4.

The sides of pieces made with the shaped 1-row method must have just the right tension or the piece will curl and pucker in an unsightly way. This is usually much looser than with rectangular knitting. When using the shaped 1-row method with 2 colors of yarn, the look of the edges will depend on the stitch pattern and may or may not be pleasing. A seed–stitch selvedge is an approach that is reversible in 2 colors and looks nice.

Washing and Blocking

There are many ways to wash and block, and delicate fibers like cashmere need more care than superwash merino.

My normal approach after a piece is complete, is to soak it in soapy water for up to 24 hours, rinse it thoroughly, and then spin it by hand in a wire basket to remove most of the water. I carefully pin the piece to a large blocking board, aim a fan at it, and let it dry overnight.

Weaving in Ends

Try to use large skeins so there are not extra ends to weave in. Some projects like the Colormill Prototype on page 352 used over 40 pieces of yarn. In these cases join the new yarn by knitting it together with the old yarn for 3-5 stitches. After washing and blocking, trim the ends flush.

The more complex the stitch pattern, the more forgiving the pattern in terms of hiding yarn joins. Plain stockinette is the least forgiving stitch pattern.

REFERENCES

Invention or unvention? Given the simplicity of Sequence Knitting it seems like many of these fabrics must have been created by past knitters, but the written records that I have been able to find tell a more limited tale. The fabrics created with the 1-row method with very short sequences like [K1, P1], [K2, P1], [K2, P2], and [K3, P1] are well represented, but as the sequences become more complex the number of references falls off dramatically. The exceptions are broken garters and swirls.

In the table on the facing page I have included the references I could find for the **fabrics** that can be created with Sequence Knitting, whether or not that's how they were created in the source. Much of the time the fabrics are given either as multi-row pattern or as a chart - very rarely are they described as a Sequence Knit. Ribbing is not included in the table because all varieties are common.

Pattern	Sequence	References
Accordion	K3,P1	Burns, p. 50; 400 Knitting Stitches, p. 17; The Harmony Guides. Knit & Purl: 250 Stitches to Knit, p. 151; Klopper, p. 34; Phildar, p. 16; Walker, Second Treasury, p. 7
	K7,P1	The Harmony Guides. Knit Edgings & Trims, p. 35
Broken Garter	K2,P2	The Harmony Guides. Knit & Purl: 250 Stitches to Knit, p. 79
	K3,P1	Mason, p. 27
	K3,P2	Burns, p. 70
	K4,P1	Burns, p. 58
	K3,P3	Burns, p. 62; Eaton, p. 90; Radcliffe, p. 138; Shangold - pp. 13, 20; Thomas, Mary Thomas's Book of Knitting Patterns, p. 20
	K5,P1	Stanfield p. 26
	K5,P2	Burns, p. 66
	K4,P4	Berry, Basic Knitting. p. 89; The Harmony Guides. Knit & Purl: 250 Stitches to Knit, p. 88; Leapman, Color Knitting the Easy Way, p. 56
	K5,P5	Berry, Basic Knitting, pp. 72, 93; Berry, Beyond Basic Knitting, p. 93
	K11,P11	Hiyashi, pp. 20, 76-77
Mistake Ribbing	K2,P1	Many, usually called Farrow Rib
	K3,P1,K1,P1	Walker, Second Treasury, p. 4
Mock Ribbing	K3,P1	The Harmony Guides. Knit & Purl: 250 Stitches to Knit, p. 49; The Harmony Guide To Knitting, Techniques and Stitches, p. 62
Swirl	K1,P2	Ruhe, p. 105
	K2,P1	Gibson-Roberts, p. 257; Ruhe, p. 123
	K2,P2	Phildar. p. 25; The Harmony Guides. Knit & Purl: 250 Stitches to Knit, p. 54; Ruhe, pp. 97, 99
	K3,P1	The Harmony Guides. Knit & Purl: 250 Stitches to Knit, p. 38; 60 Quick Baby Blankets, p. 138; Mezgimo Menas, p. 38
	K2,P3	Ruhe, pp. 85, 89
	K3,P2	The Harmony Guides. Knit & Purl: 250 Stitches to Knit, p. 73; Ruhe, p. 82; Thompson, p. 111
	K4,P1	Bernard, p. 31; Ruhe, pp. 54, 79, 82
	K2,P4	Ruhe, p. 95
	K3,P3	Albright, p. 87; Carron, p. 16; Leapman, Knit Stitch, p. 33; Mezgimo Menas, p. 38; Phildar, p. 24
	K4,P2	Ruhe, pp. 82, 87; Taylor, Rita p. 19
	K5,P1	The Harmony Guides. Knit & Purl: 250 Stitches to Knit, p. 254; Kose, p. 8; Phildar, p. 24
	K4,P2	Ruhe, pp. 55, 60
	K4,P4	Walker, Treasury, p. 24
	K5,P1,K1,P1	The Harmony Guides. Knit & Purl: 250 Stitches to Knit, p. 67
	K5,P3	Albright, p. 42; The Harmony Guides. Knit & Purl: 250 Stitches to Knit, p. 83
	K7,P2	Seto, p. 10
	K3,P3,K3,P1,K1,P1	Stanfield, p. 35

BIBLIOGRAPHY

When the concept of Sequence Knitting was coming together, I could not believe that it was not already documented in the knitting literature, so I sought to find all the references I could. This bibliography includes the books I investigated as part of my research not only for the stitch patterns, but also for other aspects of the project including color work, book design, and general commentary on knitting.

Albers, Josef. Interaction of Color, 50th Anniversary Edition. Yale University, 2013. (Originally published: Yale University, 1963)
Albright, Barbara. Odd Ball Knitting: Creative Ideas for Leftover Yarn. New York: Potter Craft, 2005.
Baber, M'Lou. Double Knitting: Reversible Two Color Designs. Pittsville, Wisconsin: Schoolhouse Press, 2008.
Barr, Lynne. Reversible Knitting: 50 Brand-New Groundbreaking Stitch Patterns. New York: STC Craft/ A Melanie Falick Book, 2009.
Bartlett, Roxana. Slip-Stitch Knitting: Color Pattern the Easy Way. Loveland, Colorado: Interweave Press, 1998.
Bernard, Wendy. Up, Down, All-around Stitch Dictionary. New York: Stewart, Tabori & Chang, 2014.
Berry, Leigh Ann, ed. Basic Knitting. Mechanicsburg, PA: Stackpole Books, 2004.
––––––––. Beyond Basic Knitting. Mechanicsburg, PA: Stackpole Books, 2008.
Bryant, Laura Militzer. Artful Color, Mindful Knits. Sioux Falls, SD: XRX, Inc., 2013.
Burns, Missy; Kaisler, Stephanie Blaydes; Tosten, Anita. Knitting with Hand-dyed Yarns. Woodinville, WA: Martingale & Company, 2004. *This book includes a discussion on broken garter starting on p. 56.*
Carron, Cathy. Spiral Pullover. *knit purl*, fall/winter 2014, pp. 16-17, 26.
Chinchio, Connie Chang. Textured Stitches: Knitted Sweaters & Accessories with Smart Details. Loveland, CO: Interweave Press, 2011.
Christoffersson, Britt-Marie. Pop Knitting: Bold Motifs Using Color & Stitch. Loveland, CO: Interweave Press, 2010.
Crompton, Claire. The Knitter's Bible Stitch Library. England: David & Charles, 2010.
Eaton, Jan. 200 Stitch Patterns for Baby Blankets. Concord, CA: C&T Publishing, Inc., 2006.
Epstein, Nicky. Knitting On the Edge. New York: Sixth & Spring Books, 2004.
Fassett, Kaffe. Glorious Knits. New York: Clarkson N. Potter, 1985.
––––––––. Lecture. Kaleidoscope of Colour. Vogue Knitting Live LA, Century City, CA. 12-1 PM, September 24, 2011.
––––––––. Gala Dinner Speech. Vogue Knitting Live LA, Century City, CA. September 24, 2011.
400 Knitting Stitches. New York: Potter Craft, 2007.
Gardiner, Kay and Shayne, Ann. Mason Dixon Knitting. New York: Potter Craft, 2006.
––––––––. Knitting Outside the Lines. New York: Potter Craft, 2008.
Hamilton, Cornelia Tuttle. Noro: Meet the Man Behind the Legendary Yarn: Knit 40 Fabulous Designs. New York: Sixth & Spring, 2009.
The Harmony Guides. The Harmony Guide To Knitting, Techniques and Stitches. New York: Harmony Books, 1992.
––––––––. Knit & Purl: 250 Stitches to Knit. Loveland, CO: Interweave 2007.
––––––––. Knit Edgings & Trims: 150 Stitches. Loveland, CO: Interweave 2009.
––––––––. Vol. 1, Knitting Techniques: All You Need to Know About Hand Knitting. London: Collins & Brown, Ltd., 1998. Originally published by Lyric Books, 1986.
––––––––. Vol. 2, 450 Knitting Stitches. London: Collins & Brown, Ltd., 1998. Originally published by Lyric Books, 1986. Same as The Harmony Guide to Knitting Stitches. London: Lyric Books Limited, 1983.
––––––––. Vol. 3, 440 More Knitting Stitches. London: Collins & Brown, Ltd., 1998. Originally published by Lyric Books, 1987.
––––––––. Vol. 4, 250 Creative Knitting Stitches. London: Collins & Brown, Ltd., 1998. Originally published by Lyric Books, 1990.
Haxell, Kate. The Knitter's Palette, A Workbook of Color and Texture Techniques and Effects. Hove, England: Quid Publishing, 2013.
Hiatt, June Hemmons. The Principles of Knitting. First ed. New York: Simon & Schuster, 1989.
––––––––. The Principles of Knitting. Second ed. New York: Simon & Schuster, 2012.
Hemingway, Karen. Super Stitches Knitting. New York: Watson-Guptill Publications, 2007.

Hiyashi, Kotomi. Let's Enjoy Circular Needle Knitting!! Japan: Graphics, Inc., 2012. ISBN978-4-7661-2408-8. In Japanese.

Høxbro, Vivian. Shadow Knitting. Loveland, Colorado: Interweave Press, 2004.

Ihnen, Lori. Colorwork for Adventurous Knitters. Minneapolis, MN: Creative Publishing International Inc., 2012.

Klopper, Gisela. Beautiful Knitting Patterns. New York: Sterling Publishing Co., Inc., 2005.

The Knitting Dictionary, 1030 Stitches and Patterns. Paris: Mon Tricot, 1972.

Kose, Chie. 500 Knitting Pattern World of Chie Kose. Japan: Bunka Publishing Bureau, 2010. ISBN 978-4-579-11297-5. In Japanese.

Landra, Maie. Knits from a Painter's Palette. New York: Sixth & Spring, 2006.

Leapman, Melissa. Color Knitting the Easy Way. New York: Potter Craft, 2010.

––––––––. The Knit Stitch Pattern Handbook. New York: Potter Craft, 2013.

––––––––. Mastering Color Knitting. New York: Potter Craft, 2010.

Lowe, Catherine. The Ravell'd Sleeve: The Journal of the Couture Knitting Workshop. Catherine Lowe, 2009.

Menz, Deb. Color in Spinning. Loveland, CO: Interweave Press, 2005.

Mezgimo Menas. Latvia: Mezgimo Menas, 2000.

Miser, Lorna. The Knitter's Guide to Hand-Dyed and Variegated Yarn. New York: Watson-Guptill, 2010.

Neighbors, Jane F. Reversible Two-Color Knitting. New York: Charles Scribner's Sons, 1974.

New, Debbie. Unexpected Knitting. Pittsville, WI: Schoolhouse Press, 2003.

Newhall, Susan. Color and Fiber: The Untold Story Class. Madrona Fiber Arts, Tacoma, WA. February 15, 2014.

Phildar. Hand Knitting Stitches. Paris: Phildar, 1985.

Phillips, Mary Walker. Knitting. New York: Franklin Watts, 1977.

––––––––. Step-by-Step Knitting: A Complete Introduction to the Craft of Knitting. New York: Golden Press, 1967.

Pobedinskaya, Olga. Knitting Pleats: Stunning Garments and Accessories. Bothell, WA: Martingale Company, 2011.

Radcliffe, Margaret. The Essential Guide to Color Knitting Techniques. North Adams, MA: Storey Publishing, 2008.

Ruhe, Stella. Dutch Traditional Ganseys: Sweaters from 40 Villages. Baarn, The Netherlands: Forte Uitgevers BV, 2013.

Schreier, Iris. Reversible Knits: Both Sides Right. Asheville, NC: Lark Books, 2009.

Seto, T. Knitting Patterns 500. Japan: Tankobon Hardcover, 1989. ISBN 978-4-529-01588-2. In Japanese.

60 Quick Baby Blankets. New York: Sixth & Spring Books, 2013.

Stanfield, Lesley. The New Knitting Stitch Library. Ashville, NC: Lark Books, 1992.

Stanley, Montse. Reader's Digest Knitter's Handbook. Pleasantville, NY: Reader's Digest Association, 2001.

Thomas, Mary. Mary Thomas's Knitting Book. New York: Dover Publications, 1972.

––––––––. Mary Thomas's Book of Knitting Patterns. New York: Macmillan Publishing Co., 1945. Originally published London: Hodder and Stoughton Ltd., 1943.

Thompson, Gladys. Patterns for Guernseys, Jerseys & Arans: Fishermen's Sweaters from the British Isles. Third ed. New York: Dover Publications, 1979.

Tillotson, Marjory. The Complete Knitting Book. London: Sir Isaac Pitman & Sons, Ltd., 1934.

Torii, Setsuko. Hand-knit Works. Kyoto, Japan: Maria Shobo, 2006. (ISBN4-89511-382-5, in Japanese).

––––––––. Zoom on Knit Texture. Kyoto, Japan: Avril, 2010/2011.

The Editors of Vogue Knitting Magazine. Vogue Knitting, the Ultimate Knitting Book. New York: Sixth & Spring Books, 2002.

––––––––. Vogue Knitting Stitchionary: Volume 1 Knit & Purl. New York: Sixth & Spring Books, 2005.

Walker, Barbara G. A Treasury of Knitting Patterns. Pittsville, Wisconsin: Schoolhouse Press, 1996. Originally published New York: Charles Scribner's Sons, 1968.

––––––––. A Second Treasury of Knitting Patterns. Pittsville, Wisconsin: Schoolhouse Press, 1998. Originally published New York:

Charles Scribner's Sons, 1970.

———————. Charted Knitting Designs: A Third Treasury of Knitting Patterns. Pittsville, Wisconsin: Schoolhouse Press, 1998. Originally published New York: Charles Scribner's Sons, 1972.

———————. A Fourth Treasury of Knitting Patterns. Pittsville, Wisconsin: Schoolhouse Press, 2001. Originally published New York: Charles Scribner's Sons, 1973.

Zimmerman, Elizabeth. Knitting Without Tears: Basic Techniques and Easy-to-Follow Directions for Garments to Fit All Sizes. New York: Fireside, 1971.

SOURCES

Aslan Trends
www.aslantrends.com

Beaverslide Dry Goods
www.beaverslide.com

Biggan Designs
www.biggandesign.com

Brooklyn Tweed
www.brooklyntweed.net

Cascade Yarns
www.cascadeyarns.com

Catherine Lowe
www.catherine-lowe.com

Habu Textiles
www.habutextiles.com

Hillesvåg Ullvarefabrikk AS (Hifa yarns)
www.hifa.no

Isager Aps
www.isagerstrik.dk

Joyce's Knitwear
www.joycesknitwear.com

Karbella Yarns
www.karabellayarns.com

Koigu Wool Designs
www.koigu.com

Lisa Souza Knitwear and Dyeworks
www.lisaknit.com

Madelinetosh Hand Dyed Yarns
www.madelinetosh.com

Mountain Colors Hand-painted Yarns
www.mountaincolors.com

Noro Yarns
www.knittingfever.com

Östergötlands Ullspinneri AB
www.ullspinneriet.com

Prism Arts Inc.
www.prismyarn.com

Prochemical and Dye, Inc.
www.prochemicalanddye.com

Quince & Co.
www.quinceandco.com

Rowan Yarns
www.rowanyarns.co.uk

School Products Yarns
www.schoolproductsyarns.com

String Yarns
www.stringyarns.com

Studio Donegal
www.studiodonegal.ie

Sunshine Yarns
www.sunshineyarns.com

Western Sky Knits
www.westernskyknits.com

Wool2Dye4
www.wool2dye4.com

Woolfolk
www.woolfolkyarn.com

CAST-ONS FOR DIFFERENT PATTERN MULTIPLES

Cast On	2	3	4	5	6	7	8	9	10	11	12
20	2+0	3+2	4+0	5+0	6+2	7+6	8+4	9+2	10+0	11+9	12+8
21	2+1	3+0	4+1	5+1	6+3	7+0	8+5	9+3	10+1	11+10	12+9
22	2+0	3+1	4+2	5+2	6+4	7+1	8+6	9+4	10+2	11+0	12+10
23	2+1	3+2	4+3	5+3	6+5	7+2	8+7	9+5	10+3	11+1	12+11
24	2+0	3+0	4+0	5+4	6+0	7+3	8+0	9+6	10+4	11+2	12+0
25	2+1	3+1	4+1	5+0	6+1	7+4	8+1	9+7	10+5	11+3	12+1
26	2+0	3+2	4+2	5+1	6+2	7+5	8+2	9+8	10+6	11+4	12+2
27	2+1	3+0	4+3	5+2	6+3	7+6	8+3	9+0	10+7	11+5	12+3
28	2+0	3+1	4+0	5+3	6+4	7+0	8+4	9+1	10+8	11+6	12+4
29	2+1	3+2	4+1	5+4	6+5	7+1	8+5	9+2	10+9	11+7	12+5
30	2+0	3+0	4+2	5+0	6+0	7+2	8+6	9+3	10+0	11+8	12+6
31	2+1	3+1	4+3	5+1	6+1	7+3	8+7	9+4	10+1	11+9	12+7
32	2+0	3+2	4+0	5+2	6+2	7+4	8+0	9+5	10+2	11+10	12+8
33	2+1	3+0	4+1	5+3	6+3	7+5	8+1	9+6	10+3	11+0	12+9
34	2+0	3+1	4+2	5+4	6+4	7+6	8+2	9+7	10+4	11+1	12+10
35	2+1	3+2	4+3	5+0	6+5	7+0	8+3	9+8	10+5	11+2	12+11
36	2+0	3+0	4+0	5+1	6+0	7+1	8+4	9+0	10+6	11+3	12+0
37	2+1	3+1	4+1	5+2	6+1	7+2	8+5	9+1	10+7	11+4	12+1
38	2+0	3+2	4+2	5+3	6+2	7+3	8+6	9+2	10+8	11+5	12+2
39	2+1	3+0	4+3	5+4	6+3	7+4	8+7	9+3	10+9	11+6	12+3
40	2+0	3+1	4+0	5+0	6+4	7+5	8+0	9+4	10+0	11+7	12+4
41	2+1	3+2	4+1	5+1	6+5	7+6	8+1	9+5	10+1	11+8	12+5
42	2+0	3+0	4+2	5+2	6+0	7+0	8+2	9+6	10+2	11+9	12+6
43	2+1	3+1	4+3	5+3	6+1	7+1	8+3	9+7	10+3	11+10	12+7
44	2+0	3+2	4+0	5+4	6+2	7+2	8+4	9+8	10+4	11+0	12+8
45	2+1	3+0	4+1	5+0	6+3	7+3	8+5	9+0	10+5	11+1	12+9
46	2+0	3+1	4+2	5+1	6+4	7+4	8+6	9+1	10+6	11+2	12+10
47	2+1	3+2	4+3	5+2	6+5	7+5	8+7	9+2	10+7	11+3	12+11
48	2+0	3+0	4+0	5+3	6+0	7+6	8+0	9+3	10+8	11+4	12+0
49	2+1	3+1	4+1	5+4	6+1	7+0	8+1	9+4	10+9	11+5	12+1
50	2+0	3+2	4+2	5+0	6+2	7+1	8+2	9+5	10+0	11+6	12+2
51	2+1	3+0	4+3	5+1	6+3	7+2	8+3	9+6	10+1	11+7	12+3
52	2+0	3+1	4+0	5+2	6+4	7+3	8+4	9+7	10+2	11+8	12+4
53	2+1	3+2	4+1	5+3	6+5	7+4	8+5	9+8	10+3	11+9	12+5
54	2+0	3+0	4+2	5+4	6+0	7+5	8+6	9+0	10+4	11+10	12+6
55	2+1	3+1	4+3	5+0	6+1	7+6	8+7	9+1	10+5	11+0	12+7
56	2+0	3+2	4+0	5+1	6+2	7+0	8+0	9+2	10+6	11+1	12+8
57	2+1	3+0	4+1	5+2	6+3	7+1	8+1	9+3	10+7	11+2	12+9
58	2+0	3+1	4+2	5+3	6+4	7+2	8+2	9+4	10+8	11+3	12+10
59	2+1	3+2	4+3	5+4	6+5	7+3	8+3	9+5	10+9	11+4	12+11
60	2+0	3+0	4+0	5+0	6+0	7+4	8+4	9+6	10+0	11+5	12+0
61	2+1	3+1	4+1	5+1	6+1	7+5	8+5	9+7	10+1	11+6	12+1
62	2+0	3+2	4+2	5+2	6+2	7+6	8+6	9+8	10+2	11+7	12+2
63	2+1	3+0	4+3	5+3	6+3	7+0	8+7	9+0	10+3	11+8	12+3
64	2+0	3+1	4+0	5+4	6+4	7+1	8+0	9+1	10+4	11+9	12+4
65	2+1	3+2	4+1	5+0	6+5	7+2	8+1	9+2	10+5	11+10	12+5
66	2+0	3+0	4+2	5+1	6+0	7+3	8+2	9+3	10+6	11+0	12+6
67	2+1	3+1	4+3	5+2	6+1	7+4	8+3	9+4	10+7	11+1	12+7
68	2+0	3+2	4+0	5+3	6+2	7+5	8+4	9+5	10+8	11+2	12+8
69	2+1	3+0	4+1	5+4	6+3	7+6	8+5	9+6	10+9	11+3	12+9
70	2+0	3+1	4+2	5+0	6+4	7+0	8+6	9+7	10+0	11+4	12+10
71	2+1	3+2	4+3	5+1	6+5	7+1	8+7	9+8	10+1	11+5	12+11
72	2+0	3+0	4+0	5+2	6+0	7+2	8+0	9+0	10+2	11+6	12+0
73	2+1	3+1	4+1	5+3	6+1	7+3	8+1	9+1	10+3	11+7	12+1
74	2+0	3+2	4+2	5+4	6+2	7+4	8+2	9+2	10+4	11+8	12+2
75	2+1	3+0	4+3	5+0	6+3	7+5	8+3	9+3	10+5	11+9	12+3
76	2+0	3+1	4+0	5+1	6+4	7+6	8+4	9+4	10+6	11+10	12+4
77	2+1	3+2	4+1	5+2	6+5	7+0	8+5	9+5	10+7	11+0	12+5
78	2+0	3+0	4+2	5+3	6+0	7+1	8+6	9+6	10+8	11+1	12+6
79	2+1	3+1	4+3	5+4	6+1	7+2	8+7	9+7	10+9	11+2	12+7
80	2+0	3+2	4+0	5+0	6+2	7+3	8+0	9+8	10+0	11+3	12+8
81	2+1	3+0	4+1	5+1	6+3	7+4	8+1	9+0	10+1	11+4	12+9
82	2+0	3+1	4+2	5+2	6+4	7+5	8+2	9+1	10+2	11+5	12+10
83	2+1	3+2	4+3	5+3	6+5	7+6	8+3	9+2	10+3	11+6	12+11
84	2+0	3+0	4+0	5+4	6+0	7+0	8+4	9+3	10+4	11+7	12+0

Cast On	2	3	4	5	6	7	8	9	10	11	12
85	2+1	3+1	4+1	5+0	6+1	7+1	8+5	9+4	10+5	11+8	12+1
86	2+0	3+2	4+2	5+1	6+2	7+2	8+6	9+5	10+6	11+9	12+2
87	2+1	3+0	4+3	5+2	6+3	7+3	8+7	9+6	10+7	11+10	12+3
88	2+0	3+1	4+0	5+3	6+4	7+4	8+0	9+7	10+8	11+0	12+4
89	2+1	3+2	4+1	5+4	6+5	7+5	8+1	9+8	10+9	11+1	12+5
90	2+0	3+0	4+2	5+0	6+0	7+6	8+2	9+0	10+0	11+2	12+6
91	2+1	3+1	4+3	5+1	6+1	7+0	8+3	9+1	10+1	11+3	12+7
92	2+0	3+2	4+0	5+2	6+2	7+1	8+4	9+2	10+2	11+4	12+8
93	2+1	3+0	4+1	5+3	6+3	7+2	8+5	9+3	10+3	11+5	12+9
94	2+0	3+1	4+2	5+4	6+4	7+3	8+6	9+4	10+4	11+6	12+10
95	2+1	3+2	4+3	5+0	6+5	7+4	8+7	9+5	10+5	11+7	12+11
96	2+0	3+0	4+0	5+1	6+0	7+5	8+0	9+6	10+6	11+8	12+0
97	2+1	3+1	4+1	5+2	6+1	7+6	8+1	9+7	10+7	11+9	12+1
98	2+0	3+2	4+2	5+3	6+2	7+0	8+2	9+8	10+8	11+10	12+2
99	2+1	3+0	4+3	5+4	6+3	7+1	8+3	9+0	10+9	11+0	12+3
100	2+0	3+1	4+0	5+0	6+4	7+2	8+4	9+1	10+0	11+1	12+4
101	2+1	3+2	4+1	5+1	6+5	7+3	8+5	9+2	10+1	11+2	12+5
102	2+0	3+0	4+2	5+2	6+0	7+4	8+6	9+3	10+2	11+3	12+6
103	2+1	3+1	4+3	5+3	6+1	7+5	8+7	9+4	10+3	11+4	12+7
104	2+0	3+2	4+0	5+4	6+2	7+6	8+0	9+5	10+4	11+5	12+8
105	2+1	3+0	4+1	5+0	6+3	7+0	8+1	9+6	10+5	11+6	12+9
106	2+0	3+1	4+2	5+1	6+4	7+1	8+2	9+7	10+6	11+7	12+10
107	2+1	3+2	4+3	5+2	6+5	7+2	8+3	9+8	10+7	11+8	12+11
108	2+0	3+0	4+0	5+3	6+0	7+3	8+4	9+0	10+8	11+9	12+0
109	2+1	3+1	4+1	5+4	6+1	7+4	8+5	9+1	10+9	11+10	12+1
110	2+0	3+2	4+2	5+0	6+2	7+5	8+6	9+2	10+0	11+0	12+2
111	2+1	3+0	4+3	5+1	6+3	7+6	8+7	9+3	10+1	11+1	12+3
112	2+0	3+1	4+0	5+2	6+4	7+0	8+0	9+4	10+2	11+2	12+4
113	2+1	3+2	4+1	5+3	6+5	7+1	8+1	9+5	10+3	11+3	12+5
114	2+0	3+0	4+2	5+4	6+0	7+2	8+2	9+6	10+4	11+4	12+6
115	2+1	3+1	4+3	5+0	6+1	7+3	8+3	9+7	10+5	11+5	12+7
116	2+0	3+2	4+0	5+1	6+2	7+4	8+4	9+8	10+6	11+6	12+8
117	2+1	3+0	4+1	5+2	6+3	7+5	8+5	9+0	10+7	11+7	12+9
118	2+0	3+1	4+2	5+3	6+4	7+6	8+6	9+1	10+8	11+8	12+10
119	2+1	3+2	4+3	5+4	6+5	7+0	8+7	9+2	10+9	11+9	12+11
120	2+0	3+0	4+0	5+0	6+0	7+1	8+0	9+3	10+0	11+10	12+0
121	2+1	3+1	4+1	5+1	6+1	7+2	8+1	9+4	10+1	11+0	12+1
122	2+0	3+2	4+2	5+2	6+2	7+3	8+2	9+5	10+2	11+1	12+2
123	2+1	3+0	4+3	5+3	6+3	7+4	8+3	9+6	10+3	11+2	12+3
124	2+0	3+1	4+0	5+4	6+4	7+5	8+4	9+7	10+4	11+3	12+4
125	2+1	3+2	4+1	5+0	6+5	7+6	8+5	9+8	10+5	11+4	12+5
126	2+0	3+0	4+2	5+1	6+0	7+0	8+6	9+0	10+6	11+5	12+6
127	2+1	3+1	4+3	5+2	6+1	7+1	8+7	9+1	10+7	11+6	12+7
128	2+0	3+2	4+0	5+3	6+2	7+2	8+0	9+2	10+8	11+7	12+8
129	2+1	3+0	4+1	5+4	6+3	7+3	8+1	9+3	10+9	11+8	12+9
130	2+0	3+1	4+2	5+0	6+4	7+4	8+2	9+4	10+0	11+9	12+10
131	2+1	3+2	4+3	5+1	6+5	7+5	8+3	9+5	10+1	11+10	12+11
132	2+0	3+0	4+0	5+2	6+0	7+6	8+4	9+6	10+2	11+0	12+0
133	2+1	3+1	4+1	5+3	6+1	7+0	8+5	9+7	10+3	11+1	12+1
134	2+0	3+2	4+2	5+4	6+2	7+1	8+6	9+8	10+4	11+2	12+2
135	2+1	3+0	4+3	5+0	6+3	7+2	8+7	9+0	10+5	11+3	12+3
136	2+0	3+1	4+0	5+1	6+4	7+3	8+0	9+1	10+6	11+4	12+4
137	2+1	3+2	4+1	5+2	6+5	7+4	8+1	9+2	10+7	11+5	12+5
138	2+0	3+0	4+2	5+3	6+0	7+5	8+2	9+3	10+8	11+6	12+6
139	2+1	3+1	4+3	5+4	6+1	7+6	8+3	9+4	10+9	11+7	12+7
140	2+0	3+2	4+0	5+0	6+2	7+0	8+4	9+5	10+0	11+8	12+8
141	2+1	3+0	4+1	5+1	6+3	7+1	8+5	9+6	10+1	11+9	12+9
142	2+0	3+1	4+2	5+2	6+4	7+2	8+6	9+7	10+2	11+10	12+10
143	2+1	3+2	4+3	5+3	6+5	7+3	8+7	9+8	10+3	11+0	12+11
144	2+0	3+0	4+0	5+4	6+0	7+4	8+0	9+0	10+4	11+1	12+0
145	2+1	3+1	4+1	5+0	6+1	7+5	8+1	9+1	10+5	11+2	12+1
146	2+0	3+2	4+2	5+1	6+2	7+6	8+2	9+2	10+6	11+3	12+2
147	2+1	3+0	4+3	5+2	6+3	7+0	8+3	9+3	10+7	11+4	12+3
148	2+0	3+1	4+0	5+3	6+4	7+1	8+4	9+4	10+8	11+5	12+4
149	2+1	3+2	4+1	5+4	6+5	7+2	8+5	9+5	10+9	11+6	12+5

Cast On	2	3	4	5	6	7	8	9	10	11	12
150	2+0	3+0	4+2	5+0	6+0	7+3	8+6	9+6	10+0	11+7	12+6
151	2+1	3+1	4+3	5+1	6+1	7+4	8+7	9+7	10+1	11+8	12+7
152	2+0	3+2	4+0	5+2	6+2	7+5	8+0	9+8	10+2	11+9	12+8
153	2+1	3+0	4+1	5+3	6+3	7+6	8+1	9+0	10+3	11+10	12+9
154	2+0	3+1	4+2	5+4	6+4	7+0	8+2	9+1	10+4	11+0	12+10
155	2+1	3+2	4+3	5+0	6+5	7+1	8+3	9+2	10+5	11+1	12+11
156	2+0	3+0	4+0	5+1	6+0	7+2	8+4	9+3	10+6	11+2	12+0
157	2+1	3+1	4+1	5+2	6+1	7+3	8+5	9+4	10+7	11+3	12+1
158	2+0	3+2	4+2	5+3	6+2	7+4	8+6	9+5	10+8	11+4	12+2
159	2+1	3+0	4+3	5+4	6+3	7+5	8+7	9+6	10+9	11+5	12+3
160	2+0	3+1	4+0	5+0	6+4	7+6	8+0	9+7	10+0	11+6	12+4
161	2+1	3+2	4+1	5+1	6+5	7+0	8+1	9+8	10+1	11+7	12+5
162	2+0	3+0	4+2	5+2	6+0	7+1	8+2	9+0	10+2	11+8	12+6
163	2+1	3+1	4+3	5+3	6+1	7+2	8+3	9+1	10+3	11+9	12+7
164	2+0	3+2	4+0	5+4	6+2	7+3	8+4	9+2	10+4	11+10	12+8
165	2+1	3+0	4+1	5+0	6+3	7+4	8+5	9+3	10+5	11+0	12+9
166	2+0	3+1	4+2	5+1	6+4	7+5	8+6	9+4	10+6	11+1	12+10
167	2+1	3+2	4+3	5+2	6+5	7+6	8+7	9+5	10+7	11+2	12+11
168	2+0	3+0	4+0	5+3	6+0	7+0	8+0	9+6	10+8	11+3	12+0
169	2+1	3+1	4+1	5+4	6+1	7+1	8+1	9+7	10+9	11+4	12+1
170	2+0	3+2	4+2	5+0	6+2	7+2	8+2	9+8	10+0	11+5	12+2
171	2+1	3+0	4+3	5+1	6+3	7+3	8+3	9+0	10+1	11+6	12+3
172	2+0	3+1	4+0	5+2	6+4	7+4	8+4	9+1	10+2	11+7	12+4
173	2+1	3+2	4+1	5+3	6+5	7+5	8+5	9+2	10+3	11+8	12+5
174	2+0	3+0	4+2	5+4	6+0	7+6	8+6	9+3	10+4	11+9	12+6
175	2+1	3+1	4+3	5+0	6+1	7+0	8+7	9+4	10+5	11+10	12+7
176	2+0	3+2	4+0	5+1	6+2	7+1	8+0	9+5	10+6	11+0	12+8
177	2+1	3+0	4+1	5+2	6+3	7+2	8+1	9+6	10+7	11+1	12+9
178	2+0	3+1	4+2	5+3	6+4	7+3	8+2	9+7	10+8	11+2	12+10
179	2+1	3+2	4+3	5+4	6+5	7+4	8+3	9+8	10+9	11+3	12+11
180	2+0	3+0	4+0	5+0	6+0	7+5	8+4	9+0	10+0	11+4	12+0
181	2+1	3+1	4+1	5+1	6+1	7+6	8+5	9+1	10+1	11+5	12+1
182	2+0	3+2	4+2	5+2	6+2	7+0	8+6	9+2	10+2	11+6	12+2
183	2+1	3+0	4+3	5+3	6+3	7+1	8+7	9+3	10+3	11+7	12+3
184	2+0	3+1	4+0	5+4	6+4	7+2	8+0	9+4	10+4	11+8	12+4
185	2+1	3+2	4+1	5+0	6+5	7+3	8+1	9+5	10+5	11+9	12+5
186	2+0	3+0	4+2	5+1	6+0	7+4	8+2	9+6	10+6	11+10	12+6
187	2+1	3+1	4+3	5+2	6+1	7+5	8+3	9+7	10+7	11+0	12+7
188	2+0	3+2	4+0	5+3	6+2	7+6	8+4	9+8	10+8	11+1	12+8
189	2+1	3+0	4+1	5+4	6+3	7+0	8+5	9+0	10+9	11+2	12+9
190	2+0	3+1	4+2	5+0	6+4	7+1	8+6	9+1	10+0	11+3	12+10
191	2+1	3+2	4+3	5+1	6+5	7+2	8+7	9+2	10+1	11+4	12+11
192	2+0	3+0	4+0	5+2	6+0	7+3	8+0	9+3	10+2	11+5	12+0
193	2+1	3+1	4+1	5+3	6+1	7+4	8+1	9+4	10+3	11+6	12+1
194	2+0	3+2	4+2	5+4	6+2	7+5	8+2	9+5	10+4	11+7	12+2
195	2+1	3+0	4+3	5+0	6+3	7+6	8+3	9+6	10+5	11+8	12+3
196	2+0	3+1	4+0	5+1	6+4	7+0	8+4	9+7	10+6	11+9	12+4
197	2+1	3+2	4+1	5+2	6+5	7+1	8+5	9+8	10+7	11+10	12+5
198	2+0	3+0	4+2	5+3	6+0	7+2	8+6	9+0	10+8	11+0	12+6
199	2+1	3+1	4+3	5+4	6+1	7+3	8+7	9+1	10+9	11+1	12+7
200	2+0	3+2	4+0	5+0	6+2	7+4	8+0	9+2	10+0	11+2	12+8
201	2+1	3+0	4+1	5+1	6+3	7+5	8+1	9+3	10+1	11+3	12+9
202	2+0	3+1	4+2	5+2	6+4	7+6	8+2	9+4	10+2	11+4	12+10
203	2+1	3+2	4+3	5+3	6+5	7+0	8+3	9+5	10+3	11+5	12+11
204	2+0	3+0	4+0	5+4	6+0	7+1	8+4	9+6	10+4	11+6	12+0
205	2+1	3+1	4+1	5+0	6+1	7+2	8+5	9+7	10+5	11+7	12+1
206	2+0	3+2	4+2	5+1	6+2	7+3	8+6	9+8	10+6	11+8	12+2
207	2+1	3+0	4+3	5+2	6+3	7+4	8+7	9+0	10+7	11+9	12+3
208	2+0	3+1	4+0	5+3	6+4	7+5	8+0	9+1	10+8	11+10	12+4
209	2+1	3+2	4+1	5+4	6+5	7+6	8+1	9+2	10+9	11+0	12+5
210	2+0	3+0	4+2	5+0	6+0	7+0	8+2	9+3	10+0	11+1	12+6
211	2+1	3+1	4+3	5+1	6+1	7+1	8+3	9+4	10+1	11+2	12+7
212	2+0	3+2	4+0	5+2	6+2	7+2	8+4	9+5	10+2	11+3	12+8
213	2+1	3+0	4+1	5+3	6+3	7+3	8+5	9+6	10+3	11+4	12+9
214	2+0	3+1	4+2	5+4	6+4	7+4	8+6	9+7	10+4	11+5	12+10

Cast On	2	3	4	5	6	7	8	9	10	11	12
215	2+1	3+2	4+3	5+0	6+5	7+5	8+7	9+8	10+5	11+6	12+11
216	2+0	3+0	4+0	5+1	6+0	7+6	8+0	9+0	10+6	11+7	12+0
217	2+1	3+1	4+1	5+2	6+1	7+0	8+1	9+1	10+7	11+8	12+1
218	2+0	3+2	4+2	5+3	6+2	7+1	8+2	9+2	10+8	11+9	12+2
219	2+1	3+0	4+3	5+4	6+3	7+2	8+3	9+3	10+9	11+10	12+3
220	2+0	3+1	4+0	5+0	6+4	7+3	8+4	9+4	10+0	11+0	12+4
221	2+1	3+2	4+1	5+1	6+5	7+4	8+5	9+5	10+1	11+1	12+5
222	2+0	3+0	4+2	5+2	6+0	7+5	8+6	9+6	10+2	11+2	12+6
223	2+1	3+1	4+3	5+3	6+1	7+6	8+7	9+7	10+3	11+3	12+7
224	2+0	3+2	4+0	5+4	6+2	7+0	8+0	9+8	10+4	11+4	12+8
225	2+1	3+0	4+1	5+0	6+3	7+1	8+1	9+0	10+5	11+5	12+9
226	2+0	3+1	4+2	5+1	6+4	7+2	8+2	9+1	10+6	11+6	12+10
227	2+1	3+2	4+3	5+2	6+5	7+3	8+3	9+2	10+7	11+7	12+11
228	2+0	3+0	4+0	5+3	6+0	7+4	8+4	9+3	10+8	11+8	12+0
229	2+1	3+1	4+1	5+4	6+1	7+5	8+5	9+4	10+9	11+9	12+1
230	2+0	3+2	4+2	5+0	6+2	7+6	8+6	9+5	10+0	11+10	12+2
231	2+1	3+0	4+3	5+1	6+3	7+0	8+7	9+6	10+1	11+0	12+3
232	2+0	3+1	4+0	5+2	6+4	7+1	8+0	9+7	10+2	11+1	12+4
233	2+1	3+2	4+1	5+3	6+5	7+2	8+1	9+8	10+3	11+2	12+5
234	2+0	3+0	4+2	5+4	6+0	7+3	8+2	9+0	10+4	11+3	12+6
235	2+1	3+1	4+3	5+0	6+1	7+4	8+3	9+1	10+5	11+4	12+7
236	2+0	3+2	4+0	5+1	6+2	7+5	8+4	9+2	10+6	11+5	12+8
237	2+1	3+0	4+1	5+2	6+3	7+6	8+5	9+3	10+7	11+6	12+9
238	2+0	3+1	4+2	5+3	6+4	7+0	8+6	9+4	10+8	11+7	12+10
239	2+1	3+2	4+3	5+4	6+5	7+1	8+7	9+5	10+9	11+8	12+11
240	2+0	3+0	4+0	5+0	6+0	7+2	8+0	9+6	10+0	11+9	12+0
241	2+1	3+1	4+1	5+1	6+1	7+3	8+1	9+7	10+1	11+10	12+1
242	2+0	3+2	4+2	5+2	6+2	7+4	8+2	9+8	10+2	11+0	12+2
243	2+1	3+0	4+3	5+3	6+3	7+5	8+3	9+0	10+3	11+1	12+3
244	2+0	3+1	4+0	5+4	6+4	7+6	8+4	9+1	10+4	11+2	12+4
245	2+1	3+2	4+1	5+0	6+5	7+0	8+5	9+2	10+5	11+3	12+5
246	2+0	3+0	4+2	5+1	6+0	7+1	8+6	9+3	10+6	11+4	12+6
247	2+1	3+1	4+3	5+2	6+1	7+2	8+7	9+4	10+7	11+5	12+7
248	2+0	3+2	4+0	5+3	6+2	7+3	8+0	9+5	10+8	11+6	12+8
249	2+1	3+0	4+1	5+4	6+3	7+4	8+1	9+6	10+9	11+7	12+9
250	2+0	3+1	4+2	5+0	6+4	7+5	8+2	9+7	10+0	11+8	12+10
251	2+1	3+2	4+3	5+1	6+5	7+6	8+3	9+8	10+1	11+9	12+11
252	2+0	3+0	4+0	5+2	6+0	7+0	8+4	9+0	10+2	11+10	12+0
253	2+1	3+1	4+1	5+3	6+1	7+1	8+5	9+1	10+3	11+0	12+1
254	2+0	3+2	4+2	5+4	6+2	7+2	8+6	9+2	10+4	11+1	12+2
255	2+1	3+0	4+3	5+0	6+3	7+3	8+7	9+3	10+5	11+2	12+3
256	2+0	3+1	4+0	5+1	6+4	7+4	8+0	9+4	10+6	11+3	12+4
257	2+1	3+2	4+1	5+2	6+5	7+5	8+1	9+5	10+7	11+4	12+5
258	2+0	3+0	4+2	5+3	6+0	7+6	8+2	9+6	10+8	11+5	12+6
259	2+1	3+1	4+3	5+4	6+1	7+0	8+3	9+7	10+9	11+6	12+7
260	2+0	3+2	4+0	5+0	6+2	7+1	8+4	9+8	10+0	11+7	12+8
261	2+1	3+0	4+1	5+1	6+3	7+2	8+5	9+0	10+1	11+8	12+9
262	2+0	3+1	4+2	5+2	6+4	7+3	8+6	9+1	10+2	11+9	12+10
263	2+1	3+2	4+3	5+3	6+5	7+4	8+7	9+2	10+3	11+10	12+11
264	2+0	3+0	4+0	5+4	6+0	7+5	8+0	9+3	10+4	11+0	12+0
265	2+1	3+1	4+1	5+0	6+1	7+6	8+1	9+4	10+5	11+1	12+1
266	2+0	3+2	4+2	5+1	6+2	7+0	8+2	9+5	10+6	11+2	12+2
267	2+1	3+0	4+3	5+2	6+3	7+1	8+3	9+6	10+7	11+3	12+3
268	2+0	3+1	4+0	5+3	6+4	7+2	8+4	9+7	10+8	11+4	12+4
269	2+1	3+2	4+1	5+4	6+5	7+3	8+5	9+8	10+9	11+5	12+5
270	2+0	3+0	4+2	5+0	6+0	7+4	8+6	9+0	10+0	11+6	12+6
271	2+1	3+1	4+3	5+1	6+1	7+5	8+7	9+1	10+1	11+7	12+7
272	2+0	3+2	4+0	5+2	6+2	7+6	8+0	9+2	10+2	11+8	12+8
273	2+1	3+0	4+1	5+3	6+3	7+0	8+1	9+3	10+3	11+9	12+9
274	2+0	3+1	4+2	5+4	6+4	7+1	8+2	9+4	10+4	11+10	12+10
275	2+1	3+2	4+3	5+0	6+5	7+2	8+3	9+5	10+5	11+0	12+11
276	2+0	3+0	4+0	5+1	6+0	7+3	8+4	9+6	10+6	11+1	12+0
277	2+1	3+1	4+1	5+2	6+1	7+4	8+5	9+7	10+7	11+2	12+1
278	2+0	3+2	4+2	5+3	6+2	7+5	8+6	9+8	10+8	11+3	12+2
279	2+1	3+0	4+3	5+4	6+3	7+6	8+7	9+0	10+9	11+4	12+3

Cast On	2	3	4	5	6	7	8	9	10	11	12
280	2+0	3+1	4+0	5+0	6+4	7+0	8+0	9+1	10+0	11+5	12+4
281	2+1	3+2	4+1	5+1	6+5	7+1	8+1	9+2	10+1	11+6	12+5
282	2+0	3+0	4+2	5+2	6+0	7+2	8+2	9+3	10+2	11+7	12+6
283	2+1	3+1	4+3	5+3	6+1	7+3	8+3	9+4	10+3	11+8	12+7
284	2+0	3+2	4+0	5+4	6+2	7+4	8+4	9+5	10+4	11+9	12+8
285	2+1	3+0	4+1	5+0	6+3	7+5	8+5	9+6	10+5	11+10	12+9
286	2+0	3+1	4+2	5+1	6+4	7+6	8+6	9+7	10+6	11+0	12+10
287	2+1	3+2	4+3	5+2	6+5	7+0	8+7	9+8	10+7	11+1	12+11
288	2+0	3+0	4+0	5+3	6+0	7+1	8+0	9+0	10+8	11+2	12+0
289	2+1	3+1	4+1	5+4	6+1	7+2	8+1	9+1	10+9	11+3	12+1
290	2+0	3+2	4+2	5+0	6+2	7+3	8+2	9+2	10+0	11+4	12+2
291	2+1	3+0	4+3	5+1	6+3	7+4	8+3	9+3	10+1	11+5	12+3
292	2+0	3+1	4+0	5+2	6+4	7+5	8+4	9+4	10+2	11+6	12+4
293	2+1	3+2	4+1	5+3	6+5	7+6	8+5	9+5	10+3	11+7	12+5
294	2+0	3+0	4+2	5+4	6+0	7+0	8+6	9+6	10+4	11+8	12+6
295	2+1	3+1	4+3	5+0	6+1	7+1	8+7	9+7	10+5	11+9	12+7
296	2+0	3+2	4+0	5+1	6+2	7+2	8+0	9+8	10+6	11+10	12+8
297	2+1	3+0	4+1	5+2	6+3	7+3	8+1	9+0	10+7	11+0	12+9
298	2+0	3+1	4+2	5+3	6+4	7+4	8+2	9+1	10+8	11+1	12+10
299	2+1	3+2	4+3	5+4	6+5	7+5	8+3	9+2	10+9	11+2	12+11
300	2+0	3+0	4+0	5+0	6+0	7+6	8+4	9+3	10+0	11+3	12+0
301	2+1	3+1	4+1	5+1	6+1	7+0	8+5	9+4	10+1	11+4	12+1
302	2+0	3+2	4+2	5+2	6+2	7+1	8+6	9+5	10+2	11+5	12+2
303	2+1	3+0	4+3	5+3	6+3	7+2	8+7	9+6	10+3	11+6	12+3
304	2+0	3+1	4+0	5+4	6+4	7+3	8+0	9+7	10+4	11+7	12+4
305	2+1	3+2	4+1	5+0	6+5	7+4	8+1	9+8	10+5	11+8	12+5
306	2+0	3+0	4+2	5+1	6+0	7+5	8+2	9+0	10+6	11+9	12+6
307	2+1	3+1	4+3	5+2	6+1	7+6	8+3	9+1	10+7	11+10	12+7
308	2+0	3+2	4+0	5+3	6+2	7+0	8+4	9+2	10+8	11+0	12+8
309	2+1	3+0	4+1	5+4	6+3	7+1	8+5	9+3	10+9	11+1	12+9
310	2+0	3+1	4+2	5+0	6+4	7+2	8+6	9+4	10+0	11+2	12+10
311	2+1	3+2	4+3	5+1	6+5	7+3	8+7	9+5	10+1	11+3	12+11
312	2+0	3+0	4+0	5+2	6+0	7+4	8+0	9+6	10+2	11+4	12+0
313	2+1	3+1	4+1	5+3	6+1	7+5	8+1	9+7	10+3	11+5	12+1
314	2+0	3+2	4+2	5+4	6+2	7+6	8+2	9+8	10+4	11+6	12+2
315	2+1	3+0	4+3	5+0	6+3	7+0	8+3	9+0	10+5	11+7	12+3
316	2+0	3+1	4+0	5+1	6+4	7+1	8+4	9+1	10+6	11+8	12+4
317	2+1	3+2	4+1	5+2	6+5	7+2	8+5	9+2	10+7	11+9	12+5
318	2+0	3+0	4+2	5+3	6+0	7+3	8+6	9+3	10+8	11+10	12+6
319	2+1	3+1	4+3	5+4	6+1	7+4	8+7	9+4	10+9	11+0	12+7
320	2+0	3+2	4+0	5+0	6+2	7+5	8+0	9+5	10+0	11+1	12+8
321	2+1	3+0	4+1	5+1	6+3	7+6	8+1	9+6	10+1	11+2	12+9
322	2+0	3+1	4+2	5+2	6+4	7+0	8+2	9+7	10+2	11+3	12+10
323	2+1	3+2	4+3	5+3	6+5	7+1	8+3	9+8	10+3	11+4	12+11
324	2+0	3+0	4+0	5+4	6+0	7+2	8+4	9+0	10+4	11+5	12+0
325	2+1	3+1	4+1	5+0	6+1	7+3	8+5	9+1	10+5	11+6	12+1
326	2+0	3+2	4+2	5+1	6+2	7+4	8+6	9+2	10+6	11+7	12+2
327	2+1	3+0	4+3	5+2	6+3	7+5	8+7	9+3	10+7	11+8	12+3
328	2+0	3+1	4+0	5+3	6+4	7+6	8+0	9+4	10+8	11+9	12+4
329	2+1	3+2	4+1	5+4	6+5	7+0	8+1	9+5	10+9	11+10	12+5
330	2+0	3+0	4+2	5+0	6+0	7+1	8+2	9+6	10+0	11+0	12+6
331	2+1	3+1	4+3	5+1	6+1	7+2	8+3	9+7	10+1	11+1	12+7
332	2+0	3+2	4+0	5+2	6+2	7+3	8+4	9+8	10+2	11+2	12+8
333	2+1	3+0	4+1	5+3	6+3	7+4	8+5	9+0	10+3	11+3	12+9
334	2+0	3+1	4+2	5+4	6+4	7+5	8+6	9+1	10+4	11+4	12+10
335	2+1	3+2	4+3	5+0	6+5	7+6	8+7	9+2	10+5	11+5	12+11
336	2+0	3+0	4+0	5+1	6+0	7+0	8+0	9+3	10+6	11+6	12+0
337	2+1	3+1	4+1	5+2	6+1	7+1	8+1	9+4	10+7	11+7	12+1
338	2+0	3+2	4+2	5+3	6+2	7+2	8+2	9+5	10+8	11+8	12+2
339	2+1	3+0	4+3	5+4	6+3	7+3	8+3	9+6	10+9	11+9	12+3
340	2+0	3+1	4+0	5+0	6+4	7+4	8+4	9+7	10+0	11+10	12+4
341	2+1	3+2	4+1	5+1	6+5	7+5	8+5	9+8	10+1	11+0	12+5
342	2+0	3+0	4+2	5+2	6+0	7+6	8+6	9+0	10+2	11+1	12+6
343	2+1	3+1	4+3	5+3	6+1	7+0	8+7	9+1	10+3	11+2	12+7
344	2+0	3+2	4+0	5+4	6+2	7+1	8+0	9+2	10+4	11+3	12+8

Cast On	2	3	4	5	6	7	8	9	10	11	12
345	2+1	3+0	4+1	5+0	6+3	7+2	8+1	9+3	10+5	11+4	12+9
346	2+0	3+1	4+2	5+1	6+4	7+3	8+2	9+4	10+6	11+5	12+10
347	2+1	3+2	4+3	5+2	6+5	7+4	8+3	9+5	10+7	11+6	12+11
348	2+0	3+0	4+0	5+3	6+0	7+5	8+4	9+6	10+8	11+7	12+0
349	2+1	3+1	4+1	5+4	6+1	7+6	8+5	9+7	10+9	11+8	12+1
350	2+0	3+2	4+2	5+0	6+2	7+0	8+6	9+8	10+0	11+9	12+2
351	2+1	3+0	4+3	5+1	6+3	7+1	8+7	9+0	10+1	11+10	12+3
352	2+0	3+1	4+0	5+2	6+4	7+2	8+0	9+1	10+2	11+0	12+4
353	2+1	3+2	4+1	5+3	6+5	7+3	8+1	9+2	10+3	11+1	12+5
354	2+0	3+0	4+2	5+4	6+0	7+4	8+2	9+3	10+4	11+2	12+6
355	2+1	3+1	4+3	5+0	6+1	7+5	8+3	9+4	10+5	11+3	12+7
356	2+0	3+2	4+0	5+1	6+2	7+6	8+4	9+5	10+6	11+4	12+8
357	2+1	3+0	4+1	5+2	6+3	7+0	8+5	9+6	10+7	11+5	12+9
358	2+0	3+1	4+2	5+3	6+4	7+1	8+6	9+7	10+8	11+6	12+10
359	2+1	3+2	4+3	5+4	6+5	7+2	8+7	9+8	10+9	11+7	12+11
360	2+0	3+0	4+0	5+0	6+0	7+3	8+0	9+0	10+0	11+8	12+0
361	2+1	3+1	4+1	5+1	6+1	7+4	8+1	9+1	10+1	11+9	12+1
362	2+0	3+2	4+2	5+2	6+2	7+5	8+2	9+2	10+2	11+10	12+2
363	2+1	3+0	4+3	5+3	6+3	7+6	8+3	9+3	10+3	11+0	12+3
364	2+0	3+1	4+0	5+4	6+4	7+0	8+4	9+4	10+4	11+1	12+4
365	2+1	3+2	4+1	5+0	6+5	7+1	8+5	9+5	10+5	11+2	12+5
366	2+0	3+0	4+2	5+1	6+0	7+2	8+6	9+6	10+6	11+3	12+6
367	2+1	3+1	4+3	5+2	6+1	7+3	8+7	9+7	10+7	11+4	12+7
368	2+0	3+2	4+0	5+3	6+2	7+4	8+0	9+8	10+8	11+5	12+8
369	2+1	3+0	4+1	5+4	6+3	7+5	8+1	9+0	10+9	11+6	12+9
370	2+0	3+1	4+2	5+0	6+4	7+6	8+2	9+1	10+0	11+7	12+10
371	2+1	3+2	4+3	5+1	6+5	7+0	8+3	9+2	10+1	11+8	12+11
372	2+0	3+0	4+0	5+2	6+0	7+1	8+4	9+3	10+2	11+9	12+0
373	2+1	3+1	4+1	5+3	6+1	7+2	8+5	9+4	10+3	11+10	12+1
374	2+0	3+2	4+2	5+4	6+2	7+3	8+6	9+5	10+4	11+0	12+2
375	2+1	3+0	4+3	5+0	6+3	7+4	8+7	9+6	10+5	11+1	12+3
376	2+0	3+1	4+0	5+1	6+4	7+5	8+0	9+7	10+6	11+2	12+4
377	2+1	3+2	4+1	5+2	6+5	7+6	8+1	9+8	10+7	11+3	12+5
378	2+0	3+0	4+2	5+3	6+0	7+0	8+2	9+0	10+8	11+4	12+6
379	2+1	3+1	4+3	5+4	6+1	7+1	8+3	9+1	10+9	11+5	12+7
380	2+0	3+2	4+0	5+0	6+2	7+2	8+4	9+2	10+0	11+6	12+8
381	2+1	3+0	4+1	5+1	6+3	7+3	8+5	9+3	10+1	11+7	12+9
382	2+0	3+1	4+2	5+2	6+4	7+4	8+6	9+4	10+2	11+8	12+10
383	2+1	3+2	4+3	5+3	6+5	7+5	8+7	9+5	10+3	11+9	12+11
384	2+0	3+0	4+0	5+4	6+0	7+6	8+0	9+6	10+4	11+10	12+0
385	2+1	3+1	4+1	5+0	6+1	7+0	8+1	9+7	10+5	11+0	12+1
386	2+0	3+2	4+2	5+1	6+2	7+1	8+2	9+8	10+6	11+1	12+2
387	2+1	3+0	4+3	5+2	6+3	7+2	8+3	9+0	10+7	11+2	12+3
388	2+0	3+1	4+0	5+3	6+4	7+3	8+4	9+1	10+8	11+3	12+4
389	2+1	3+2	4+1	5+4	6+5	7+4	8+5	9+2	10+9	11+4	12+5
390	2+0	3+0	4+2	5+0	6+0	7+5	8+6	9+3	10+0	11+5	12+6
391	2+1	3+1	4+3	5+1	6+1	7+6	8+7	9+4	10+1	11+6	12+7
392	2+0	3+2	4+0	5+2	6+2	7+0	8+0	9+5	10+2	11+7	12+8
393	2+1	3+0	4+1	5+3	6+3	7+1	8+1	9+6	10+3	11+8	12+9
394	2+0	3+1	4+2	5+4	6+4	7+2	8+2	9+7	10+4	11+9	12+10
395	2+1	3+2	4+3	5+0	6+5	7+3	8+3	9+8	10+5	11+10	12+11
396	2+0	3+0	4+0	5+1	6+0	7+4	8+4	9+0	10+6	11+0	12+0
397	2+1	3+1	4+1	5+2	6+1	7+5	8+5	9+1	10+7	11+1	12+1
398	2+0	3+2	4+2	5+3	6+2	7+6	8+6	9+2	10+8	11+2	12+2
399	2+1	3+0	4+3	5+4	6+3	7+0	8+7	9+3	10+9	11+3	12+3
400	2+0	3+1	4+0	5+0	6+4	7+1	8+0	9+4	10+0	11+4	12+4

A LITTLE MATH

How can you know how many possible sequences exist for a sequence of a given length? It is intuitive that as a sequence becomes longer, there will be more possibilities, but using math helps us to understand this better.

A sequence can be comprised of any kind of stitches, but for simplicity's sake, let's only consider knits and purls so the math is binary.

If a sequence has only 1 stitch, there are 2 possible sequences: [K1] and [P1]. If the sequence has 2 stitches there are 4 possible sequences: [K2], [K1, P1], [P1, K1], and [P2]. The total number of sequences will be 2^n where n is the sequence length. In the examples above, this is 2^1 or 2 for n=1 and 2^2 or 4 for n=2. As n increases by 1 stitch, the total number of sequences double: 2, 4, 8, 16, 32, 64, ...

The 2^n possibilities can be broken down further depending on the mix of knit and purl stitches in the sequence. The formula for the binomial coefficient below gives the number of sequences for a given sequence length and a specific mix of knits and purls:

$$\binom{n}{k} = \frac{n!}{k! * (n-k)!}$$

where n is the sequence length, and k is the number of knit stitches. n-k is the number of purl stitches.

Let's work through the simple example where n=2, because we already know the answer from above. The number of knit stitches can be 2, 1, or 0, thus there are 3 possible groups of sequences:

$$\binom{2}{2} = \frac{2!}{2!*(2-2)!} = 1\text{, the 1 sequence is [K2]}$$

$$\binom{2}{1} = \frac{2!}{1!*(2-1)!} = 2\text{, the 2 sequences are [K1, P1] and [P1, K1]}$$

$$\binom{2}{0} = \frac{2!}{0!*(2-0)!} = 1\text{, the 1 sequence is [P2]}$$

The first and last formulas each lead to the trivial sequences, [K2] and [P2]. They are trivial because they are redundant with the sequences [K1] and [P1] for n=1.

The middle formula says there are 2 sequences, [K1, P1] and [P1, K1], but since these are permutations of each other only one is unique. So in this example, only 1 of the 4 sequences is unique, [K1, P1].

There is also another factor to consider, which is that a purl is just the backside of a knit: working [P5, K1] is very similar to working [K5, P1].

Determining the unique sequences requires removing all trivial or irrelevant sequences due to:

- Already existing as a shorter sequence
- Permutations
- Purl-heavy versions

The table on the facing page summarizes this information for sequences ranging from 1 to 6 stitches. The unique sequences are shown in bold, 14 in total.

n	Total # Sequences	# knit stitches	# Sequences Per # Knit Stiches	Actual Sequences
1	2	1	1	**k**
		0	1	p
2	4	2	1	kk
		1	2	**kp**, pk
		0	1	pp
3	8	3	1	kkk
		2	3	**kkp**, kpk, pkk
		1	3	ppk, pkp, kpp
		0	1	ppp
4	16	4	1	kkkk
		3	4	**kkkp**, kkpk, kpkk, pkkk
		2	6	kpkp, pkpk, **kkpp**, kppk, ppkk, pkkp
		1	4	kppp, pkpp, ppkp, pppk
		0	1	pppp
5	32	5	1	kkkkk
		4	5	**kkkkp**, kkkpk, kkpkk, kpkkk, pkkkk
		3	10	**kkkpp**, kkppk, kppkk, ppkkk, pkkkp, **kkpkp**, kpkpk, pkpkk, kpkkp, pkkpk
		2	10	kkppp, kpppk, pppkk, ppkkp, pkkpp, kpkpp, pkppk, kppkp, ppkpk, pkpkp
		1	5	kpppp, ppppk, pppkp, ppkpp, pkppp
		0	1	ppppp
6	64	6	1	kkkkkk
		5	6	**kkkkkp**, kkkkpk, kkkpkk, kkpkkk, kpkkkk, pkkkkk
		4	15	**kkkkpp**, kkkppk, kkppkk, kppkkk, ppkkkk, pkkkkp, **kkkpkp**, kkpkpk, kpkpkk, pkpkkk, kpkkkp, pkkkpk, kkpkkp, kpkpkp, pkkpkk
		3	20	**kkkppp**, kkpppk, kpppkk, pppkkk, ppkkkp, pkkkpp, **kkpkpp**, kpkppk, pkpkkp, kppkkp, ppkkpk, pkkpkp, **kkppkp**, kppkpk, ppkpkk, pkpkkp, kpkkpp, pkkppk, kpkpkp, pkpkpk
		2	15	kkpppp, kppppk, ppppkk, pppkkp, ppkkpp, pkkppp, kpkppp, pkpppk, kpppkp, pppkpk, ppkpkp, pkpkpp, kppkpp, ppkppk, pkppkp
		1	6	kppppp, pkpppp, ppkppp, pppkpp, ppppkp, pppppk
		0	1	pppppp

INDEX

INDEX

1-row method, 5-6, 10-11, 25-95
—, chart, viii, 28
—, classes, 29
—, repeat, stitch 4, 10-13
—, repeat, row 28
—, permutations, 10-12, 54-55
—, selvedges, 54-55
2x2 squares, 122-123, 132, 308
Abbreviations, 361
Accordion, 10, 28-31, 46-49, 56-57
Aesthetically reversible, see Reversible, aesthetic
Albers, Josef, 346
Algorithm, 3
Andrus, 8-9, 114-115, 344-345
Artful Color, Mindful Knits, Bryant, 335
Askin, 8-9
Bach, 112-113
BG 1, 2, 3, 5, 7, and 11, 40-41
Bibliography, 368-376
Blocking, 364-365
Bordhi, Cat, vii
Box pleat(s), 29-31, 50-51, 53
Brioche, 46
Broken garter, 10-11, 29-31, 36-45, 199, 205, 344-345, 350-353
Bryant, Laura, 335
Butterfly, 14, 364
Carron, Cathy, 196
Casting on and off, 14, 364-365
Cast-on table, 372-373
Castro, 350-351
Cellular Automaton Knitting, 23
Chain link, 173, 286-287, 312-313
Chaos theory, 23
Charts, viii, 28
Classes, general 29-30
—, 1-row fabrics, 29-30
—, serpentine method, 98
—, spiral method, 196
Color in Spinning, Menz, 335
Color(s)
—, adjacent, 340-341

—, CMYK vs. RYB, 340-341
—, mixing, 338-343, 346-349
—, primary, 340-341
—, secondary, 340-341
—, wheel(s), 340-341
—, values, 338-341, 346-349, 352-355
Colormill, 44-45, 344-345, 352-353, 365
Contrast, 338, 341-353
Cowl pattern, 120-121, 202-203
Delta Wing, 288-289
Derain, 48-49
Disrupted garter, 102-103
Dogpatch, 350-351
Drape, 332
Drewes, 8-9
Dutch ganseys, 196
Dyeing yarn, 335-337
Enders, 8-9
Fabric types, 56-57, 122-127, 204, 206-207
Fabrics, specific
—, accordion
 —, 1-row method, 65, 69, 80, 83, 85-86
 —, serpentine method, 191
—, all over
 —, serpentine method, 130-151, 153-189, 192
 —, shaped 1-row, 296-307, 309-311, 313-317, 318-323, 324-329
 —, spiral method, 196, 234, 236, 253, 257, 263, 269, 271, 276, 278
—, broken garter
 —, 1-row method, 62, 64, 67, 70, 72, 74, 76, 79, 82, 87, 90
 —, spiral method, 217, 225, 250
—, mistake ribbing
 —, 1-row method, 28-35, 56-57, 63, 66, 71, 73, 75, 77-78, 81, 88-89, 91-94
 —, serpentine method, 152, 190, 193
 —, spiral method, 199, 254, 258, 265, 270, 272, 277, 279
—, mock ribbing, spiral method, 222, 237-238, 242, 245-246, 275
—, ribbing

—, 1-row method, 61, 68, 84, 95
—, spiral method, 216, 218, 220, 223, 226, 229, 232, 235, 239, 243, 247, 251, 255, 259, 266, 273
Faggoting, vii
Falbo, 8-9
Fassett, Kaffe, 352
Fiber choice, 332-333
Fiber(s), mixing, 344-345
Finishing, 364-365
Flood, Jared, 350
Garter, 3, 14, 60, 102-103, 196, 333
—, disrupted, 102-103
—, reversibility, 36-39
Gauge, 14-15, 333, 344
Gravel, 285-287
Hadrians Wall, 106-107
Handwarmers pattern, 210-211
Harlin, 212-213
Hat pattern, 42-43, 208-209, 212-213
Hellsten, Ulla-Karin, 116
Hiatt, June Hemmons, 209, 364
Intarsia, 343
Interaction of Color, Albers, 346
Interweave Knitting Lab, 354
Irregular fabrics, 56-57
Kaidan, 118-119
Kenner, 8-9
Knitting, Fair Isle, 343
Knitting, Bohus, 343
Kozak, 42-43
Lowe, Catherine, vii, 286, 344, 364
Lyden, 8-9
Mably, Brandon, 352
Marchant, Nancy, vii
Marlett, 8-9
Mayes, 100-101
Menz, Deb, 335
Method, 1-row, see 1-row method
Method, serpentine, see Serpentine method
Method, spiral, see Spiral method
Mirror images, 16-17, 20, 56

PAGE 378

Miser, Lorna, 335
Mistake ribbing, 29-35, 56-57, 199
Mixing color(s), 340-341
Mixing fibers, 342-345, 348-349
Mock ribbing, 28, 98, 199, 206
Morant, 8-9
Mountain Colors Mountain Goat, 53
Murley, 8-9
Nebraska Winter, 52-53
New, Debbie, 23
Norberg, Börje, 116
Noro, Eisaku, 350
Northfirst, 116-117
Östergötlands Ullspineri, 116
Parallelogram(s), 282
—, 1x1, 290-291
—, 2x2, 290-293
Pattern multiple(s), 4
—, remainder, 4-5, 10-15, 108, 122-124, 126, 199, 204-209, 285
—, specific, 1-row method
  —, 1, 60
  —, 2, 61
  —, 2+1, 62
  —, 3+1, 63
  —, 3+2, 64
  —, 4, 68
  —, 4+1, 65, 69
  —, 4+2, 66, 70
  —, 4+3, 67
  —, 5+1, 73, 75
  —, 5+2, 76
  —, 5+3, 71, 74, 77
  —, 5+4, 72
  —, 6, 78, 81-82, 84, 88, 91, 93
  —, 6+1, 79, 83, 85, 90, 92, 94
  —, 6+2, 80, 86, 95
  —, 6+3, 87
—, specific, serpentine method
  —, 3+1, 130
  —, 4+1, 131-132
  —, 5+1, 133, 135, 137
  —, 5+2, 134, 136, 138

  —, 6+1, 139, 141
  —, 6+2, 140, 142
  —, 7+1, 143-144
  —, 7+2, 145
  —, 7+3, 146
  —, 8+1, 147-148, 150
  —, 8+2, 149, 151-152
  —, 9+1, 153-154, 159
  —, 9+2, 155, 160
  —, 9+3, 156-157, 161-162
  —, 9+4, 158, 163
  —, 10+1, 164
  —, 10+2, 165-166, 168, 170, 172, 174
  —, 10+4, 167, 169, 171, 173, 175
  —, 11+1, 176
  —, 11+2, 177
  —, 11+3, 178
  —, 11+4, 179
  —, 11+5, 180
  —, 12+1, 181, 186, 189
  —, 12+2, serpentine, 187, 188
  —, 12+3, 182-183, 190-191
  —, 12+4, 184-185, 192-193
—, specific, shaped 1-row method
  —, triangle
    —, 1, 1x1, 295-302
    —, 1, 1x2, 303-307
    —, 2, 2x2, 308, 310, 312
    —, 2+1, 2x2, 309, 311, 313
  —, parallelogram
    —, 12, 1x1, 314, 318-319, 324, 327
    —, 12-1, 2x2, 316-317, 322-323, 326, 329
    —, 12, 2x2, 315, 320-321, 325, 328
—, specific, spiral method
  —, 1, 215
  —, 2, 216
  —, 2+1, 217
  —, 3, 218
  —, 3+1, 219
  —, 4, 220, 223
  —, 4+1, 221, 224
  —, 4+2, 222, 225

  —, 5, 226, 229, 232
  —, 5+1, 227, 230, 233
  —, 5+2, 228, 231, 234
  —, 6, 235, 239, 243, 247, 251, 255
  —, 6+1, 236, 240, 244, 248, 252, 256
  —, 6+2, 237, 241, 245, 249, 253, 257
  —, 6+3, 238, 242, 246, 250, 254, 258
  —, 12, 259, 266, 273
  —, 12+1, 260, 267, 274
  —, 12+2, 261, 268, 275
  —, 12+3, 262, 269, 276
  —, 12+4, 263, 270, 277
  —, 12+5, 264, 271, 278
  —, 12+6, 265, 272, 279
—, triangle(s), 285
Pattern
—, cowl, 120-121, 202-203, 342-343
—, hand warmers, 210-211
—, hat, 42-43, 207-209, 212-213
—, scarf, 8-9, 34-35, 40-41, 44-45, 48-49, 52-53, 100-101, 106-107, 110-119, 292-293, 350-351
—, shawl, 44-45, 52-53, 286-289
Pearl-McPhee, Stephanie, vii, 26
Perfectly reversible, see Reversible, perfect
Permutations, 10-13, 54-58, 104-105, 122-127, 199
  —, 1-row method, 10-13, 54-58
  —, serpentine method, 104-105, 122-127
  —, spiral method, 199
Photography to measure contrast, 338-339, 354-355
Piland, 8-9
Pooling, 332, 335-337
Principles of Knitting, Hiatt, 209, 364
Ravelry, 332, 350
References, 366-367
Regular fabrics, 56-57
Repeat, see also Pattern Multiple
—, round, 199, 206
—, row, 28, 104-105, 125-127
—, stitch, 16

Reversible, 16-22, 36-39, 125-127, 209, 363
—, aesthetic, 16, 21-22, 46-47, 50, 125
—, broken garter, 36-39
—, garter, 36-39
—, perfect, 16, 18, 26, 28
—, shift, 16, 19, 26, 28, 32, 36-39, 46-47, 50, 104-105, 205
—, shift-flip, 16, 20
Rib and Seed Diamonds, 108-111, 128, 137, 144, 159, 176
Ribbing, 2, 8-18, 22, 28-33, 54-55, 196-200
Robson, 292-293, 348-349, 354-355
Row repeat(s), 28, 126-127, 199
Ruddock, 8-9
Ryd-Dups, Biggan, 354
Scarf pattern, see Pattern, scarf
Seed stitch, 3, 14-15, 23, 26, 29, 38, 40-41, 49, 104, 108-109, 201, 285
Self-assembled, 23
Selvedge(s), 10-11, 54-55, 58, 124, 364-365
Sequence
—, definition, 3
—, knitting, 2-7
—, knitting and science, 23
—, length, 3-4, 10, 26, 32, 50, 56, 58, 98, 124, 126-127, 196-201, 204-206, 374-375
Sequences, specific
—, 2(K1, P1), K1, 77
—, 2(K1, P1), K2, P2, 33
—, 2(K1, P1), P1, K1, 93-95
—, 2(K2, P2), 2(K1, P1), 206-209, 266-272
—, 2(K2, P2), K1, P1, 174-175
—, 2(K2, P2), K2, 9
—, 2(P1, K1), P2, K2, 33
—, 3(K1, P1), 3(P1, K1), 2(K1, P1), S1WYIF, 49
—, 3(K1, P1), K2, 9
—, 3(K1, P1), K2, 9
—, K1, 3, 60, 215
—, K1, 2(K1, P1), 38-39, 75-76, 108, 128, 137-138, 232-234

—, K1, 3(K1, P1), 108, 128, 144-146
—, K1, 4(K1, P1), 108-111, 128, 159-163
—, K1, 5(K1, P1), 108-109, 128, 176-180
—, K1, P1, 3-4, 14-15, 23, 30, 33, 38, 40-41, 61-62, 199-201, 205, 216-217, 295
—, K1, P1, 2(P1, K1), 91
—, K1, P1, K2, P2, 9, 33
—, K1, P2, K3, P2, K1, 100
—, K1, P3, 4(K1, P1), 273-279
—, K10, P10, 38
—, K10, P2, K2, P2, 51
—, K11, P1, K3, P1, 51
—, K11, P11, 38, 41
—, K12, P12, 38
—, K2, 2(P1, K1), see K3, P1, K1, P1
—, K2, 4(P1, K1), P2, 285-287, 312-313
—, K2, P1, 19, 32, 63-64, 102, 130, 199-201, 218-219, 296
—, K2, P1, K1, P1 see K1, 2(K1, P1)
—, K2, P1, K1, P2, 33, 93-95, 251-254
—, K2, P1, K2, P3, 51
—, K2, P1, K3, 80
—, K2, P2, 2, 5, 10-13, 18, 20, 33, 38, 41, 43, 46-47, 68-70, 122-123, 132, 196, 199, 205, 223-225, 282, 290, 297, 303, 308-309
—, K2, P2, 3(K1, P1), 172-173
—, K2, P2, K1, P1, 33, 91-92, 142, 202, 255-258
—, K2, P2, K2, 82
—, K3, 3(K1, P1), K3, 324-326
—, K3, 3(K1, P1), P3, 327-329
—, K3, P1, 9, 30-31, 33, 46-47, 65-67, 102, 122-123, 131, 201, 220-222, 298
—, K3, P1, K1, P1, 9, 33, 88-90, 243-246
—, K3, P1, K2, see K5, P1
—, K3, P1, K2, P2, K1, P3, 211
—, K3, P1, K3, P1, K8, 30
—, K3, P1, K3, P5, 51
—, K3, P1, S1WYIB, P1, 212-213
—, K3, P2, 33, 73-74, 135-136, 229-231
—, K3, P2, K3, P4, 51
—, K3, P3, 4-7, 20, 26, 28, 33, 38-39, 41, 46, 54-55, 84-87, 141, 199, 205, 247-250, 310-311
—, K3, P3, 2(K1, P1), 170-171
—, K3, P3, 3(K1, P1), 189-193, 292-293, 302, 314-317
—, K3, P3, K1, P1, 21, 33, 116-119, 125, 150-152
—, K3, P3, K2, P2, 168-169
—, K3, P3, K3, see K6, P3
—, K3, P4, K2, P2, K1, see K4, P4, K2, P2
—, K3, P6, K3, see K6, P6
—, K3, S1WYIB, P3, S1WYIB, K3, P5, 52-53
—, K4, P1, 71-72, 102-103, 133-134, 201, 204, 226-228
—, K4, P1, K4, P7, 51
—, K4, P2, 33, 46, 81-83, 140, 239-242
—, K4, P2, K4, P6, 51
—, K4, P3, K4, P5, 51
—, K4, P4, 30-31, 33, 38, 46
—, K4, P4, K1, P1, 166-167, 350-351
—, K4, P4, K2, P2, 34, 104-106, 186-188, 259-265
—, K4, P4, K3, P3, K2, P2, K1, P1, 196
—, K5, P1, 22, 30, 46, 56-57, 78-80, 102-103, 139, 201, 206, 235-238
—, K5, P1, K1, P1, 51
—, K5, P3, 46, 148-149
—, K5, P5, 38, 41, 44, 350-351
—, K5, S1WYIF, P5, S1WYIB, 288-289, 306-307
—, K6, 3(K1, P1), 301
—, K6, P1, 102, 143
—, K6, P2, 9, 46
—, K6, P3, 9, 154-158
—, K6, P6, 9, 38, 114, 299-300, 304-305, 318-323
—, K7, P1, 46, 102-103, 147
—, K7, P2, K1, P2, 51
—, K7, P7, 38, 41
—, K8, P1, 102-103, 153
—, K8, P1, K2, P1, 51
—, K8, P2, 120-121, 165
—, K8, P4, 112-113, 181-185

—, K8, P8, 38
—, K9, P1, 102-103, 164
—, K9, P3, K1, P3, 51
—, K9, P9, 38
—, P1, 3
—, P1, K1, P2, K2, 33, 95
—, P1, K3, P1, 9
—, P3, K1, P1, K3, see K3, P3, K1, P1
—, P3, K3, P1, K1, 33
—, P5, K5, see K5, P5
Serpentine method, 5-7, 10-11, 98-193
—, blocking, 98
—, pattern multiples, 122-127
—, permutations, 104-105, 122-123, 126-127
—, reversibility, 125-127
—, row repeat(s), 125-127
—, selvedges, 98
—, types, 122-123, 126-127
Serra, 206-209
Shaped 1-row method, 5, 16, 281-329, 364-365
Shawl pattern, see Pattern, shawl
Shift reversible, see Reversible, shift
Shift-flip reversible, see Reversible, shift-flip
Sources, 371
Spiral method, 5-7, 12-13, 16-17, 195-279
—, asymmetric even sequences, 206
—, classes, 196-199
—, odd sequences, 204
—, permutations, 12-13, 198-199
—, properties, 198-199
—, reversibility, 198-199
—, symmetric even sequences, 205
Stitch dictionary
—, 1-row method, 58-95
—, Serpentine method, 128-193
—, Shaped 1-row method, 294-329
—, Spiral method, 214-279
—, Stockinette, 3, 54, 196, 199, 215, 333, 335, 365
Sundbø, Annemor, viii

Swirl, spiral method, 6-7, 12-13, 196-207, 219, 221, 224, 227-228, 230-231, 233, 236, 240-241, 244, 248-249, 252, 256, 260-262, 264, 267-268, 274-275
Tenderloin, 350-351
The Knitter's Guide to Hand-dyed and Variegated Yarn, Miser, 335
The Ravell'd Sleeve, Lowe, 364
Torii, Setsuko, 344
Triangle(s), 282, 284-285, 295-313
Twigs, 285-287
Types, fabric, see Fabric types
Unexpected Knitting, New, 23
Vogue, 352, 364
Washing, 365
Weaving in ends, 365
Wegner, 120-121
Welden, 202-203, 342-343
Wilde, 34-35
Winterwork, 210-211
Woolston, 110-111
Wortham, 8-9
Yarn, viii, 14, 332-355
—, contrast, 338-355
—, silk-mohair, 333, 344-345, 348-349
—, supplier
 —, Aslan Trends, 40-43, 120-121, 339
 —, Beaverslide, 339
 —, Biggan Designs, 354
 —, Blue Mountain Fiber Arts, 333
 —, Brooklyn Tweed, 100-101, 110-111, 288-289, 333, 339
 —, Cascade, 58, 208-209, 212-213, 333
 —, Catherine Lowe Bespoke, 286-287, 344
 —, Hifa, 339
 —, Isager, 342-343
 —, Karabella, 112-113
 —, Koigu, 49, 333, 335, 339
 —, Lisa Souza, vi, 52-53, 114-115
 —, Louet, 333
 —, Madelinetosh, 202-203
 —, Miss Babs, 333

 —, Noro, 350-351
 —, Östergötlands Ullspinneri, 116-117
 —, Quince & Co., 339
 —, Rohrspatz & Wollmeise, 44
 —, Rowan, 344-345, 348-349
 —, Studio Donegal, 106-107
 —, Sunshine Yarns, 339
 —, Western Sky Knits, 339
 —, Wool2Dye4, 333
 —, Woolfolk, 339
—, Variegated, 34, 44, 49, 114, 292, 332-351
Zig zag(s), 98, 100, 135, 155, 169
Zimmerman, Elizabeth, vii, 332

SCARVES, SHAWLS, AND COWLS

Marlett
Page 9

Enders
Page 9

Morant
Page 9

Lyden
Page 9

Piland
Page 9

Ruddock
Page 9

Askin
Page 9

Murley
Page 9

Kenner
Page 9

Drewes
Page 9

Wortham
Page 9

Falbo
Page 9

SCARVES, SHAWLS, AND COWLS

SCARVES, SHAWLS, AND COWLS

Hadrians Wall
Page 106

Woolston
Page 110

Bach
Page 112

Northfirst
Page 116

Kaidan
Page 118

Wegner
Page 120

Welden
Page 202, 343

Twigs
Page 286

Gravel
Page 286

Delta Wing
Page 289

Robson
Page 292, 348, 354

Castro, Dogpatch, Tenderloin
Page 350

HATS
HANDWARMERS

Kozak
Page 43

Serra 1
Page 209

Serra 2
Page 209

Serra 3
Page 209

Serra 4
Page 209

Serra 5
Page 209

Serra 6
Page 209

Harlin
Page 212

Winterwork
Page 211

ABOUT THE AUTHOR

Cecelia Campochiaro is a knitter who lives and works in Silicon Valley. *Sequence Knitting* is her first publication outside the sciences. She grew up in a family of artists and has been knitting since she was 12.